A Hakka Woman

By

Di Lebowitz

Grosvenor House
Publishing Limited

All rights reserved
Copyright © Di Lebowitz, 2024

The right of Di Lebowitz to be identified as the author of this work has been asserted in accordance with Section 78 of the Copyright, Designs and Patents Act 1988

The book cover is copyright to Di Lebowitz

This book is published by
Grosvenor House Publishing Ltd
Link House
140 The Broadway, Tolworth, Surrey, KT6 7HT.
www.grosvenorhousepublishing.co.uk

This book is sold subject to the conditions that it shall not, by way of trade or otherwise, be lent, resold, hired out or otherwise circulated without the author's or publisher's prior consent in any form of binding or cover other than that in which it is published and without a similar condition including this condition being imposed on the subsequent purchaser.

A CIP record for this book
is available from the British Library

ISBN 978-1-80381-779-8
eBook ISBN 978-1-80381-778-1

To the strongest woman I know, my grandmother.

A NOTE ABOUT THE LANGUAGE

Paupau doesn't speak English. She speaks in a mishmash of Hakka, Tung Ping Chau dialect and Hong Kongese. Whilst writing this book, I was concerned how I could portray Paupau's voice as authentically as possible and adamant she doesn't come across as a stereotype or caricature of what a Chinese woman 'ought to sound like'. Every effort has been made to try and preserve my grandmother's voice and in doing so, certain Hakka or Hong Kongese words that don't quite translate into English have been used. A glossary of these terms can be found at the end of this book.

Some people might find it odd that I have chosen to use 'Hong Kongese' rather than 'Cantonese' when referring to the language spoken in Hong Kong. This was a deliberate choice and one that aims to highlight the subtle but significant differences between Hong Kong Cantonese and the Cantonese spoken in mainland China, Macau or Singapore. Due to Hong Kong's British colonial influence, Hong Kong Cantonese employs many more English terms that have been absorbed into its everyday speech, words that even some local Hong Kong people may not be fully aware are in fact English. There are also variants in how certain words are pronounced as well as colloquialisms that exist solely in Hong Kong. It was important for me to maintain this distinction in this story which is why readers will see the term 'Hong Kongese' when referring to Hong Kong Cantonese.

In Cantonese, the transliteration for maternal grandmother is 'Popo' or 'Porpor'. I have chosen not to use either but instead write it as 'Paupau'. Originally this was not intentional but simply due to how my family have always and still 'spell out' Paupau. For me, it became natural, as the 'au' seems to emphasise the *au* sound. I had been made aware of this when a fellow Hongkonger pointed out my alternative way of spelling. But 'Popo' sounds too much like the police and I didn't like the association of the police with my beloved grandmother. 'Porpor' also sounds odd to me, like 'poor-poor', so I have decided for this retelling of my grandmother's story, she will be Paupau.

Prologue

April 2019, Hong Kong

'Ah-yah! Didi! Where are your slippers?' scolds Paupau. 'Ha? You do the same in England? Put your slippers on!' she grumbles.

She elbows me away from the kitchen sink and I almost lose my balance. How is my barely five-foot, eighty-six-year-old grandma this strong? Before I can protest, she placed a pair of garishly embroidered pink slippers on the tiled kitchen floor.

'Here, put them on,' she instructs.

'But Paupau, do I have to? You know I hate wearing them! They're like feet-prison.' I sulk, as if I were a little girl again.

Paupau flashes me a look, a warning that she's ready to start nagging and I immediately know it would be pointless to argue with her. Some grandmothers have a talent for knitting or sewing. Some have a talent for baking breads or cakes. Mine has a talent for nagging. It doesn't matter how young or old you are, if Paupau wants you to do something, she'll nag you until you surrender. Who needs UN Conflict Resolution Officers when you could get my grandma, who has the power to badger dictators until they cry for mercy?

'Put your slippers on! So ugly to have big wide feet! Why don't you put them on? Ha? They are new slippers! Very pretty, I bought them in the market, see? Aren't they pretty? And only fifty dollars – a good deal, right? Come, put them on. Didi, put them on,' she continues as she nudges the slippers closer to me.

I catch a glimpse of my grandmother's feet – feet of a lifetime of labour, rough and leathery.

'You don't like them? Ha? I bought them especially for you! See, they are pink – young women like pink, right? Come on, put them on. No one likes a woman with wide, ugly feet! Come, put them on, Didi,' she continues.

I feel the heat rise in the back of my neck, my face scrunches up and lips curl, ready to argue back like I did as a child, but this time, I don't. This time, my body lets out a loud chuckle.

'Ha? What's so funny? I said something funny?' Paupau mutters. She presses her lips together and furrows her brow, but the glint in her eyes reveals she is feigning annoyance. It's a little game we have played all my life: she nags, I argue back, she pretends to be irritated, I play along and then eventually comply. In a battle of wills or rather stubbornness, Paupau always won, and yielding to her was the easiest way to shut her up and leave me alone. But now, as a grown woman, on my annual visit to Hong Kong, I simply give in without a fight.

I study her face – it's a face I know better than my own. I can't help but notice the many more lines etched onto it since my last trip. My favourite eighty-six-year-old looks older than I allow myself to remember. Something pricks in my eyes.

'Okay, okay. I'll put them on. See, happy now?' I say gently with a smile as I slide into the slippers – a perfect fit.

'Good girl. See, isn't that much better? Now your feet won't look so ugly, now they look correct,' she says with a triumphant grin and opens the fridge. She squats down and pulls out a red plastic bag filled with mangosteens.

'My favourite!' I exclaim, surprised she remembered.

'Ah, yes . . . yes, your favourite. Yes, that's right,' she mumbles with no eye contact as she takes the bag of fruit and dashes out of the kitchen.

That's odd. Has she forgotten mangosteen is my favourite? It wouldn't surprise me. I do only get to see her once a year. But then, why try to hide it? Everyone forgets things. It's no big deal. Shrugging off the thought, I continue to wash the rest of the melamine bowls and dishes from dinner. I think back to all those times Paupau used to tell me off when I was a little girl, prancing around our living room barefoot as I did my best Anita Mui and Madonna impressions. She really hated it when I was barefoot.

I let out a deep sigh as a tear rolls down my cheek and drops into the sink. I never understood that Paupau's nagging was directly proportional to how much she cared and loved. The more she loved, the more she nagged. Being the granddaughter who was nagged the most, I guess I should wear it as a badge of honour. I like that thought. A smile tugs at the corners of my mouth. I am still Paupau's favourite granddaughter although it's been years since I left Hong Kong; Paupau's rebellious grandchild, the one with the wide, flat feet just like hers. May my feet take me back to her, back to my roots.

'Didi, what is taking you so long? Don't worry about the dishes, I will do them later. You never wash them clean enough, anyway! Come and eat some mangosteen,' Paupau calls out to me.

The dining table is lined with bubble wrap. It's her favourite form of tablecloth. 'Easy wiping,' she would claim, despite my cousin and me telling her how bad it is for the environment.

'Here, eat. Very fresh and sweet!' She pushes an open mangosteen with its juicy white flesh into my face.

'Thank you, Paupau.'

I gobble the segments of fruit and it glides down my throat, cooling me in the April heat. I'm reminded of all the times Paupau had especially gone to the best fruit stalls to buy me mangosteen. This is the taste of my childhood, the taste of her love.

'You left these on the sofa.' Paupau gestures to a small stack of old photographs I had compiled. 'And also those boxes. What will you do with them?' She points to the three large plastic storage boxes of photographs I took out before dinner.

'Oh, don't worry, I'll put them away later. I haven't finished with them yet.'

'What you want with all those old photographs, anyway? Every time you come back, you always go through those old photo boxes.'

'Well, I can't take you with me, can I?' I smile.

The thought has crossed my mind more than once.

'You cheeky girl. I'm so old. Even if you take me to London with you, what would I do there? Ha? I'd be a burden to you.'

She shakes her head as she sits at the dining table.

'You're not *that* old, Paupau. You are still in great shape!'

There is a long pause. My grandmother sits upright and flicks through the stack of photos.

'What kind of photo is this? Who would take a photo of photos?'

A frown creases her face as she points to a photograph, one I haven't seen in a long time. It was a photo I took of all her passport-sized portraits tiled next to each other in chronological order.

'It was me, I took it . . . but I don't remember what it was for. Maybe a school history project?'

'Hmmm. I remember! These are for my Hong Kong ID card. You see here? I'm not smiling in any of them. I look so serious! Serious face for serious business.' She nods proudly.

'So, which one is for your Hong Kong ID card now?'

Without warning, Paupau springs up out of her chair, wipes her mouth with the back of her hand and fetches her purse.

'This one.'

She hands me her identification card.

'You see this one? It has a special chip in it, so fancy! Your Auntie Yin helped me apply for the new version.'

'Can I see?'

I study the small portrait. The face in it has an equally grim and serious expression to all the other passport-sized photos. I would never understand why someone who loves to pull faces and beam a smile full of crooked teeth could always look so solemn in all her document photos.

'That's odd. Paupau, it's got only your birth year written on it.'

I point to the section where it's supposed to have a full birth date – day, month, year.

'Yes, I know,' she says, without glancing at her ID card.

'But that can't be right. Where's the rest of it? Where's the rest of your birth date?'

'They didn't know it and I don't know it either,' she says, completely unfazed.

'Who's they? And what do you mean you don't know your birth date? Have you forgotten? We celebrate it every year.'

I wave her ID card in my hand in protest.

'I didn't forget! Of course, I know my birth date!' She stomps her wide, flat feet on the parquet floor.

'Okay, okay. You didn't forget. But I don't understand why there's only your birth year?' I take another look at the ID card, wondering why I've never noticed this before, and stand up to hand it back to Paupau.

An enormous sigh leaves my grandmother's sturdy frame as she shakes her head at me. Paupau must have told me about her ID card before, but I was too young to understand or simply didn't pay any attention. She sits back at the table, and I watch her glance over at the photographs.

'Didi, come and sit down.' She pulls out a chair for me. 'Sit, and I will explain. You know, there are so many things that you don't understand, so many things that you young people take for granted. But I will tell you. I will tell you everything before it all falls out of my head, and I forget even my name.'

If feet are the roots of a woman, let them be strong and planted firmly on the soil so that she may grow into a robust and beautiful tree.

Part 1

I am Hakka

For most of my life, I didn't know what my birth date was in what you would call the 'sun calendar'. I only knew the year: 1932, the year of the water monkey.

You saw on my Hong Kong ID card, right? You saw how it has just the year 1932 on it and perhaps you find it funny or strange – no month, no date. But there is nothing funny or strange about it; actually it's quite sad. I never had a birth certificate nor any documentation to mark my birth. Certificates and documents were for the wealthy, and we were merely poor farmers living off the land. So, when it was time to apply for a Hong Kong ID card back in the seventies, I had nothing to hand to the officer. I had nothing to prove my name or my birth date. In fact, I couldn't prove my existence to the officer, so I gave him my lunar birth date.

'Ah Sum,' he said. 'We use the Western calendar now. Do you know what it is?'

'Erh . . . I am sorry, sir. I only know the year,' I said as I shook my head, embarrassed that I couldn't tell him. 'But I know the lunar birth date!'

'Listen, Ah Sum, they are two different calendars. How am I supposed to know what it is on the Western date? Ha?' the officer barked at me impatiently.

'Oh, I see,' I said as I lowered my head, but really, I didn't see. How was I supposed to know the difference? Or that we had stopped using our own calendar? There was no way I could convert my lunar birth date – the months were all different! Our months are shorter, with twenty-eight or twenty-nine days. Our year cycle follows the moon, like the cycle of a woman's body.

'So, what should I put down, ha?' the officer snapped at me.

I wanted to shout back at him but didn't dare.

'I . . . I don't know. I was born in 1932,' I mumbled.

So that is how I ended up with just the year 1932 printed on my shiny plastic ID card, but it's okay. At least my photograph came out nice and clear.

***

Most poor people didn't know how to read or write back then, so we had to rely on family members to remember our birth dates and other important dates. Sometimes people would get confused, mix up the dates and then tell you the wrong one so you'd end up living your entire life with the wrong birth date. Imagine that! Lucky for me, my parents were literate and also had excellent memories so they could remember it and tell me.

A few years ago, your Auntie Yin converted my birth date to the sun calendar for me and it's 7 March, but this doesn't feel right, it doesn't feel like it belongs to me. I would rather stick with the lunar version because that's the one I know – the first day of the second month, the very start of spring – the month of new beginnings.

I was born at a time before the Japanese invasion, before Mao, before Communism in China and everything else that came with it. My parents were Hakka people – a people who have a long-standing reputation for being reliable hard workers. There are sayings about Hakka women and how we are built like ox – strong, obedient, unbreakable and cheap to keep. I tell you, if I hadn't been born Hakka, there was no way I could have endured so much. I have been fighting with monsters all my life and now my mind and body are getting exhausted and old. Sometimes when I see my face in the mirror in the morning, I cry out, ah-yah! Who is this old, wrinkly woman, with so many deep lines across her face? How did I get so ugly with my giant nose, leathery skin and greying hair? Did you know old people shrink? Yes! I am shrinking! Each year when you come back to visit me, you notice I am getting shorter. Soon I will be so small you won't be able to see me because I will have withered away. Didi, you must look after your body. You must honour it because this is the only body you have – you cannot ask for an exchange or refund, understood? Remember that.

With my old age, when I talk about one thing, my mind drifts and I end up talking about something else. Ah, yes, I was telling you where I came from. My father was called Lam Yun and my mother, Dai Tsing. They were farmers who lived in a small, quiet Hakka village called Lau Kwok near Daya Bay, not so far from Shenzhen in mainland China. The entire area used to be a beautiful, serene blanket of green, dotted with little wooden and stone houses. Now I hear it's all gone, smothered by big factories, high rises and motorways. They call this development, but what is development when everything looks so grey and sad?

I was born the fifth child in my family. I am told that when Mother saw she had given birth to another girl, she shook her head and sighed with disappointment. She did this not because she didn't love me, but because she knew to be a daughter is to become someone else's property – a wife and daughter-in-law, whose Fate would lie in another family's hands.

The six of us – Big Sister, Big Brother, Second Sister, Second Brother, me and Little Sister – lived in a small stone house with a mezzanine connected by a wooden ladder. My parents, two brothers and little sister slept upstairs whilst my older sisters and I slept downstairs, right by the kitchen. We didn't have enough room for a wooden platform and mattress like my parents, so the three of us slept on the floor on top of woven bamboo mats lined with quilts my mother had sewn. Oh, how I loved my little corner by the stove that kept me warm at night, especially during the winter when the cold damp would seep up through the floor and into my bones. I've always hated the cold and would wrap myself like a thick dumpling and curl up right next to the stove to soak up all the heat.

'Ah Ping,' Big Sister would call out. 'Don't get too close to the stove or you will burn yourself!'

Reluctantly, I would shuffle away, only to wiggle my way back to the source of heat like a little silkworm as soon as Big Sister fell asleep.

That was how we slept on the hard floor. I remember when I came to visit you for your graduation in London and we stayed in a hotel, ah yah! That Western-style mattress was so soft, I thought I was going to sink into it! I couldn't sleep on such a soft mattress, and it made my back ache each morning.

There wasn't much space. Our kitchen was a small bench with a clay stove. We didn't have a magic cooker where you can flick a switch for gas or electricity. Oh no, it was hard work to cook back then! You had to put hay, grass and wood – whatever you could find – to make the fire and you had to stay with it the whole time to make sure it didn't go out otherwise your rice wouldn't cook. Or worse, the fire would be too strong, your rice would burn and everything would go to waste. But you know what? The rice tasted better back then . . . If I close my eyes right now, I can still smell the fragrance of my mother's rice.

There was no indoor plumbing and no magic tap with running water – there wouldn't be for many, many years. Every morning and evening, someone had to collect water from the village well and store it in wooden buckets, to be used sparingly. Our shower was a bucket and ladle in the courtyard outside; there was no privacy and all we had for curtains were a few old cloths hung on bamboo rods. But at that age, it didn't matter to me.

There was always something drying outside our home in the courtyard – clothes, vegetables, mandarin peel, seeds, rice, fish.

'Ah Ping, you see all these foods drying here?' my mother would ask as she spread the tangerine peel and salted fish on the bamboo baskets in the sun.

I nodded.

'The sun has special powers. It makes food last longer, so it doesn't go bad. That way we can keep it for the winter.'

This is how I will always remember the outside of our house. It is the smell of dried salted fish and tangerine peel baking under the sun's magical rays. But the inside of the house smelt differently. It smelt of the incense that my parents offered daily to Kwun Yum – the goddess of mercy and compassion.

Like so many other households in the village, our family were Buddhists and had a small altar in the corner of our house. Instead of Buddha statues or Bodhisattvas, we had a faded statuette of Kwun Yum, who watched over us. Every evening before dinner, I studied how my mother offered incense and prayers to the goddess and I absorbed every detail – the way she lit three joss sticks and planted them in the holder, how the smoke danced in front of her face as she uttered prayers of petition to Kwun Yum to take care of us. When my mother was finished, she would kowtow three times before standing up slowly with a smile of calm serenity. I miss that smile.

***

Everyone in the family had a job. Sitting around at home and doing nothing was unthinkable; it was even considered immoral. From a young age, we understood that everyone in the family had to contribute in any way they could; doing nothing was the same as letting your family down. If we didn't work, we didn't eat. If we didn't eat, we'd die. Everyone had to work no matter the age or gender and that is why Hakka people never bound their daughters' feet. How are you supposed to work in the paddy fields or take care of your siblings at home with those ridiculous-looking lotus feet? Impossible! Bound feet were for the wealthy girls and women who had plenty of servants to do all their running around for them, not us.

My mother, father and brothers rose every morning before dawn to tend the rice paddy fields whilst my older sisters stayed at home, taking turns on household chores and caring for Little Sister and me. I didn't see my father much except during dinner time, but even then, he rushed his meal so he could dash off to the village school – he was a teacher there. He worked day and night to support his family and to be a useful member of society, and I knew, at that age, that I wanted to be like him. I wanted to be useful.

'Father, I want to go to work with you,' I said one evening during dinner time.

'Go to work? You mean in the rice paddy fields? Hmm, well it's very hard work. I don't think you're ready. You are too small. The water will be much too deep for you.'

'Father, I don't want to stay at home. It's so boring. And I want to do something. I want to be like you.' I crossed my arms.

'My cheeky water monkey, always up to something! Well, if you really want to help . . . I guess you could help me look after our cow. Your sisters are so busy with housework, I'm sure they could do with some help. Why don't you take over? You'll need to take the cow out every day to graze and bring her back.'

'Yes! Yes! I can do that. See!'

I bounced off my stool and pretended to walk our cow around the house.

'All right, all right. That's enough.' My father chuckled. 'Very good. So that will be your job from now on. Remember, cows are sacred to us farmers. They are our friends because they help us till the land and carry our loads. Be sure to take care of her,' he said calmly.

'Yes, Father!' I jumped up and down with pure excitement. I was a big girl now, a big girl with a job.

I could barely sleep that night. As soon as dawn broke, I sprang out of bed, hastily got ready and hurried outside to greet our cow. I had seen her plenty of times, but suddenly standing so close next to her with no adults around, she looked enormous. Her breath felt hot and wet on my face as my hands trembled to grab her lead.

'Now Mrs Cow,' I said, trying to sound as confident as possible. 'I'm taking you to graze. Father told me to look after you, so you must listen to me.' My voice shook.

I did not know what I was doing as I led the cow through the hills that surrounded our village, following the other girls who had been tasked with the same chore. All the girls looked older than me and were clearly much more experienced. They never seemed to flinch as their cows roamed freely on the big patch of green. For weeks I didn't dare leave my cow alone and kept close to her as I whispered kind words to her, so she wouldn't trample on me. I guess it worked, as before long, Mrs Cow and I were like two friends going on a walk together.

But little girls get distracted. Little girls prefer to play with their friends. One morning after taking Mrs Cow to graze, I wandered off with the others, singing Hakka songs and collecting berries. Time slipped away and when I realised it was late morning and time to return home, my stomach knotted. Did my cow graze her belly full? I didn't know because I wasn't paying attention. I had neglected my duties and knew my father would be so angry and disappointed with me if he were to find out! Quickly, I grabbed the cow's lead and headed back, hoping Father wouldn't notice. When I brought her home, in time for our family lunch, my father stopped me.

'Ah Ping, did you take the cow for grazing today?' he said with a raised eyebrow.

'Yes, Father,' I said, shoulders hunched. I had never lied to him or anyone before. I didn't know what a lie was.

'Hmm. Really? Then why does our cow's belly look so skinny? Hmm?'

My eyes shot up at my father as I took a big gulp.

'You were too busy playing, weren't you?' He raised an eyebrow.

I nodded admittedly and bowed my head, ready to be told off and punished.

'Ah-yah! Ah Ping, my little lazy monkey!' said my father in a stern tone, but as soon as I saw the curl of his lips, he erupted into laughter. 'My lazy water-monkey! What a cheeky little thing you are! I bet you were too distracted playing with those other girls!' He laughed.

Why was he laughing instead of scolding me? I didn't understand. For the next few days, my father continued to tease me, calling me 'lazy water-monkey' but not once did he raise his voice at me. All that teasing made me feel so guilty for having disappointed a man who worked so hard that I never once dared to bring our cow home hungry again. I couldn't stand being called lazy because to be lazy is to be useless, to let your family down.

***

Those were simpler times and despite having little, we had everything we needed. We had a roof over our head, enough food to eat, clothes on our back and most importantly, we had each other. When I think back to my childhood home and those precious memories, there is a dull ache in my heart that hums for what I can never get back. My Hakka home is a dream from a long time ago that keeps moving further and further away from me, as if I have been homesick my whole life.

I CAN WRITE MY OWN NAME

Didi, do you know you are very lucky? You got to go to school and become a master of your own Fate – that is the power of education. But for me and my sisters, life was very different.

Every evening when I was a little girl, I watched my brothers shovel rice from bowl to mouth, gobbling every morsel in a hurry. I listened to the slams of their chopsticks and bowls on the table before dashing out the door, heading for night-school. And every evening I would wonder why it was only my brothers who went to school and not my sisters. They were certainly old enough to attend, so why didn't they go? What was it that my brothers were doing and learning that we weren't?

In the afternoons, during the quiet hour right before dinner, I would pester Big Brother the second he returned home from the paddy fields.

'Big Brother, please teach me some characters! Please! You're not doing anything now. Teach me,' I nagged.

'Ah Ping, you're too young. You won't understand any of it, anyway.'

'I'm not too young! I'm almost seven! Please, Big Brother. Teach me, teach me, teach me.'

I stomped my feet, sulking, with my arms crossed. I guess you could say, even at that age, I was stubborn.

'Fine, I'll show you!' he huffed. 'I don't know why you need to learn, anyway. Girls don't need to read or write.'

'Not true! Mother knows! She knows her characters.'

My mother was one of the few women in the entire village who was completely literate.

'Mother is different. And stop being so cheeky!' he grumbled.

'Well, are you coming outside or not?'

'Yes! Coming!' I called as I ran outside to our courtyard with Big Brother.

With a small tree branch in his hand, I watched Big Brother mark characters on the ground. What was he drawing? This was incredible! The artful play of his wrist that looked like magic mesmerised me.

'What's that?' I asked.

'These are characters. See here? That's "mother". That one there says "father". And this one is "little sister" – that's you.'

It was incredible how a few flicks of the wrist could make words, and each of those words has a specific meaning. In that precise moment, I was hooked.

I must learn to make magic like that too.

***

'Father, can I go to school?' I asked.

It was during dinner and one of the few moments I got to see my father.

'Ha? School? Ah Ping, why would you want to go to school?' His face scrunched up in confusion.

'Big Brother and Second Brother go to school.'

'Yes, but girls don't go to school. Girls stay at home or work,' he said, still shovelling rice into his mouth.

'But I want to go. I want to learn.'

'Hmmm.'

There was a long pause, as though my father hadn't heard me – perhaps if he said nothing, he could pretend I had never asked.

'I want to go to school. I want to go to school!' I sulked.

I figured if it worked on Big Brother, my methods of persuasion would work on Father too.

'Ah Ping, none of your sisters go to school.' His voice was soft and calm, as usual.

'Please, Father! Please! I want to go. Please!'

I tried to stomp my feet on the floor, but my legs were too short.

'Listen, Ah Ping.' My father placed his chopsticks down on the table and looked straight at me. 'School is for boys, not girls. You know we need you at home to help look after your little sister.'

'But I want to go!' I cried.

I had never raised my voice like that to my father, but in that moment, I didn't care. He had to say yes.

'That's enough, Ah Ping.' My father flashed a look at me and immediately I was silenced.

I had crossed the line by sulking like that and making demands. A good girl is supposed to be silent and obedient, and to never argue – especially not with her father. But I didn't give in that easily and badgered my father every evening until he would give in. But every evening he gave me the same response: 'No, Ah Ping. Girls don't go to school. You can't go, it's not possible.'

School was for sons, not daughters. Our place was at home or on the rice paddy fields next to our mothers and grandmothers, with baby siblings strapped to our backs. Besides, there was nothing to read on the rice fields anyway, so what use would a girl have for reading and writing? What a waste of time and money! God forbid a girl would learn to think for herself and learn to ask questions. She could rebel against her family, her in-laws, or her husband! No! No! No! That could never happen. It would be too dangerous!

Sounds ridiculous, even infuriating, right? But that was how it was back then, unless you were lucky enough to be born into a rich family. Some rich families would educate their daughters so they could be matched to a more suitable husband, but their education was restricted to 'womanly' affairs. Girls like me – we didn't stand a chance. Maybe there was another way?

As the only schoolteacher and one of the few literate people in the village, my father was a highly respected man. People would come with letters sent from relatives in neighbouring villages, beseeching my father to decipher the characters. He happily obliged and often refused the gifts or money they offered him, telling them it's his honour and duty to help others.

Everyone adored my father. Rice, dried salted fish, dried mandarin peel, woven bamboo baskets – those were just a few of the things the villagers gifted my father to show their reverence for him. Seeing how much the villagers venerated my father made me even more eager to be his student. But when I got rejection after rejection, my dreams of attending school so I could learn how to write like my brothers turned into nothing more than a silly childish wish.

'Son, take Ah Ping with you to school tonight,' my father said to Big Brother.

Dinnertime. My brothers' familiar routine of shovelling rice in a race against each other to get to school faster.

'Ha?' Big Brother said, almost choking on his food. 'But Father, she's a girl! She can't go to school!'

'Take her to school with you and make sure you take good care of her,' said my father.

Big Brother's eyes widened as he pursed his lips before nodding in compliance.

What? Am I dreaming? I'm going to school?

I sat there, barely daring to breathe, afraid that the slightest movement would shatter this dream or cause my father to change his mind.

'Ah Ping, finish your dinner or you'll be late for your first day,' said Father.

With that, I stuffed the rest of my rice into my mouth in one go. Before I had even swallowed it, I had leapt out of my stool and dashed out of the house where Big Brother was waiting.

I had walked past the village school many times but had never been inside, so I didn't know what to expect, what a school would look like. Four walls, a roof and a large open space stuffed with wooden stools and tables – that was it, one big classroom where everyone was taught together, regardless of age or level. At the front was an old blackboard covered in scratches and framed with worn edges.

The second I stepped inside, everyone stopped talking. I think I heard someone gasp. So many eyes on me. All eyes of boys and all staring at me. Some of the boys were as small and as young as me, whilst others looked much taller and seemed more like men than boys. I hadn't really understood what my father and Big Brother had meant when they said school wasn't a place for girls until I was the only girl in a room full of forty boys.

'Ah Ping, go and sit over there near the back and don't embarrass me,' said Big Brother as he gave me a little nudge towards the back of the classroom, where I would be less visible.

I looked around for a spare seat. The classroom was packed, and every stool was taken. Some students sat on the floor in between rows, so I copied them and found a spot at the back. Their tables and chairs felt like towers next to me. Boys whispered and giggled as they pointed at me with their judgemental fingers.

'Isn't that Teacher Lam's daughter?'

'What is a girl doing here?'

'Doesn't she know girls aren't allowed?'

'She looks too young to be here.'

I knew I was not welcomed.

Suddenly, everyone sprung up and stood at attention. *What's going on? Why is everyone standing up?* I copied. With all those rows of heads in front of me covering my view, I couldn't see what was going on. I hopped up and down and swivelled my head from side to side, trying to catch a glance.

Right there, at the front of the classroom, was the schoolteacher – my father. Watching everyone bowing to greet him good evening filled me with awe and wonder at the command he had over an entire class. I couldn't wait to start learning.

***

For the next three nights, I gobbled my dinner as quickly as humanly possible before racing my brothers to get to school. I was worried that if I didn't eat fast enough, if my legs were too slow to keep up, they would leave me behind but that never happened. Ah Ping the Water Monkey was faster than that! I sprinted down the narrow mud lanes through the village so I could take my seat as an equal among a sea of sons. What a feeling, one I would never forget. In all my life, I had never felt more fortunate, more special, than when I was allowed to go to school. I think those were the happiest times of my life.

On the fourth night, as I hurried to leave the house, my father called out to me.

'Ah Ping, you will stay here tonight,' said my father.

'But I have to go to school,' I said, my mouth still full of rice.

'No school tonight. Tonight, you must stay here.'

'Oh.' I tilted my head. 'But can I go tomorrow?'

'No. You must stay here tomorrow night as well.'

'Oh . . . What about after the night that? Can I go after that?'

'Ah Ping.' He sighed. 'You cannot go to school with your brothers anymore.'

'But . . . I thought . . . what about school?'

'That's enough.'

My father never snapped at me. Maybe I did something wrong? Perhaps I was a bad student and couldn't keep up with the rest of the class? Why couldn't I go anymore?

My toes curled against the stone floor, stopping me from stomping in a tantrum as hot, angry tears gushed out of eyes and down my face.

It's not fair! It's not fair.

I wanted to scream in protest, but all I could do was stay silent because isn't that what good little girls did? I was confused by my father's instructions, but I also didn't want to get into trouble. Silence would later become a language that I would speak better than anything else. Silence could become a marker of my obedience and submission.

I bowed my head and dragged myself to my corner of the house where I slept and balled up against the wall, sobbing.

'Ah Ping, it's all right. No need to cry,' Big Sister soothed. 'At least you got to go to school for three nights. That's better than me – I never got to go and I'm your Big Sister. You were really very lucky.'

She wiped the snot and tears off my face with her palm that had been roughened by years of manual labour.

'No need to cry, little one. Father must have a reason for this, and we must respect and obey him,' she said.

Indeed, there was a reason.

The older students had gone home protesting to their fathers about how a girl was in the class with them, learning right next to them, sharing their space and not just any girl – Teacher Lam's daughter. We had broken an unwritten rule and my mere presence caused an uproar in the village. Fathers came complaining, objecting to my own father's mindless decision, worried what allowing me to attend would eventually mean.

We know she is your daughter, but you know better than anyone, that girls don't go to school.

What use does a girl have with an education? Especially one so young?

What if all the other girls start asking to go to school too? What then?

Can you imagine? Empty homes, chores undone, rice fields unattended and disobedient girls who'll make their future husbands lose face!

No, no, no! Not possible. It cannot continue.

Those were some of the snippets I had overheard when fathers, uncles, grandfathers came knocking on our door. I knew my father had no choice but to comply. I would never set foot in that school ever again.

***

I went to school for only three nights, but I had learnt the most valuable lesson I could: how to write my name. Your name is the most precious thing you own and carries with it your heritage, your roots. It is the first thing your parents give you when you are born and the one thing that is left after you die.

Names are important, and I was lucky enough to be given one that had meaning. Many village children came from illiterate families, so their parents couldn't give them a meaningful name and sometimes they were given numbers – Sister One, Brother Two, Daughter Three. But not me. It was my father who named me.

林平妹

You see this character here:

林

This is Lam. 'Lam' means forest, and that is my family name. For us, the surname always comes first, and that's because family comes first. This is our root and without our roots, we are nothing, just a dead plant with no support, belonging nowhere.

平妹

That is my given name, Ping Mui. 'Ping' means equal or average but can also mean peace and 'Mui' means little sister, so altogether my name means 'little peaceful sister in the forest'. Isn't that beautiful? And it is so easy to write, anyone could do it. But for short, everyone called me 'Ah Ping'. Sadly, no one ever calls me that now . . . everyone I know who used to call me Ah Ping has all since passed on.

From time to time, I still wonder how my life would have turned out if I had got an education or at least been taught how to read and write. What kind of person would I have become? Would I have been as successful as Big Brother who later became a dai fu – a

Chinese traditional herbalist – or as well-versed as Second Brother who became a schoolteacher in China? Perhaps I could have been a nurse or a businesswoman with my own shop selling Hakka dumplings? Could you imagine? A lifetime of opportunities that were never realised. I guess this is what people mean by Fate.

Video call 1 : 24 December 2019
Christmas Eve, 4:30pm Hong Kong time

'Eh, Didi! Have you eaten yet?'

My grandmother's eyes are peeled back as if the wider she opens them, the better she can see me. Why doesn't she have her glasses on?

'Yes, Paupau. What about you? Can you hear me clearly?' I am speaking ten times louder than I usually do, enunciating every syllable even though she's always had perfect hearing.

'Hmm.' She leans over to touch the screen. 'Why is your face so small?'

'It's the screen, don't touch it or the phone will fall.'

It's my cousin's iPhone. Paupau doesn't know how to use a smartphone; she barely manages with her standard flip phone and its specially designed big buttons for seniors. *Too small. Buttons are too small!* This is how we've been communicating – my cousin pops over to Paupau's one-bedroom flat so I can video-call her in between my annual Hong Kong visits.

'I went for yum cha this morning after church. You know it's Mr Jesus' birthday, right? Have you been to church today? They don't use pushcarts any more – you have to order by ticking boxes on a piece of paper.' She scrunches her nose disapprovingly.

'What, pushcarts at church? You mean at the restaurant?' I ask, a little confused by Paupau's jumbled thoughts.

'Of course, at the restaurant. How can anyone see when it's so small? Ha? You don't even know what you're ordering.' She frowns and shakes her head as if nothing in this world could be big enough for her ageing eyes.

Dim sum restaurants stopped using steel pushcarts almost two decades ago so why does she mention this now? Has she forgotten I've been back home many times since emigrating?

'Yes, it's all tick-boxes now. A shame really . . . but you can't read the menu anyway, so why does that matter? Just tell the waiter what you want, and they'll write it down for you.'

'Ha? I cannot read but I can still recognise the characters. And it's too small! How can people read what they are getting? I'm old not stupid.' She scowls. Paupau's illiteracy is a touchy subject – it always has been.

'Yes, you're right. It is too small. Eh, Paupau, do you remember when I was a little girl, we would go for yum cha together?' I ask, trying to change the subject to a happier time. 'Do you remember that neither of us could read the menu on those pushcarts!'

'Ah yes! Yes, I remember. What a sight we must have been – an old Hakka woman and a gwai mui. We couldn't read a single word between us, but we still managed.' She beams as she sits back on the sofa. Her smile lines look thicker than the last time I saw her face to face.

'Of course! We always found a way. Eh, Paupau, did you receive my Christmas card?'

'What card? You sent a card? To me? When?' She scratches the front of her hand and picks at the skin around her thumb.

'I sent you a Christmas card about three weeks ago. Hasn't it arrived yet?'

'Really? A Christmas card for me? I don't know . . . You sent it here?' She tilts her head as her eyebrows raise in confusion. Paupau has always forgotten things, even when she was younger – 'no-brain moment' she would call it, but it never used to bother her.

There is a long pause. I can hear my cousin in the background rummaging through my grandmother's pile of correspondence – a pile she never touches. Why would she? It belongs to a world she can never access, so she chooses to ignore it. I'd do the same.

'Is it this one?' My cousin puts it in front of the screen.

'Yes, that's the one.' I replied, embarrassed at how juvenile my handwriting looks on the red envelope. I had especially written

Paupau's name in Chinese characters so she could at least recognise it was for her and then open it herself. Why hadn't she noticed it?

'Ah-yah! That's my name. Did you write this, Didi?'

'Yes, that's my handwriting.' I nod.

'How did you know how to write my name?' She is still studying the envelope with the many UK stamps affixed.

'You taught me, Paupau. Remember?'

'Really? I did? I taught you? When?'

I was eight or nine, perched against the dining table as I watched Paupau clumsily balance a blue Biro in her right hand and draw out three characters in big, unsteady handwriting. I had seen my grandmother hold a lot of things before – a meat cleaver, chopsticks, a wok, rosary beads, my school backpack, but I had never seen her hold a pen until then.

'Oh, it was a long time ago, I was just a little girl.'

'But when . . . when did I teach you? You know . . . I . . . I don't remember. My mind, it. . .' She stares straight at the screen blankly as if her eyes are searching for an answer beyond me. I bite my lip to hold back my frown.

'Why don't you open it up in front of your granddaughter? Hmm?' suggested my cousin, hoping to break Paupau's negative train of thought.

'Ah, yes, good idea,' she replies with a spark of anticipation in her voice.

She squints down to look for the envelope seal and, with her thick thumb nail that's tough enough to cut through choi sum, she tears open the envelope and pulls out the card.

'Whah, so beautiful. And look!' She gestures at my cousin. 'See, Didi also put a picture of us in it. Look. Thank you, Didi, such a good girl.' She holds the photograph close to her chest.

I watch her scan the card for words she might recognise or know. Her head tilts.

'Oh, and I see my name here.' She points at the card. 'It's my name. Look, Didi wrote my name.'

'Do you still know how to write it – your name?' I ask but as soon as the words slip out, I purse my lips. What if she's forgotten? Me and my big mouth as always.

'Ha? You think I'm so old that I would forget how to write my name? Of course, I can.' She leaps off from the sofa and is out of frame. I hear her mumbling something to my cousin about getting a pen and paper – items not usually present in her home.

'Okay, are you paying attention?' She reappears, waving a pen at me whilst a piece of paper rests on a cushion on her lap. With a deep breath, she writes her name, her hand wobbling. When she is finished, she proudly holds up the paper to the screen and I exhale with relief that she still remembers this:

林平妹

'See, this one is Lam. This is my family name,' she says, pointing to the first character. 'See these two – Ping Mui, this is my name.' Her face is radiant. It's a face I want etched into my memory no matter how many times I've seen it.

I study her handwriting. Messy strokes with uneven character sizes, the handwriting of a child.

'Now, Didi, do *you* remember how to write *your* name? Hmm?' she smirks.

I grin back at her. These are the little games we play with each other. Despite her age, she still enjoys teasing me so much that I wonder: in another life, could we have been best friends?

'Of course!' I fumble around my desk for pen and paper.

'Ha? A lefty? How can you even hold a pen properly being left-handed?' She laughs.

I pause and my head jerks back. What? But she's always known I'm a lefty. Ever since I was barely able to hold chopsticks, she would mock-scold me for using the 'wrong' hand. Being left-handed wasn't 'proper', especially for a girl.

'Lefties can still write. Hang on a second and you'll see,' I say and ignore her earlier comment. Another no-brain moment perhaps? After all, when was the last time she saw me write? Over twenty years ago, maybe more – a schoolgirl sprawled across the living room, doing my homework on the parquet floor whilst watching Sailor Moon.

'See!' I held up my name and Paupau bursts out laughing. 'What's so funny?' I glance back at my writing. Is it really that bad?

'Us! We are. What a ridiculous sight – one illiterate old woman and a gwai mui chai trying to write,' she chuckles.

I couldn't feign annoyance any more; seeing her laugh like that with her jagged-teeth-grin that's been stained by too much Vita lemon tea. She jiggles. When Paupau laughs, she doesn't just laugh with her mouth, or even face. She laughs with her whole body.

'Look at my writing. It's so ugly!' She glances back at her piece of paper and chortles. 'And yours is so big and fat.'

I'm in hysterics watching Paupau laugh uncontrollably as all shame and embarrassment dissolve. In that moment of shared joy, I think back to how my grandmother never allowed the everyday challenges she faced get in the way of taking care of me. No matter how many times her sense of self-worth was tested, even by the simplest of things like ordering food, she never let it stop her from encouraging me to be the best I could. It didn't matter that neither of us could read; we were a team and the two of us always managed because we had each other.

'It's not that bad, right?' I try to defend my poor penmanship.

'Hmmm. And how many years have you studied for? Ha?' She raises a brow and curls her lips.

I want to interject and remind her that no one ever taught me how to write in my native tongue and just like her, any characters I do know have been self-taught.

'I only went to school for three nights. Three! What's your excuse, hmm?' She smirks proudly. And she should be proud.

Life is a series of natural and spontaneous changes. Don't resist them – that only creates sorrow. Let reality be reality. Let things flow naturally forward in whatever way they like.

— Lao Tzu

Reality can flow naturally when you are privileged enough for it to do so. For the poor, the othered, the forgotten, reality is always an uphill battle.

The Japanese are Coming

I was seven years old when the Japanese invaded my village.

It started with nothing more than hushed rumours and whispers. No newspapers or radio – we were cut off from the rest of the country and didn't know of the atrocities that were occurring in the big cities or towns. News passed from mouth to ear through travellers and merchants, but so much of what they said was either out of date or thought to be unreliable. No one wanted to believe that China was at war or if there was one, it could never reach us.

But as the news of war came to us far too frequently to ignore, the quiet gossips of aunties and uncles in the village quickly turned into loud public exclamations of worry and alarm. I had never seen adults like that before – faces pulled back by fear and eyes that seemed to stare into the distance but didn't see. The adults talked incessantly about places called Shanghai and Nanking, about the Japanese and their brutality, about the terrifying sharpness of their blades.

Who are the Japanese? What did they want from us?

Until then, I had never heard of other countries or people. I didn't know other places beyond the next village even existed. My entire world was the village, my family, my home, my cow, but now all that was about to change.

I couldn't help but notice my parents' long and pale faces that hung with anxiety. I had never seen them like that before and I too, became unsettled, fearing something awful was going to happen.

'Father, the villagers are talking about the Japanese, that there is war going on in other parts of China. I hear these rumours . . . about the Japanese. It's awful what they are doing to us. Is war coming?' asked Big Brother.

'Don't worry, son. These are rumours. You know, most of the time what we hear isn't completely true. Besides, the war is happening in the big cities. That's where the Japanese are. They wouldn't come here. What would they want with us farmers, anyway? Don't worry.'

Big Brother and I exchanged glances. It was the first time my father's voice had ever trembled.

***

It was ten days before the Winter Festival, which in your sun calendar is around 21 December, so you can imagine how cold it already was, but that morning was especially chilly, so my mother wrapped me in a heavily padded cotton jacket. It was so thick I could barely squat on the floor with it on as I huddled with the other girls in the village square. We clumped together for warmth as we competed in jacks, throwing small pebbles up and down, our knuckles red raw. It was my favourite childhood game.

Without warning, screams and shouts shattered the air, drowning out our mischievous laughter.

'The Japanese are here! The Japanese are here! Run! Run for your lives! The Japanese are here!' a voice screeched.

The two older girls sprung up and dashed away, leaving me and the others frozen in confusion.

What is happening? Where did they go?

My eyes scanned everywhere for an answer, but all I could see were frenzied eyes and ashen faces of men and women running away. Big loud noises like thunder tore through the sky. I looked up and saw giant metal birds – aeroplanes zooming closer and closer to us.

'Run! Run away! Run! Run for your lives!' someone cried out.

Screams came from every direction.

What do I do? What is happening?

I sprung off the ground and ran as fast as my stubby legs could take me, but the more I ran, the fewer people I saw. My eyes darted around, searching for something recognisable as my heart hammered in my chest, but I was all alone.

Ma! I need to find Ma. I'd be safe with her.

Without thinking, I turned around and ran back towards the village, towards home.

Distorted faces, arms clutching at bundles of possessions, but none were of my mother. I searched and searched but found nothing except the remains of panic and fear – bunches of clothes, upturned bamboo baskets, discarded wooden clogs.

Wait, what is that?

I stopped and looked down. Tiny arms swung frantically as the air filled with their cries. I knelt on the muddy floor and as soon as I spotted the faded pink and red of their swaddling cloths, the hairs on the back of my neck stood up. Baby girls, they were all baby girls.

I gasped and fell back.

Where are their mothers? Why did they leave them here like that?

'Ah Ping! What are you still doing here? You've got to run! If the Japanese find you, they'll kill you. Go!'

I looked up, it was an auntie.

Maybe she knows where my parents are?

'Wait, Auntie. Wait for me!' I scurried towards her.

I tried to call out to her again, but the metal birds in the sky muted my cries for help.

No! Please don't go. Please wait for me. Wait!

But it was too late, she had disappeared into the distance. When I looked around, there was no one there, and I realised I was all alone in a deserted village. Without thinking, I ran in the same direction as the auntie until my little legs took me to the bank of a wide river.

Villagers with their children and anything else they could carry were scrambling to cross the river. My eyes searched their faces for my mother, for someone I could recognise.

'Ma! Ma! It's Ah Ping! Ma! Are you there?' I called out.

No one answered. No one turned around.

With hesitant steps, I approached the river's edge and looked down at what seemed like a bottomless stream of water. I looked around and saw there was no one else left to cross the river but me, I knew I had to cross it. I took a deep breath, biting the inside of my cheek, and stepped in.

Whah!

The cold water pierced every part of me like a thousand needles, and my insides recoiled inwards to find some inch of heat. The water reached up to my chest as my feet kept slipping on the rocks at the bottom. I stood still, too petrified to move in case the current would drag me to my certain death. To this day, I don't know how to swim.

My body bobbed up and down, feeling weightless as it battled the river. My hands tried to grab at the water, to grab at anything to help me get across as I cried for my mother to come and help me.

Ma, I am so cold. I am so afraid. Ma!

A glimmer of hope flickered in front of me when I spotted an uncle I recognised from our village. He was wading through the water with his adult son and a cow.

'Uncle. Uncle! Please help me cross. The river is so cold and deep,' I pleaded.

He stopped his cow and looked down at me.

'Help you? Ha! I'd rather help my cow cross than help you,' he spat out.

I wish I knew how to answer back, to demand he tell me why he thought a cow was more worthy than a girl, but he had already gone. Trailing behind him was his adult son.

'Brother, please help me. Please.' I begged.

He didn't even look at me and lowered his eyes as he trudged through the water as if he had never seen me.

Why wouldn't they help me?

That moment in the freezing water taught me everything I needed to know about my worth as a poor girl, which was next to nothing. Cows were worth more than us because cows weren't abandoned on the roadside by their mothers and left to die.

The icy water soaked through my thick jacket, weighing me down as the cold penetrated deep into my body.

Keep going. I am almost there. I can see the other side, I can almost touch it.

But then, out of nowhere, *dhak-dhak-dhak-dhak* sounds ripped through the air as big, loud splashes pounded all around me. I didn't dare move. Bullets from the Japanese aeroplanes shot through the air, striking the water below. *Dhak-dhak-dhak-dhak-dhak*. There were so many bullets – it was a miracle they all missed me.

When the planes left, the air was quiet again. I looked down at the water, mesmerised by the glimmer of finger-length pieces of something. I reached as far as I could into the water and grabbed a handful of them.

What are they? They are so beautiful. They must be worth a lot of money.

You know what they were? Bullet shells! I was playing with bullet shells.

Suddenly, I snapped out of my trance and looked up. I was the last one left in the river and everyone else had gone far ahead. Instinct took hold as I waded against the current, desperate to get to the other side, but the riverbank was too high for my arms and legs to crawl up. I grabbed onto the rocks and weeds in front of me, but they were slippery from moss and algae. Every time I tried to climb out, *BOOM!* I skidded and fell straight back into the water.

I don't know how many attempts it took until I finally managed to crawl out of the river. My shivering body was covered in mud and pruned hands were red raw. The villagers looked like mere dots in the distance.

'Wait for me!'

The villagers were all huddled together in silence at the bottom of a steep hill as if waiting for someone to take charge.

'Quickly,' commanded an uncle. 'We need to get up that hill so we can hide in the bushes. Hurry. Hurry!'

One by one, they clambered up the hill with their children on their backs. Those old enough had to make the climb themselves.

When it was my turn, I looked around and saw I was once again the last one. I took a big gulp.

There's no way I can get up there...

The hill may as well have been a mountain. It felt ten times higher than the riverbank, but I knew I couldn't stay behind. My tiny hands gripped onto whatever branches and weeds were in front of me as I pulled myself up.

Step. Grab. Step. Grab.

Little cuts of crimson formed in my palms and between my fingers, but I didn't stop. I had to reach the top. Just as I was about to make my last step to the top, *BAM!*

What was that?

A powerful kick. A loss of balance. A stumble.

I skidded and fell all the way back down the hill. When I looked up, I saw none other than the cruel man who had refused to help me across the river earlier. What a pok gai ham ga chaan. Why would anyone do something like that – to kick a small harmless girl? If he didn't want to help me then fine, but to have kicked me like that? There's a special place in Hell for people like him.

How will I get up there again? And why did you have to kick me, Uncle?

As I stood alone at the bottom, my fear boiled into an angry determination. This time I climbed up the hill faster than before and I knew I was going to make it to the top.

Where is everyone? Are they playing hide-and-seek?

My eyes scanned the area, hoping to recognise a familiar face, but all I spotted were villagers hiding in bushes and behind rocks, squatting and hunched over in solemn silence. Suddenly, the terrifying truth struck me: I was really alone. No mother, father, siblings, no one. I was all by myself. My body trembled.

'Eh, you there. What are you doing? Hide!' a man's voice called out.

A tug pulled at my back and jerked me into the bushes. I craned my neck to see who it was and it was none other than the same pok gai who had kicked me down the hill. I was so unlucky to have to hide next to him.

'Be quiet!' the man spat.

With no means to dry off or warm up, I had no choice but to stay in my soaked clothing. The thick cotton-padded jacket my mother had so lovingly put on me felt like an ice pack around my shivering body as the cold winter wind blew without mercy. By the evening, I was burning up as my chest tightened. A cough had developed at the worst possible time. My lungs heaved for air as I coughed and coughed.

Ouch! What was that?

Hard knuckles – the knuckles of a man – struck my head as I whimpered like a helpless kitten.

Cough.

Thump.

Sharp knuckles hit me again. You know who it was? That same ham ga chaan.

'Uncle, why did you hit me?' I asked.

'Shut up! Stop your coughing or I will beat you to death!'

Another cough slipped out and his razor-like knuckles struck me again, but this time, he did it much harder. Every part of me wanted to cry out, but I didn't dare. Instead, I bit down on my lips to contain my whelps. Pain tastes metallic.

Ma! Ma!

My mind screamed out for her, for anyone, to come and help me or to soothe me with the lie that all was going to be okay.

When the temperature plummeted at night, the air was even colder, making it harder to breathe without coughing. That pok gai was still next to me, knuckles at the ready.

Cough.

Thump.

Cough.

Thump.

Eventually, I stuffed my fist into my mouth to mute the sounds, hoping he couldn't hear me and beat me. If I cried, he would hit me harder.

I remember staring at the night sky, begging for Kwun Yum to send out a signal to my mother so she could find me and save me.

I didn't sleep that first night. I stayed up the whole time wondering when it would be morning so I could go back home to my mother.

Eight days on water

I hid up in the hill with the other villagers, learning to make myself small, practically invisible. There was nothing to eat and if there was, no one had shared it with me. A girl without her family is a nobody – she has no importance or value. No need to waste precious food on her.

For the first two days, all I could think about was how hungry I was as my tummy grumbled with increasing ferocity. Stomach acid churned away my insides throughout the day whilst my hunger pangs gnawed at me throughout the night, keeping me up as I drifted in and out of sleep. By the second day, I was so hungry I thought about eating the grass. *Cows eat grass so maybe I can eat it too?* But I was too afraid that it would make me sick.

The worst wasn't the hunger, but the thirst. It had consumed me, turning the days into one endless and feverish nightmare. My mouth was ash.

'Eh! There's a stream of fresh water just on the other side of those trees,' whispered one of the uncles.

Water? Did someone say water?

One by one, the villagers peeled themselves off the ground and scurried towards the water source like animals as I followed closely by. I watched them pick the larger leaves off the trees and use them to scoop up the water into their mouths. I copied.

The water was so cold. Each gulp hurt my chest, but still, I drank. I drank and drank until my belly blew up like a winter melon, giving me momentary relief from my hunger, but it wasn't enough to fool it. Every day, I snuck over to the stream to fill my belly that could never be satisfied, as my stomach bloated with emptiness. I was like a hungry ghost, fading in and out, all the while wondering why my mother and father hadn't found me yet. *Maybe the Japanese caught them? Are they even alive?*

A HAKKA WOMAN

Eight days. This is how long I had to survive drinking hill-water and nothing else whilst I had to hide in my damp clothes that never wanted to dry, squatting, and waiting. For eight days, I coughed and coughed, and yet no one offered to help me. No one checked if I was all right. The same people who had known me since I was born, the same people who smiled and praised my father with lip service, the same so-called neighbours – all strangers. People show their true face during times of adversity.

No rice means no energy. The hushed whispers and gossip among the villagers had quickly disappeared into a lifeless silence. All I could hear were the grumblings of empty stomachs and restless bodies. I wondered if I would be stuck on that hill, destined to drink nothing but hill-water forever. Then, out of nowhere, voices in the distance started to call out.

'The Japanese have left. Come out everyone. It's safe! The Japanese have left!'

I didn't dare move. My eyes darted to the others who didn't move either, as if in a trance.

'It's safe. They've gone. The Japanese have left. Come out!'

No, that can't be. That can't be true. I must be dreaming.

I squeezed my eyes shut and huddled into a ball, too afraid to believe those words. It must be a trick – a trick from the Japanese to kill us all.

Again, the voice called out, but this time louder. It was definitely in our Hakka dialect.

How could the Japanese know our language? That wasn't possible.

I opened one eye and peeked around to see a man warily stepping forward with his head ducked low, as if avoiding bullets that never came. Slowly, with every step, his curved back gradually straightened.

'Come out! It's true. Come, they've gone. We're safe. Come, come!' he called over and over, waving for us to join him.

First the men peeled themselves off the ground and stood up, tiptoeing out of hiding, scanning the area for signs of the Japanese.

When they were certain it was safe, they gestured for their women, children and elderly to get up.

Is it all over? Could I go home now? Will I see Ma and Ba?

With renewed energy, I leapt off my patch of ground, ready and eager to return home. Assembling their belongings, the others shuffled around while we began our slow descent down the hill.

My little legs couldn't keep up as I tried to walk as fast as I could, but the faster I moved, the bigger gasps of cold air I had to take. Each breath sliced through my lungs, squeezing my insides.

I can't breathe! I can't breathe!

Heaving and coughing, I struggled to catch my breath and slumped to the ground. I could no longer keep going. I had given up.

'Ah Ping! Ah Ping!'

It was a man's voice somewhere in the distance.

Who is calling me? Did I fall asleep?

'Ah Ping, your mother is calling for you!'

There was that voice again, but this time it seemed closer. I felt a nudge and then a light tug at my jacket.

'Get up, Ah Ping. Your mother – she is calling for you. She is down the hill. Come on, you need to get up. You can't stay here. Ah Ping!'

My eyes peeled open to the sight of a middle-aged man's face, which I immediately recognised.

'Uncle? Do I . . . do I know you?' I asked, still lying on the damp ground.

'Yes, I know your parents. Ah Ping, your mother has been looking everywhere for you for days. Come! I'll take you to her. Hurry, let's go.'

'My mother? My mother!' I cried out and sprung off the floor, ready to run down the hill.

'Wait, Ah Ping. You're going the wrong way. This way!'

It didn't matter if I slipped and fell or how tired I was or how badly I was coughing with every step. I didn't care about any of that because I had to find my mother; I had to find home again. I ran and ran, hoping if I passed one more tree or one more corner, I'd find her waiting for me.

'Ah Ping, Ah Ping, where are you?'

I know that voice!

I scurried towards the sound, my eyes searched frantically for my mother, but there was so much foliage, I couldn't see her.

'Ma? Ma! I'm here. Ma! I'm here!' I cried.

'My darling girl is that you? Where are you? Ah Ping? Ah Ping!'

I kept screaming out to her over and over until my voice became coarse. Then, as if by sheer will or magic, she was there – her unmistakable slender frame appeared through the trees.

'Ma!'

I charged towards her as my arms and legs wrapped around her body like an octopus, squeezing her as tightly as I could. I refused to let go because if I did, I might lose her again. Tears sprayed out of my eyes uncontrollably as I wailed into her arms. They were tears I had been too afraid to cry. Tears that wanted to tell her everything that had happened over the last eight days: getting lost; the baby girls; that horrible man who kicked me, who thumped me on the head day after day; the cold; the cough; drinking freezing water . . . but everything came out all at once in garbled sounds and cries.

'It's all right, Ah Ping. You are safe now. It's all right. Nothing to be afraid of. I'm here. It's all right,' my mother soothed, wiping my tears and snot with the sleeve of her jacket.

'I . . . I am sorry, Ma,' I mumbled.

'Sorry? What is there to be sorry for, silly girl? It's all right, Ah Ping. No need to cry. Hmm? Come, everyone is waiting to see you. We were all so worried.' Her voice was tender.

My mother took me by the hand and led us the rest of the way down the hill. I gripped onto her so tightly that my knuckles turned white.

I'm never letting you go. I'm not losing you again.

When we reached a clearing at the bottom of the hill, everything felt like a strange dream.

'Look everyone, it's Ah Ping. Ah Ping, you're back! Thank Kwun Yum you are safe,' exclaimed Father.

Everyone was there: my father, my brothers and my sisters, all huddled around me cheering in celebration that they had found me.

Am I dreaming? Is this my family in front of me or am I still sleeping in those bushes . . . or worse? Am I dead? Is this Hell?

I began to cry. Big Sister leapt out and hugged me so hard she wrung out all the horrific memories of the last eight days.

'Ah Ping, I was worried about you, my dear little sister.' Her voice broke.

Just like that, she had snapped me out of my confusion, and I knew it was real and I was finally safe.

'Come, we must return to the village and see what is left,' said my father.

ALL THOSE BABIES

I will never forget the smell. It was the smell of blood and charcoaled houses mixed with burning pigskin. It was the reek of something unspeakable that had happened in our village. The fire had eaten everything – the trees, the crops and the houses. Nothing was spared.

Baht-baht-baht-baht!

Sounds like corn popping broke through the eerie silence, but there was no corn, just homes and belongings still burning and crackling. Smoke rose to the sky like an offering to the Heavens, but this was not a good offering, this was a tragic sacrifice.

'Ah Ping, don't look. Close your eyes. Don't look!' shouted my mother.

But it was too late, I looked down.

Why are there so many arms and legs of dolls on the ground?

I stared at the pile but could not register what I was seeing until the horrific realisation hit me. Discarded infant girls half-wrapped in their pink swaddling cloths, drenched in crimson. A body here. A head there. All cut in half, sliced like watermelon. I shrieked, but I couldn't move or look away. Suddenly an arm jerked me back, and a hand covered my eyes.

'Don't look, Ah Ping.' cried my mother.

'Who would do such a thing?!' exclaimed Big Brother.

'Those poor baby girls!' screamed Big Sister.

'The Japanese. It's the Japanese,' said my father.

He was practically emotionless. What emotion could anyone possibly convey in the face of such horror?

'We cannot stay here. We must keep moving,' he said.

***

The moment we arrived where our house once stood, my mother collapsed onto her knees and wailed. Our little stone house, the only home I had ever known, had been reduced to charred stones and soot. There was nothing left, just rubble and buried memories.

'What are we going to do now? What are we going to do?' My mother screamed as she banged her fists against the soil.

I had never seen my mother cry before. As we stood next to her, our tears dropped to the earth, forming a pool of our collective grief. If we stayed there long enough, would the pool of our tears drown us?

'Come, we have to go. We can't stay here,' said Father.

'But where will we go? There is nothing here, nothing in the village,' said Big Brother, whose eyes never once looked away from the remains of our home.

There was a long pause, punctuated by the sound of my mother's sobs.

'Tung Ping Chau. It's an island. I heard some villagers are heading over there. It's part of Hong Kong, so we should be safe from the Japanese.'

'Where is it?'

'I think it's over those hills, across the sea. We will need to head back to the hills. If we keep walking, we should get to the seafront.' My father gestured towards the mountains behind us.

'Ma, come, we have to go.' Second Sister pulled my mother off the ground.

Ma wasn't ready to leave, her fists clenched tightly onto the soil of our home.

'It's all gone. All gone!' screamed Mother.

We had nothing except for the clothes on our backs and our cow – the same cow I had spent so many mornings taking out to graze. I can't remember how the cow came to be with us. Perhaps my father had enough foresight to take it with him when they first fled from the Japanese.

One foot in front of the other, we hiked over hills and mountains, the silence only broken by the rustling of leaves, making us jump at every sound, anxious it was the Japanese waiting to ambush us.

'Big Brother, help me. I'm so tired. I can't walk anymore.' I tugged at my brother's sleeve.

My legs were as soft and useless as cheung fun jiggling on a plate. I hadn't eaten in over eight days. In one swoop, Big Brother lifted me up effortlessly and piggybacked me most of the way. Nestled on his back with my head between his shoulder blades, my mind wandered to steaming bowls of rice piled with all the delicious foods my mother would make. My mouth drooled, leaving imprints of my foolish fantasies on my brother's back.

Stop or you'll feel worse.

But I couldn't, all I could think about was rice.

***

By that evening we reached a Hakka village that looked very much like mine, but they were luckier because the Japanese never found them. It remained untouched, safe.

'Are we here? Is this our new home?' I asked Big Sister.

'No, this village is called Ha Sa. We will stay here for the night.'

Everything that followed was a daze: the family that welcomed us, the home we sat in and the congee with dried salted fish they fed us. I remember gobbling up that warm bowl of congee so quickly that it burned my tongue. I welcomed the burn. It was a reminder that I was still alive as each spoonful soothed my throat and embalmed my body with warmth.

The next morning, as we got ready to leave, I noticed Second Sister wasn't with us.

'Big Sister, where is Second Sister?' I asked.

She kept her head down, avoiding eye contact and choosing not to speak.

'Where is she? Did something happen to her? I asked.

Still no response, so I turned to my mother.

'Ma, where is Second Sister?'

'Eh, well, your sister won't be coming to Tung Ping Chau with us. She will stay here with this family,' Mother stuttered.

'But why? Doesn't she want to come with us? Why isn't she coming?' I tilted my head.

'Ah Ping!' scolded Big Sister.

I had asked the very question a girl is never to ask: **why**. To ask why is to question, to question is to think for yourself and to think for yourself is to be disobedient. A girl's mind belonged to her family, not to herself. There is no **why** for us.

'It's all right,' Father interjected. 'Ah Ping, your sister will stay here. She will be this family's san pou chai. They will give her a place to stay and food to eat. Understood?'

I nodded, but I did not know what he meant by being a san pou chai, nor why Second Sister couldn't come with us.

Why did she have to stay with this family? Didn't she want to be with us anymore?

I wanted to ask more questions, but I knew I would get into trouble so kept quiet.

The whole time we walked towards the seafront, I was all too aware that someone —my sister – was missing. Someone had broken off a piece of our family and given it away.

VIDEO CALL 2 : 5 FEBRUARY 2020
Lunar New Year Day One, 4:30pm Hong Kong time

'Gong hei fat choi, Paupau!' I exclaim at my iPhone screen.

Paupau is wearing the same burgundy wool jumper she has worn every Lunar New Year for the last thirty years.

'Eh, Didi. Have you eaten yet? Such a good girl for calling me on New Year's Day! Gong hei fat choi!' She smiles.

'Yes, Paupau, I have eaten,' I lie. I learnt many years ago never to tell Paupau I haven't eaten – she'd force me to hang up and only call her once I've had my belly filled.

'How did you know it's Lunar New Year? I didn't know they celebrate in America.'

'Paupau, I live in England, remember? You know, the one with the Queen?'

I've lived in London for longer than I want to accept and Paupau knows that, so why does she think I'm in the States? None of our family live there.

'Oh, yes, of course I know! I know the Queen. Her head was on our coins for so long. Nice hairstyle – good look for an old woman. Very tidy.' She nods as if agreeing with herself.

'So, what are your plans for Lunar New Year? Anyone coming to visit you?'

'Hmmm, not much.' She drops her head. 'You've seen the news, right? You know what's going on in Hong Kong . . . not so safe anymore, especially for an old woman like me. What a big mess out there.' She sighs, scratching the skin on the back of her hand with her thumb.

'Have you got enough face masks? They are so hard to come by these days, but I can get some and send them over to you?'

'Yes, yes, I have some. Thanks to your Auntie Han – you remember, the one who lives in Japan? I can't believe she went from shop to shop just to get some masks for me and then she had them airmailed to me all the way from Tokyo! Must have been very expensive, but she says Japanese masks are better. She's lived in Japan for so long, I'm surprised she hasn't forgotten how to speak our tong hua.' Paupau huffs as she rubs her face.

'How long has Auntie Han lived in Japan for? Over thirty years?'

'Something like that. I still remember when she told me she was going to marry a Japanese man, I thought she was going to send me to an early grave.'

'But that was over thirty years ago. You still remember that?'

'Of course! How can I forget? After everything I have taught her, after all that she knows about what the Japanese did.'

'But Uncle has got nothing to do with the war. He wasn't even born yet.' I try to soothe and reason with her but I know it's pointless – Paupau is the most stubborn person I know.

'No, you don't understand, Didi.' Her jaw tightens as if vivid memories of her fleeing the Japanese are still too sharp to take out without slicing her.

'I thought you went to their wedding, didn't you? I remember seeing photographs – you were in them, you went to Japan.'

'Yes, I went. In the end, I had to go.' Paupau shuffles closer, her face fills up the whole screen.

I can see every wrinkle, every liver spot, in high definition.

'How could I let my daughter be on her own with no relatives for her wedding, especially in a foreign land? Ha? I couldn't do that to her. I wouldn't be able to live with myself. It wouldn't have been right. So, I told myself I will tolerate this marriage. But that was until I saw their family shrine!' Her eyes widen.

'They are not like us with statues of Mrs Mary or Mr Jesus, not even a statue of Buddha or Kwun Yum. You know what they have instead at home? A large framed black-and-white photo of my future son-in-law's grandfather – a big portrait of a Japanese Imperial officer in his full uniform. As if that wasn't bad enough, right below the portrait was his long sword. It was the same sword the Japanese used during the war!' Paupau measures the length of the sword with her hands, eyes transfixed as if it was really in front of her. Her lips turn white, face ashen with fear.

'I froze like a corpse, totally stiff, and suddenly I couldn't breathe! All I could see were those baby girls . . . all those dead babies all chopped up and left there. My heart was beating so fast and my whole body shook like I was possessed by a demon. Oh, that sword! Those babies . . . those poor baby girls!' Paupau cries out as her jaw quivered.

'My son-in-law no doubt saw my reaction, but he couldn't understand why. You see, in Japan they don't teach the full story, the *real* story of what happened during the war. He didn't know, so your Auntie Han explained everything to him. When I had finally calmed down, he poured some tea and asked my daughter to translate. This young Japanese man kowtowed to me three times and offered me the tea as a form of apology on behalf of his grandfather and what had happened to me. He then promised that if I gave him a chance, he would spend the rest of his life repaying this blood debt by taking good care of my daughter.'

Paupau's voice breaks as a tear rolls down her leathered face before looking up at me with a deep sigh.

'How do I say no after that? He is innocent, right? As you said, he wasn't born yet, not even a thought in his father's trousers. Fate had decided he would be born Japanese, and it was destiny that he and my daughter found each other. So, I drank the tea as a sign of acceptance and attended their wedding ceremony. I sat amongst the children and grandchildren of my enemy. I ate their rice, took part in their customs, slept in their bed. I did this all for my daughter because that is what a mother does. This is what sacrifice means. You must put aside your own feelings and desires for your child.' She wipes the tears from her face with her palm and it pulls at her skin. She's always been so rough with her body that it's no wonder I'm so rough with mine, too. I had inadvertently copied the woman who raised me.

'Do you hate the Japanese?' I ask.

I've always wondered how she manages to reconcile Japan's past with its present influence, especially for someone who has so many Japanese products at home and who loves their eel donburi. How does she keep the two separate?

Paupau raises an eyebrow and exhales as her shoulders relax.

'Hate? I hate what they did, yes. But this cannot be changed. Past is past. It cannot be changed and cannot hate or blame the innocent. It's not their fault.'

Auntie Han and her husband are still married to this day.

A place called Tung Ping Chau

Maybe you were too young to remember, but I will never forget the first time you saw the sea – how your big brown eyes widened with excitement as you jumped up and down. Well, that was the same for me too.

By the late afternoon, we arrived at the seafront. A dark blue expanse of water stretched beyond my sight. It was seemingly endless. The sand felt warmed by the sun, was soft against my feet.

'We'll need to cross,' said Father.

Cross that? But how? I don't know how to swim!

The memory of crossing the freezing river alone flashed through my mind, and now the idea of crossing a sea seemed impossible.

'Look! Those fishermen over there! They seem to be helping people onto their boats,' said Big Brother. 'That's so kind of them to help.'

'Maybe. But everything has a price, son,' replied my father.

Families – all with the same exhausted grey faces of Despair – huddled in front of the sampans, offering all they had for safe passage to Tung Ping Chau. Some I recognised from the village, others I had never seen before, but all were readily handing over their possessions. Women removed their gold and jade jewellery whilst men took out banknotes and coins that had been tucked away in secret pockets in their undergarments.

As we approached a sampan, a giant of a man stepped forward. His fat belly, and thick black hairs, protruded out of his open shirt. I had never seen anyone as large as that fisherman before. I gasped.

'Please, sir, can you take us? We don't have much, but we have our cow. Would that be sufficient for safe passage for me and my family?' asked my father.

'Hmmm. A cow? That's all you've got?' The giant arched an eyebrow as he scanned our cow up and down and then kissed his teeth loudly. 'Fine. Get on,' he grunted. The fisherman's voice was thick, and his words sounded funny, as if he spoke with an accent.

The choppy water rocked the little sampan wildly from side to side, ready to throw us overboard.

Will this boat sink? If I fall into the water, will Father save me? Can he swim?

My mind shot from one thought to another, but my fear of the water was quickly drowned by the dread I began to feel as I sensed the fisherman's glare.

Why is he staring at me? Why is he looking at me like that?

I cowered behind my mother, clutching to the edges of her shirt, hoping to evade his eyes that seemed to engulf me. Every time I snuck a glimpse to see if he was still looking at me, I caught his gaze and the terrifying size of him. The giant's shoulders bulged as wide as a bull with arms thicker than both my legs combined.

Don't look at me. Stop it!

But the giant fisherman didn't stop. His shadow cast over me the entire time as he rowed us closer to Tung Ping Chau.

The low tide made Tung Ping Chau's seashore look like the enormous mouth of a monster with its jagged and broken rock, teeth ready to rip and slice.

'Is this it? Are we here?' asked Ma.

'Get off!' barked the giant.

As we clambered out of the sampan, the giant smiled at me – it was a smile of gaps and yellow stains. I shivered.

'Where do we go now?' asked Big Brother.

'Let's follow them.' Father pointed at the other refugees heading towards the island.

***

'Come in, come in. Please come in,' said a man a little older than my father. He was standing outside a large stone building in the main village, inviting us in.

'Excuse me, sir, but where are we?' asked Big Brother.

'This is our school, well, it used to be, but not anymore. Come, come inside,' replied the man.

A school? But it's huge.

It was three times the size of the school in my village, but the stones of the building were so weathered with damp moss and overgrown vines it looked more like an abandoned ghost house.

A stench filled my nostrils. It was the smell of salt and disease. It was the smell of bodies too close together, breathing uncertainly as families packed themselves inside like canned sardines on any space they could find on the floor, crammed together for warmth. As mainlanders, we were unfamiliar with this kind of cold – a cold from the sea, a cold of damp and wind, a cold that sunk deep into our bones.

'Let's rest here.' My father gestured to a small space between two families.

The floor was like ice, and we had nothing to line it with. My mother placed Little Sister on her lap whilst we sat clumped together like sticky rice.

'Are you crazy? You can't light a fire in here. You will burn us all to death!' someone shouted.

I looked up and saw a few families down was a man who had built himself a small wood fire. I caught a whiff of fire and smoke.

'You mind your damn your business. It is freezing in here. I'd rather burn to death than freeze!' the man growled.

'He's right, you're going to kill us all!' someone else yelled.

'Be quiet, you! At least it'll make us warmer.' barked another.

All at once, everyone erupted into a shouting frenzy. Their loud voices echoed and vibrated in the school hall, but as soon as the heat from the fire spread, the arguing fizzled out and we could only hear the crackle of the wood. The familiar smell of wood burning enveloped me, reminding me of home and masked the awful stench wafting from everyone else.

That first night was uncomfortably silent. All I could hear were coughs and sneezes. No one spoke, too exhausted, or traumatised by recent events. The Japanese had left scars on us that would never heal.

The next morning, some of the locals came to donate food. Simple stuff like sweet potatoes, radish or tapioca – cheap foods that could satisfy our hunger pangs quickly, but we didn't dare complain. Food was scarce during times of war, and we were deeply grateful for their generosity.

The moment someone handed me a boiled sweet potato, I stuffed the entire thing into my mouth so quickly I choked. I wanted to swallow it whole so that the emptiness I felt called Hunger could be filled.

'Ah Ping, slow down or you will choke to death,' my mother scolded.

'Eh, there's more. Here, children, eat.' My father pulled out more sweet potatoes from his jacket pockets.

'How did you get more food?' asked Big Sister.

'It's from the village chief. He gave us extra,' said Father.

'Oh?' My mother raised an eyebrow.

'That man who welcomed us yesterday, did you know he is the village chief? I was asking him about the school, and I told him I was a schoolteacher, then we got to talking and it turns out his family name is also Lam. Isn't that a coincidence? Well, as soon as he knew we have the same family name, he snuck more food for us. What a generous man. So, eat more. You'll all need your strength.'

My father placed another sweet potato in my hands and I rammed it into my mouth before I had even finished the first one, but still, my hunger did not subside.

Is there more? Can I get one more?

A HAKKA WOMAN

I looked up at Father. My eyes pleaded, hoping there was more, and he would miraculously pull out another sweet potato, but there was nothing left. As soon as I finished eating, the hall felt silent again, as if we were all waiting for something to be announced, something to happen, and if we spoke, we would miss it.

***

Except for the dying glow from the small wood fires, nightfall had blanketed the school hall. The whispers of two men rustled me out of my light sleep.

'Don't see it as selling. You need to think about this logically. You can't feed them all,' said a man's voice.

'Yes, but my wife will certainly object. They are too young,' said another who sounded a lot like my father.

'Younger is better. It would make it easier for them to adapt.'

'I suppose . . .' My father sighed.

What are they talking about? Selling? Selling what? We had nothing left to sell.

As I stayed motionless on the floor, a knot formed in my stomach, but I didn't know why. I don't think I slept that night.

Seventy Hong Kong dollars

'Ah Ping, wake up.'

I felt a nudge on my shoulder. It was my mother.

'Hurry, it's time to get up.'

Before I could ask what was happening, she was already fussing over my little sister and me like it was a festival day, scrubbing our hands and faces with a damp cloth, combing our hair and braiding it with extra care. She took us by the hand and led us up to the front of the hall, where many other children stood.

Why are they all standing there? Where are you taking me?

There were more girls than boys, but all ranged in age. Some were as young as my sister and me, and some were around eleven or twelve, but all were children instructed to stand in a straight line.

'Now, both of you stand here in this line and be very still. Don't move. Bow your head and don't talk.' My mother spoke quickly as she brushed the strayed hair from my face.

What is happening? Why do I have to stand here?

'Ma!' I called out, but she couldn't hear me. My mother had joined the crowd of people gathered in front of us.

I peered over to my left and then to my right. One of the older girls at one end was sobbing uncontrollably, as if someone had just died. I looked out in front, seeing only tanned faces and eyes of strangers staring back at me.

Chief Lam nudged each child forward, one by one, announcing their age as the crowd waved banknotes in their hands, bellowing over each other.

'Fifty dollars!'

'Seventy dollars!'

'I'll take her. Eighty for that boy there.'

'Forty for her!'

Then, each child was led away, and the line of children grew shorter and shorter.

Where are they going? Why are you taking them away?

'Ma. No, Ma! Please, please don't sell me!' screamed an older girl as she was being dragged away.

Sell? Am I being sold? Is that what I heard last night? But . . . that can't be. Father wouldn't sell me. I'm not a cow. I'm not a cow!

My eyes flashed over to the doorway, but my legs wouldn't budge as my stomach pulsated with sharp stabbing pangs. A sour taste formed in my mouth. My mother and father were nowhere to be seen.

Someone pushed me forward and as my head lifted up like a goose ready for slaughter, my eyes caught sight of him. It was the same fat, hairy belly from the boat, the same fat, hairy belly that stuck out, the same bulging shoulders and the same cold, piercing eyes.

That's the giant from the boat. What are you doing here? No, don't look at me!

'Girl, Hakka, seven years old.'

'I'll take her,' the giant grunted as he stepped forward, towering over the other locals.

'Seventy dollars.'

'Sold! To Mr Tang.'

No, no. It can't be. Please, no. Anyone but him. No!

Without any warning, an arm jerked me away from the line of remaining children. As I searched for my mother, my head spun with confusion and fear.

'Ma! Ma!'

As soon as I saw her, my hands went to grab at her jacket.

'Ah Ping,' said my mother as she knelt in front of me. 'Now listen to me very carefully, as we don't have much time. You must promise me you will be a good girl and listen to the Tang family like they are your own parents. Please be good. Ah Ping, your mother is sorry.' Her voice broke.

As my mother stood up, silent tears streamed down her face, tears she did not try to hide.

'Ma, please. Ma!' I screamed, refusing to let go of her. I had lost her once, I couldn't lose her again. I desperately clung to her with all my strength.

'Remember my daughter, you are Hakka.'

With those last words, I felt a pair of arms pull me away from her and I let go.

'Ma. Ma, please don't leave me.' I called out, but my mother turned away and disappeared into the crowd.

A middle-aged woman seemed to have come from nowhere, as she draped a red cotton dress over me and blindfolded my eyes. Suddenly, I felt I was being picked up and piggybacked.

'Let me down!' I kicked frantically, but those arms gripped me tighter.

Did my father sell me? Why would Ma agree to it? Cows get sold and I'm not a cow. I'm a girl!

As my body bobbed up and down on a stranger's back, the same thought ran through my mind, over and over – that my parents had sold me and to none other than the giant fisherman I was so terrified of. This was how I was taken to Deng Uk – Tang House, in Tai Tong Village, headed by *him* – Gong Tau.

Many years later, I would come to learn that my youngest sister was also sold, for fifty Hong Kong dollars to the Gao family. They had also blindfolded her. We all were. That way we couldn't recognise the way back if we ever ran away.

Seventy dollars. That was how much I was worth.

A child's life is like a piece of paper on which every person leaves a mark.

Chinese Proverb

Tang House

I used to love piggyback rides when I was a little girl.

I remember my brothers would put my little sister and me on their backs and race each other. 'Faster, faster!' I would order Big Brother, pretending I was riding a wild boar. Every time we would quarrel over who had won the race, only to end up in hysterical giggles on the ground. But this piggyback was different. This piggyback smelt of salt, sweat and the sea.

Without warning, I was lowered, and the blindfold removed. Everything was all *mcc,* mong chaa chaa. When I rubbed my eyes to see more clearly, I noticed the silhouette of an enormous woman with broad shoulders. I had never seen such a large woman before. In those days, being fat was a symbol of prosperity and affluence as it meant you could afford to eat and live well. Everyone wanted to be fat.

The woman was tapping her foot impatiently as if she had been waiting. As she scanned me up and down, her eyes narrowed, barking at me in sounds similar to Hakka, but I couldn't understand her. When I didn't respond, she grabbed me by my pigtails and yanked me closer to her.

'Are you stupid, mute or deaf? What do they call you?' spat the woman. I think that was what she said.

My shoulders folded inwards as I hunched my neck, trying to hide my hair so she couldn't grab them again.

'Ah Ping,' I muttered and bowed my head.

More words were barked at me, too many to make out. *Why . . . skinny . . . husband . . . stupid . . . Hakka.*

Why: this is the one I heard the most and the one I understood the least. I didn't know why I was brought to that house or why I had been sold. But what puzzled me most was why a woman I had never met could be so angry with me.

A HAKKA WOMAN

Finally, when the woman tired of shouting at me, she waved some instructions at Mrs Piggyback, who then led me to a small courtyard behind the house where I was stripped to my undergarments and scrubbed down with a wet cloth. My little hands tried to cover my body as I balled myself up to hide. I had never been naked in front of anyone who wasn't my mother or Big Sister before. Shame tastes sour – not the sour of citrus summer fruits. No, shame tastes sour like old vinegar that prunes and burns.

Satisfied that I was clean, the woman handed me a dark blue cotton jacket and trousers. Seeing how they hung on me, she rolled up my sleeves and trouser cuffs, the entire time not exchanging a single word with me. I wondered if there were other little girls like me in the house being scrubbed down and dressed in clothes they would have to grow into.

Her hand gripped the hem of my sleeve as she led me to a room smaller than a closet, then pushed me in, closed the door and left. I stood there motionless in my oversize clothes as I looked around. The room stank of damp.

'Hello? Hello?' I called out.

No one answered. I went for the door, but the handle was too high for me to reach, even on my tiptoes.

'Hello?' I cried out louder. 'Is someone there?'

No one answered.

'Ma? Ba? Anyone?'

I banged on the door repeatedly until my fists ached, but still no one answered.

'Ma? Ba? Is anyone there?'

Suddenly I realised I was locked inside this strange room, inside a stranger's house. My heart hammered in my chest as I crumbled onto the ground and sobbed. I heaved for someone to hear me and let me out. When night fell and I had stopped crying, no one had come. I found a bundle of mouldy and damp blankets in the corner and laid out a sleeping area on the floor.

Before long, darkness filled the room, except for the moonlight through the window as shadows cast monsters and demons on the walls, playing with my mind.

If I couldn't see them, they can't hurt me.

I wasn't afraid of the dark until then.

I huddled in the corner and shut my eyes, but other monsters haunted me that night. My mother's last words, the way her eyes looked when she said sorry, the absence of my father whom I had always counted on, the jagged-teeth smile of the giant when he had bought me.

I remember wondering how long I had to stay in that room, or in that house. I remember thinking I must have been a worthless daughter if my parents could sell me like that. I remember thinking I must have done something truly terrible for them not to want me.

'Ma, Ma!' I cried out to the darkness, but only silence replied. I cried myself to sleep.

***

They kept me in that dark, clammy little room for seven days and seven nights, opening the door only twice a day to bring me some thin rice congee and water.

'Auntie, please, can I leave? Do you know my mother? Can I see her?' I asked Mrs Piggyback every time she cracked open the door, but she would shake her head, not saying a word before hurrying out of my prison.

Every night I fell asleep weeping for my mother, begging for her to come and take me away. In my daze, I heard her voice reminding me, 'Ah Ping, don't cry. You cannot cry. You must pick up your tears and swallow them because crying will not help you.' Recalling her words, I wept harder. My eyes were like dried-up tangerine peels.

In between sobs I uttered childish prayers as I bargained with Nobody that if I could return to my family, I would be the perfect daughter. I made promises never to talk back, to stop asking questions, to eat less and do more. I repeated these promises like prayers over and over, but in the morning when I woke up and realised it was not a terrible dream, I cried all over again.

Around the fifth day, I understood my mother wasn't coming for me – no one was. I had to accept that I had to stay in this stranger's home, but for how long? Not knowing was like being handed a prison sentence without an end date and my crime was simple: I was born both poor and a girl.

'Get up!'

It was the woman, wearing the same disapproving frown as when she first saw me.

Was I going to be let out? Was it all over?

I had counted seven days.

I sprung off the floor and stood at attention.

'Listen carefully. My husband bought you. You're nothing but a san pou chai, you're just property. We own you and that means you will do everything we tell you. You will listen and obey. My son Tin Yeung is to be your master and when the time comes, you will be given to him as his wife. You better be worth all that money my husband spent to buy you.'

Words shot out through her clenched jaw, unflinching and unmoving. Her glare warned me what would happen if I should disappoint her.

I didn't understand everything she said, but I understood enough. There was no going back to my mother and father, no going back to my old village, and no escape from this stranger's house. From that moment on, I was Tang House's property – I was their san pou chai.

SAN POU CHAI

I had to be a fast learner. No one in Tang House spoke Hakka, and I didn't speak Tung Ping Chau dialect. Even though some words sounded similar, and I could guess their meaning, there were times, especially in the beginning, when I had no idea what Ga Pau – my mother-in-law – demanded of me.

'What a stupid girl. It's no wonder you Hakka people are cursed to be farmers all your life. Useless idiot!' she spat out.

'Hakka': this single word, one that my mother told me never to forget, became something dirty and disgusting in her mouth.

There were other times when I would simply forget and reply to Ga Pau in Hakka –the words of my mother's tongue rolled out my mouth so much easier.

'What? Stop speaking in Hakka! No one speaks Hakka here. Incompetent idiot.'

If you repeat the same thing enough times to a child, it eventually becomes true. 'Hakka' soon became synonymous with other words I learnt in Tung Ping Chau dialect: stupid, useless, idiot and incompetent. And I, being a Hakka girl, was all those things. If I forgot, there was always a slap to the back of my head to remind me.

'Ah Ping! Scrub the floors. Wash the clothes. Go to the well and fetch more water. Chop up more firewood for dinner. Air the bedding. Massage my shoulders. Wash out the mah tong.' Orders Ga Pau would bark at me, an endless list of chores I had to do without complaint.

It had always baffled me that for someone who didn't work, Ga Pau was certainly an expert at ordering me around.

What does she do all day? Doesn't she get bored? Why doesn't she work?

As I carried out my chores, I would steal glimpses of her, transfixed by her large winter melon belly that stretched out her cotton blouse. So big that I had always assumed she was pregnant.

By the time I was around nine years old, I got into a little routine. I knew exactly what time to start the wood fire for lunch and dinner, how much water I needed for the perfect rice, and when Ga Pau would fall asleep in her wooden chair for her afternoon nap.

One day, when Ga Pau was taking her usual post-lunch nap, I snuck out into the courtyard. Unless I was chopping wood or hanging laundry, Ga Pau didn't like it when I was outside in the courtyard. She wanted me nearby, at her beck and call. Early afternoons were quiet, which for a nine-year-old water monkey like me, meant boring.

A few small pebbles on the ground caught my eye; they were smooth and round enough for jacks. I hadn't played jacks in such a long time, not since the Japanese stormed my village. In fact, I had played nothing with anyone since I arrived at Tang House. I had no friends and no companions. It was just me, myself and my imagination.

I stared at the pebbles for a moment before silently picking five of the smoothest ones I could find. With the little stones in my hand, I paused.

I've done all my chores for now and Ga Pau is asleep . . . isn't she?

I peeked over my shoulder and saw Ga Pau snoring as loudly as ever. I squatted on the floor and, with a deep breath, threw the pebbles up in the air. The first time they clacked as they hit the floor, I tensed.

Did she hear me? Was that too loud?

When no one came out, I collected the pebbles again and decided to go for it. The higher I threw the pebbles, the more I giggled with my imaginary friends.

'You little lazy shit!'

A sudden yank of my pigtails jerked the back of my head and dragged me across the courtyard. It was Ga Pau!

'Please. No, please! I'm sorry, Ga Pau. I'm sorry,' I begged. My hands swung wildly as I tried to hold on to my plaits, fearful she was going to tear out all my hair.

'You want to play? Ha? You are not here for playing!'

'I'm sorry. I'm sorry. Please.'

With one hand, she pinned my right hand against the wall as she ripped off her wooden clog with the other.

'You lazy little shit. You want to play? Ha? Don't you know you're here to work?'

BAM!

She smashed her clog onto my knuckles, and I squealed like an animal.

'This will teach you to never play again!'

BAM!

My hand! Stop please. Stop!

But she was too strong, and I couldn't tear away from her grip as I cried in garbled sounds for help.

BAM!

'I better not catch you playing again, or I will chop off your hand!'

As she dropped the clog onto the ground and slipped it back on, I noticed a smirk form in the corner of her mouth. Without a second glance, Ga Pau marched back inside, her wooden clogs clacking along.

Whimpering, I collapsed onto the ground and hunched over like a helpless animal. My hand shook uncontrollably from the agonising pain that throbbed and seared through my whole body. Salty tears stung the gaping wound as I rocked myself back and forth. Cries turned into big gasps of air as each breath became a struggle. Blinded by pain, I had a terrifying thought.

What if my hand is broken and I can't work with it? What if I were to lose my hand? What then? Ga Pau would surely find some way to punish me. She always does.

There were no disinfectants back then, no first-aid kits with all those magic wipes, sterile bandages and creams. Even if we did, I wouldn't have known what to do with them, so I did what any nine-year-old would have done: I wrapped my knuckles with old rags so it wouldn't sting as much every time I washed rice or clothes.

Don't let Ga Pau see your wound.

I don't know why I didn't want her to see what she had done to me. Would she have behaved any differently if she did? I doubt it. I guess I thought if she didn't see my wounds, she wouldn't have the chance to shout at or hit me.

***

'What's wrong with your hand?'

It was Ga Pau's son, my so-called future husband.

'None of your business,' I muttered.

We were outside in the courtyard and the sun was out. Perfect weather for laundry, not so great for hanging clothes with one hand.

'You better tell me, or I'll tell my mother,' he whinged.

'Nothing,' I replied, trying to brush him off.

He was always such a brat, but I didn't trust him not to tell on me or make stuff up about what I had said or done to his mother.

'I hurt my hand,' I mumbled.

As soon as the words parted my lips, they quivered. It was all so fresh in my mind that I could still hear the thump of the clog, the crush of my knuckles.

'My mother says you're nothing but a clumsy and stupid girl. That's probably why you hurt your hand. Stupid girl.'

'I'm not stupid.'

'Of course you are. Stupid girl! My mother says you're just a san pou chai, and that means you're property.'

'Stop it!'

'Crippled Hakka girl!' He pointed at my bandaged hand, taunting me with his laughter.

I gritted my teeth so I wouldn't spit out words I'd later regret as I balled my left hand into a fist.

He doesn't look that much bigger than me, maybe about an inch or so . . . If he hits me, I could hit him back, right?

I pictured his hand being bashed repeatedly with his mother's clog so he could feel what it was like, so he could taste my pain, but all I could do was stand there mute, like the useless idiot he said I was.

***

A couple of weeks passed since the clog incident when I noticed a putrid smell following me everywhere and a yellow liquid oozing from my wound.

'What is that smell? Ah Ping, come here and let me see your hand,' said Mrs Piggyback one morning as we were preparing breakfast.

I shuffled towards her.

'Ah-yah! That smell, it is revolting. Ah Ping, undo those wraps.'

I carefully unbandaged my hand. The wound had swelled up twice in size, red and raw, thick with pus. The moment she saw my bare hand, Mrs Piggyback gasped.

'How long has it been like this? Ha? This is really infected. Stop wrapping your knuckles! You're making it worse. Listen, you need to let it dry out so it can heal. Poor girl. You see this pus? That's the infection. I'm surprised you're not sick. If it gets any worse, you'd lose your hand.'

Lose my hand? No! I can't! I only wanted to hide the wound. I didn't mean for it to get worse. What have I done? I am going to lose my hand.

Tears sprayed out of me like a burst sewage pipe. Everything I had been keeping inside me suddenly exploded all at once.

'Don't cry, Ah Ping. It will be all right, it will heal. Don't worry. Let me see if I have some alcohol for you to clean it. Hmm? I'll bring it to you later. But you must stop crying. You know Ga Pau will beat you if she heard you,' she soothed.

I was lucky to have Mrs Piggyback. She was the only person in Tang House who was ever nice to me and checked up on me to ensure I was surviving. Because that was what it was – surviving.

Mrs Piggyback returned in the evening with a bottle of alcohol and various ointments to clean my wound. Eventually, my hand healed as if it had never been injured. I ended up having beautiful hands for a Hakka woman. See, look how beautiful my hand is, even with all my liver spots.

***

'Ah Ping, come here,' commanded Ga Pau.

It was late afternoon and Ga Pau was waiting for me in her dining room, sat on a stool with one foot up as she picked her nose with her extra-long pinkie nail.

'Take those bowls and plates over there into the kitchen. They are new, so you better be careful,' said Ga Pau.

Two ceramic towers stood in front of me. I took a big gulp at the daunting task. Each tower was half my height, and I knew there was no way I could take all that. To be on the safe side, I decided to take one small pile at a time.

'What are you doing? Take them *all* to the kitchen. Come on, I haven't got all day!'

I held my breath as I wrapped my arms around the pile of china.

Don't break them. Don't lose balance!

A wobble and then . . .

Oh no!

CRACK!

A few plates had slipped from under my fingers and smashed onto the floor. I shut my eyelids, not daring to move as my shoulders hunched up, waiting for Ga Pau's hand on my head.

'You stupid, clumsy idiot!' she shouted as she grabbed the pile of china off me before I could break any more dishes.

What? Aren't you going to hit me?

I was almost shocked, but just as Ga Pau had securely placed the pile of china on the table, her thick hand walloped me across the head.

'Useless idiot!' she spat.

Another smack, but this time I tried to cower and protect my head with my arms.

'How dare you cover your head. Put your hands down. Put them down!' Ga Pau yanked my guard down. 'Stupid, useless Hakka girl.'

The strikes continued. Ga Pau spared no part of my body.

Stop hitting me. Stop it!

I don't know what came over me at the moment, but I knew I had eaten enough of her blows. I wasn't going to take anymore of her punishment and darted out of the kitchen and into the courtyard. I had to get away.

'Ah-yah, how dare you run away from me! Get back here. Get back here now!'

Ga Pau kept shouting as she chased me to a dead end. Backed into a corner and with nowhere to escape, she caught up with me easily. Her eyes widened like a deranged beast's, ready to devour her prey. Her jaw pulled back as her arm raised, ready to strike.

This is going to hurt more than usual.

I was being punished. The first strike was for breaking the plates, the second was for daring to run away. Every strike in between and after was simply the usual treatment. Eventually Ga Pau had tired herself out and stopped.

'Clean yourself up. Filthy shit,' she barked.

Before returning inside, I caught sight of her. There it was – that same smirk of satisfaction from the time she smashed my knuckles. Was it pride? I always felt she enjoyed hitting me, she relished it.

Since that day, I have never broken a single dish again. Why do you think most of my dishes are plastic? Plastic doesn't break, even if dropped ten thousand times. Good for clumsy hands like mine.

VIDEO CALL 3 : 7 MARCH 2020
Paupau's 88th birthday, 4:30pm Hong Kong time

'Happy birthday, Paupau!' I am giddy, practically singing out the words.

'Eh, Didi! It's you. Have you eaten yet?' Paupau is wearing her favourite fuchsia turtleneck and bright purple jacket with the gaudy floral pattern. I love how in all the years I have known her, she has always refused to wear plain blue or black – the traditional colours of a poor Hakka woman. For her, the brighter and the more floral, the better.

'Yes, I have, Paupau. Happy birthday. Wishing you good health and a long life!'

'But it's not my birthday. My birthday has passed.' She scowls.

'I know, but I couldn't remember the lunar one. Today is your sun calendar birthday.'

'Hmmm. Sun calendar . . . it's not the same,' she tuts. 'But anyhow, thank you for calling. Did you know I'm eighty-eight? I'm so old! How did I get this old? I'm all wrinkly. You must think I look so ugly. I look more and more like my mother.' She pulls at the loose skin under her neck like an elastic band.

I've shown pictures of her to my friends who refuse to believe she is eighty-eight. *Really? More like seventy-eight.*

'Your mother?' I raise an eyebrow. She rarely brings her mother up and when she does, it's often as a passing comment, an anecdote.

'Oh yes, she looked like a dried tangerine peel in her old age. Just like me!' She studies herself in the small square of the screen, still tugging at her no-longer elastic skin as if to measure all her wrinkles.

'Have you got any photos of her? What did she look like?' I have a vague memory of a very old photograph tucked somewhere in Paupau's room. A memory or a fabrication?

'Erh, I think so. Hang on a minute. Let me go and find it.' She jumps off the couch and dashes into her bedroom before I could get a word in. Sounds of plastic boxes being moved, furniture shuffled. Where is this photograph if she's having to move so much stuff around?

'Ah, here it is!' I hear her call out in the background.

'Paupau, you okay there?' I still can't see any sign of her.

'Look, see?' She pops a discoloured photograph in front of the screen. 'Can you see it? It's right here.'

I recognise my grandmother's unmistakable grin immediately in the photograph. Standing next to her is a skinny bright-eyed old woman with a hunched back and equally old man wearing a stern expression and their traditional dark blue Hakka clothing. Behind them is a small wooden hut surrounded by untamed foliage.

'That's . . . that's your mother?' I point to the old woman.

'Yes! Clever girl. And that there – that is my father.' Her smile fades into a slight frown as she holds the photograph closer to her face. 'This is the only picture I have of them, and this was also the last time I saw them before they died,' she laments, with her eyes still fixated on her parents.

'Paupau, can I ask you something?'

I want to ask her about her parents, how she feels about them having sold her, but how do I phrase such a question? We never talk about how we feel, not directly at least. Feelings get bundled up, woven tightly into a ball of trauma that we learn to eat and bury deep inside us. If I were to ask her, would she tell me?

'Yes, Didi. What is it?'

'It's about your parents . . . I . . . well, I mean . . .' I stutter, averting my eyes. I have never asked my grandmother such a direct question before. If I don't ask her now, she may be too old one day to want to answer, or even remember.

'What about my parents?'

'Well . . . when you were a san pou chai . . . I mean, weren't you angry with them at all? You were so young, and they sold you.

It wasn't even like an arranged marriage, they just sold you. How do you forgive something like that?'

'Ah-yah, Didi!' she admonishes me. 'They had no choice. They didn't have anything, not enough to feed themselves. How could they have taken care of me? Ha? Besides, everyone was selling their sons and daughters at the time, anyway. That was how it was, nothing special, nothing sad about it. It was the reality of life after the war.'

'But—' I try to interrupt.

'No choice!' she snaps back and slaps her hands together. 'During war, people do regrettable, terrible things. That was how things were.'

'But . . . you weren't angry at them? Not even a little bit? Really?'

Paupau takes a deep, long breath and as she exhales, her shoulders slump.

'If I were to be angry with them, what does it matter now? Being angry with them changes nothing.' Paupau's voice is calm.

Is this a coping mechanism? She has always been this way – the more painful a memory, the more stoic she appears to be, as if she refuses to feed her monsters anymore tears.

'But I do wonder from time to time what my life would have been like if the Japanese never came, if I had never been sold and I was never a san pou chai. Ah-yah . . . never mind. Past is past.'

Master-in-training

Tang Tin Yeung. I hate that name – a name that burns like acid in my mouth. Even after all these years, I cannot bring myself to refer to him by his real name. He doesn't deserve it. To me, he will always be Zeoi Mao. The origins of how he came to be known by this name will come later.

Zeoi Mao was the first-born son and spoiled as the prince of the household. He was about a year older than me and looked so much like his father with his dark skin, bulgy fisheyes and broad shoulders. When I first arrived, Zeoi Mao behaved like any other little boy – teasing me, pulling faces, yanking my hair and threatening to tell on me, but he never struck me. Things changed quickly.

'Hit her. Do it. Hit her!' Ga Pau ordered her son.

I was barely ten years old and had done something that had yet again displeased the mistress of Tang House. Who knew what it was. Ga Pau was never short of reasons to strike me.

I remember Zeoi Mao standing there motionless in front of me, his eyes not daring to meet mine as if he was ashamed. He didn't move.

'Son, she is just a stupid san pou chai, a Hakka san pou chai no less,' she said, towering behind me. 'Hit her.'

My body tensed up, ready for him to strike me. Still without making any eye contact, Zeoi Mao tapped me on my arm.

Was that it? Really? That's it?

It was nothing compared to Ga Pau's mammoth strength.

'What was that? What are you doing? Tin Yeung, you will be the man of this house one day. How can you expect to lead this family if you can't discipline your future wife? We bought her, so she is nothing more than property. Her own parents didn't want her. Don't you understand she is worthless? Now, hit her.'

Something in what Ga Pau said or how she said it woke up the monster in Zeoi Mao, a monster that was let loose on my body without any hesitation. Strike after strike, blow after blow, whilst his mother watched approvingly.

Through the sounds of beaten flesh, I could hear the old man from next door cry out, 'Oh no, Ah Ping is being hit again. Poor girl. Ah Ping is being hit again!'

A tiny spark of hope ignited.

Someone can hear what is happening. Someone will come to help me and stop this.

I gripped that bit of hope as tightly as I could tense my body, waiting for Zeoi Mao to stop.

'Enough! We still need her for all the chores. Remember, Tin Yeung, you cannot beat her to death. Who will cook and clean for us then? You?' She patted her son on the shoulder, congratulating him for his first performance. After all, wasn't it a performance of who was strong and who was weak?

As my body untensed, I felt myself letting go of something: hope. You see, Didi, when no one, not even the neighbour came to help me that day, I learnt something crucial. I learnt that hope can be a dangerous thing if it rests on others. You can never depend on anyone except yourself – you must remember that.

Ah Fong

How I used to love playing in the rain, especially when the weather was hot and sticky. I loved how the rain felt on my skin and the way the air smelt so fresh straight after. It felt like a new beginning, a reset.

Gong Tau, the head of Tang House, was hardly at home during the day whilst his sons were at school leaving me with Ga Pau. In the afternoons when Ga Pau took her post-luncheon nap, the house would be quiet and I would sneak outside into the courtyard to play, sometimes whispering to myself in Hakka so I wouldn't forget my mother tongue. Was I afraid of getting caught again and having my other hand smashed? Of course! But I couldn't help but steal those precious hours for myself, to be a little girl again.

'What are you doing?' I heard a voice from behind me.

I turned around and saw a girl around my age wearing a perplexed expression.

'I'm playing,' I replied.

'But it's raining and you're getting all wet,' she said, shaking her head as if she were imitating an adult telling off a child.

'I know.' I shrugged.

She's obviously never played in the rain. I continued my pebble game, giggling at the big splashes I was making.

'I'm Ah Fong. What do they call you?' asked the girl.

'Ah Ping.'

'Can I . . . can I play too?' She inched closer.

'Aren't you afraid you'll get wet?'

'Well, yes, but . . . you're all wet too. And it looks fun.'

'Okay.' I nodded and handed my pebbles over to her.

We took turns challenging each other to make the biggest splashes as I jumped up and down with delight. It was like muscle memory – being a child playing again and for a moment

I almost forgot where I was and who they expected me to be. I could just be me.

'Ah Ping! Ah Ping, fetch me tea. Where's my tea?' Ga Pau barked out from her room.

Panicked, I dropped the pebbles. *If Ga Pau catches me, it would be the wooden clog all over again!*

'I have to go,' I whispered as I hurried towards the house.

'Ah Ping, wait! Will you be here tomorrow? Can I come and play?' asked my new friend.

I nodded abruptly and continued to head back inside.

Just like that, Ah Fong and I started to play with each other. Around the same time every afternoon, she would wait by the gate to the courtyard whilst I checked Ga Pau was still asleep. When I was sure it was safe, Ah Fong would sneak in.

***

'You sound funny,' said Ah Fong one afternoon. We were sitting on the floor, shading ourselves under lines of laundry from the scorching afternoon sun.

'No, I don't.'

'Yes, you do. Why do you sound so strange?' She pulled a face.

'No, I don't. I can't help it. I . . . I . . .' My protest turned to mumbles.

I had been on the island for three years and was still all too aware that I sounded like an outsider, a nobody.

There was a pause as Ah Fong tilted her head.

'My grandma says that woman in the house isn't your mother. That you're a san pou chai . . . what is a san pou chai?'

'I don't know. All I know is that my parents sold me after the Japanese came. Our village was destroyed, our home . . . and we had to come here on a boat. I've been here ever since.' I craned my neck to check Ga Pau hadn't woken up and couldn't overhear me. 'That woman inside is my Ga Pau. She tells me when I am of age,

I will marry her son. They make me serve them, all of them, every day.'

'But what about your parents? Don't they come to visit you?' Ah Fong asked as she drew lines on the ground with her finger.

'I . . . I don't know. I haven't seen them since they sold me.' My head slopped.

Why did I let go of you, Ma? Why did I ever let go?

'How long have you been here?'

'Since I was seven.' I shrugged.

'How old are you now?'

'You ask a lot of questions. Girls aren't supposed to ask that many questions, at least that's what Ga Pau says . . . I'm ten. What about you?'

'Nine. Well that makes you older than me. So, from now on, you'll be my big sister!' Ah Fong beamed and stuck out her pinkie finger.

'What's this?' I asked.

'To make a pinkie promise. You don't know what a pinkie promise is?' Ah Fong chuckled. 'Here,' she took my pinkie into hers and interlocked the two, 'see? Now we are sisters. We've made a promise, that's forever and from now on we can take care of each other.'

Sisters. There was a comforting feeling hearing that word after so long and to know that I was no longer alone, I had Ah Fong – my first friend. I thought of my own sisters and wondered if they too had someone like Ah Fong.

'Ah Ping . . .' My friend's face fell in a heavy frown. 'I hear her – your Ga Pau . . . I can hear her shout at you and hit you from my house.' Her eyes lowered as if she had uncovered a great shameful secret. 'My family can hear her too . . . Does it hurt, you know, when she hits you? I mean . . . I never hear you scream or call out.'

My eyes welled up with tears as my face flushed with shame.

No, don't cry. You cannot cry. What kind of Big Sister would you be if Ah Fong can see you cry?

I shook my head and swallowed my sadness.

'Come, let's play jacks,' I said as I took her by the hand and led her to where I had stashed my best pebbles.

In those exquisite hours with Ah Fong, I pretended I was a normal girl singing songs, making jokes and playing games as I allowed myself to forget I was just a san pou chai. I could remember what it was like to be happy and I had found that happiness in the smile of my dear friend.

Ah Fong felt so much older than I was with her quick wit and sharp tongue. She loved to make fun of my Hakka accent and found how I pronounced things hilarious, but she still helped me sound more like the locals. But my favourite was whenever Ah Fong would prance around the courtyard imitating Ga Pau. She'd stuff her shirt with laundry and thump about with her hands on her hips, nostrils flaring like a dragon.

'Ah Ping go and fetch me tea. Now!' Ah Fong would mimic.

'Shhh! You'll wake her and she'll kill me.' I hushed her whilst I tried to contain my roaring laughter.

Suddenly Ah Fong stopped and looked at me with a stern seriousness.

'Ah Ping, why don't you come and sleep in my home?'

'What? You know Ga Pau would never let me.'

'So? You could sneak out when everyone is asleep. My family won't mind. Besides, my Maa Maa will love you.'

'I don't know. Sounds risky,' I replied, scratching the front of my hand with my thumb.

The memory of the knuckles incident was all too vivid, and that was just for playing jacks. Imagine what Ga Pau would do to me if she caught me sneaking out at night. But at the same time, I didn't want to say no to my friend.

Would she be offended and stop coming to play with me if I said no?

***

That night I did as Ah Fong suggested and waited impatiently until everyone was asleep before sneaking out of the kitchen. I scanned the darkness that had blanketed the courtyard. The night felt silent except for the murmurs of Ga Pau and Gong Tau snoring upstairs.

As I tiptoed carefully across the courtyard, my heart hammered inside my chest. With a deep breath, I cracked the door open and slipped away. I couldn't believe how easy it was and wondered why I hadn't thought about doing this a long time ago.

Did anyone hear me? Too late to check. If I go back inside, they will surely hear the noise and wake up. You must keep going.

'Ah Ping, I'm over here,' whispered Ah Fong, who was waiting for me on the other side. 'Come, let's go,' she said as she led me to her hut.

Even through the moonlight, I could tell Ah Fong's home was much smaller than Tang House; hers had only one large room where everyone slept in.

We snuck past her parents, two older siblings and Maa Maa before huddling next to each other on her bamboo mattress that could barely fit one. Wedged next to the wall and Ah Fong with hardly any room to turn, I felt safe because I knew no one could touch or hurt me there. From that night onwards I would steal away to Ah Fong's house, where I slept next to her until dawn, dashing back so no one would notice. But like every precious moment, that feeling of safety didn't last.

'Grandma says you can't sleep in our house anymore,' said Ah Fong one afternoon.

It was a few weeks since I had first slept over.

'She says you're Tang House's san pou chai and shouldn't be sneaking around like that. She says we'll get in big trouble if we get caught and your Ga Pau wouldn't let us off lightly. I'm sorry, Ah Ping.' Her head lowered, averting my gaze.

Silence.

'But I can still come and play with you. I can come every day like always. Don't be mad,' she pleaded.

More silence.

I didn't know what to say, what to tell her, how to respond. What was there to say? How could I be mad at my friend or her family, who had welcomed me like their own? It wasn't their fault — everyone knew the Tangs were bullies, and I didn't want to get Ah Fong's family into trouble.

'Here, Sister, you go first,' said Ah Fong as she picked up the jacks to comfort me.

My heart crumbled.

The footbath

Like Hakka women, the women on the island didn't bind their daughters' feet either. Most of the girls and women worked alongside their men on the sampans or as farmers . . . I said *most*.

Despite having the biggest and flattest feet I had ever seen, Ga Pau didn't do a single day's work. Her feet were bound in other ways – a strange rotting disease had infected both her feet, which had to be washed then wrapped in special medicinal leaves daily to reduce the infection. Infection? Ha! She was so damn lazy she was cursed with that foot disease. What's the use of feet if they are never used?

This woman's feet stank, and I mean *stank*! They were like rotting corpses festering in the sun, worse than raw sewage. Once that stench filled your nostrils, it stuck inside your nose and that is all you could smell all day. On hotter days, the smell would trail behind her. Anyone could tell if she was nearby just by the stench. At least I had a warning of her whereabouts. In the daytime, Ga Pau would sit at her chair with one foot up at a time and pick at her rotten feet with her long claw-like nails, then sniff them. *Why is she doing that? Does she like the smell? Yuck.* My eyes would fixate on her, revolted yet transfixed by the sight of it.

Every afternoon, Ga Pau sent me out to search for medicinal leaves, which I had to boil until they were tender enough to use as bandage wraps. The leftover water was kept to use as a footbath for Ga Pau to wash her feet. Every evening after dinner, when I had finished cleaning up, this lazy fat woman would sit up at her bed and call out for me to change her wraps. The smell was so putrid that I could almost taste it, and no amount of time could make me become accustomed to it. No matter how hard I tried, the stench of the room filled my nostrils. Whenever I felt the urge to vomit, I would race through my tasks to get outside and inhale the crisp, clean air.

To this day, I can still feel the gag reflex that was triggered by the overwhelming odour.

'Ah Ping, footbath!' ordered Ga Pau one day, sucking her teeth to remove the remnants of dinner.

As usual, I trudged heavy, reluctant footsteps into the kitchen and readied myself for her pus-covered feet. *That can't be right . . . where are the leaves?* My throat tightened and my stomach lurched, like a banana leaf winding around a dumpling.

No, it can't be. I didn't forget, did I? I did! I forgot to go out this afternoon. This can't be happening.

I rummaged through every part of the kitchen as sweat dripped down my face uncontrollably.

'Ah Ping, what is taking you so long? Hurry up!'

I loitered in the kitchen, fearing the worst. My eyes darted at the cupboards, contemplating how I might hide in them. *Perhaps I could run away? No, she'll find me, and it would be worse. I . . . I have to tell her, I don't have a choice; I have to confess and maybe she will be more lenient on me . . . Everyone forgets, right?*

'Ga Pau,' I muttered with my head hunched low. 'Please forgive me but I forgot to collect fresh leaves today. It's my fault. I am useless, as you say. I am so, so sorry.' I humbled myself, not daring to look up at her.

My whole body tensed up, ready for my beating, but she remained eerily silent for what felt like the longest pause.

'Such incompetence! What am I supposed to wash my feet with now? Ha? Stupid little shit. Do you have some old leaves?'

I nodded profusely.

'Well? What are you waiting for? Go and prepare the old ones!' She waved me away impatiently.

What? Did I catch her words correctly? She didn't hit me . . . why didn't she hit me?

A wave of relief washed over me as I processed her words, and I tried to control my elation as I walked back towards the kitchen. *Had Ga Pau finally decided to stop hitting me? Have I finally done enough for her to be spared?* As I worked quickly to prepare her bandages and footbath, I could feel my heart pounding. All these years, it was as if I had been waiting to exhale and now suddenly; I felt like I could breathe. I'm not useless, *I'll show you, I'm not useless*.

Just as I had done every evening previously, I brought the large bucket of softened leaves and warm water by her feet and knelt on the floor in front of her. As I held my breath, I unwrapped her bandages that were thick with yellow pus and dead skin. Disgusting, but it had to be done.

Without warning, I felt Ga Pau's hand wrap around my pigtails and force my head back, and with her other hand she shoved the pus-filled bandages into my mouth.

'Eat it. Eat my pus!' Ga Pau spat. 'Eat it. I want you to eat it all!' she roared.

My arms swung frantically, trying break free from her grip as I gagged and choked, but she was too strong. Her hand clutched my hair, nails dug into my scalp.

'Swallow it all. Swallow it! You're not allowed to vomit. Swallow it! I forbid you to vomit. Swallow it!' she shouted as she clamped my mouth shut and squeezed my nostrils closed. Unable to breathe, I gulped it all down. The instant she let go, everything spewed out of me – the pus, the dead skin, the little food I had inside me, all of it sprayed across her bedroom floor. The taste of bile and rancid acid in my mouth.

'Look at this mess you made, you fucking shit,' she barked at me.

With a single push, she threw me into the mess I had made and went into a fury that didn't stop until she was out of breath, and I no longer had the strength to react.

'When I return, this better be all cleaned up.' She stood up and marched out, leaving me battered and soaked in my own vomit.

***

Hatred has a taste, and it is found in the reek of Ga Pau's pus, in her rotten bandages, in her forcing me to eat them and in the blows that she dished out on someone who had no means to defend herself. Every night since that incident, I prayed incessantly for horrid things to happen to Ga Pau. I prayed for Ga Pau's feet to fall off, for her to eat so much that her stomach would explode and kill her. I prayed for lightning to strike her and her ghost to be sent to the lowest depths of Hell, to be tormented ten thousand times worse than how she tormented me. As I prayed, a boiling rage filled me unlike anything I had experienced before. This wasn't childish anger, this was Rage. Before that night, I had still hoped that people, including Ga Pau, were inherently good, that given the chance, she would change. But when I vomited out her pus, I had also thrown up those childish beliefs – my innocence. What remained was a promise that I made to myself: no matter what, I must and will survive. She cannot win.

Why I hate the rain

The rain in Tung Ping Chau somehow always seemed to be heavier than anywhere else that I can remember. As soon as the skies opened, a torrential downpour of hot rain cascaded over everything, leaving it drenched.

One mid-summer evening, when the rain was thick and relentless and the sky was angry with thunder, water seemed to come from nowhere. From the courtyard, I watched a river of mud burst through the village like a hungry water-dragon.

But I can't swim. Look at all this water. What am I going to do?

Panicked, I rushed back inside, to find the kitchen had started to flood. My blankets and my only other change of clothes were soaked. The water was creeping in until it had reached my knees. My only stool bobbed up and down whilst rain and wind battered against the walls of Tang House.

Ah Fong! Her home is so tiny. How would it withstand such a storm? I hope you are going to be all right.

The water-dragon swept up many items and blocked my way towards her house. I could go no further. I sat up all night on my stool, surrounded by water, worried about my friend but too afraid to venture outside.

In the morning light, the storm had passed, leaving behind a sticky, muddy landscape. I tidied up the kitchen as quickly as I could, then rushed to prepare a breakfast of congee and fish for Gong Tau's workers so I could sneak away and see how my friend was doing.

'What a big mess it is out there. Have you seen anything like it? So many houses and huts have collapsed!' said one worker as the men talked about the havoc the storm had wreaked.

'Did you see the mudslides? Any house on poor foundations wouldn't have survived.' said another.

'We were lucky. Imagine those poor families in those huts. Did you hear what happened to that family next door? The entire house fell on top of all of them!' exclaimed one of the men.

'Terrible. Really terrible. Any survivors?'

'Hard to say. Some villagers have been there since dawn trying to rescue whoever they can and they're still there.'

Next door? Could they be talking about Ah Fong's house? What if something happened to her?

I slammed the tray of food onto the table and dashed outside. I would have to deal with the consequences Ga Pau would no doubt inflict on me later. My friend was more important.

People talk about mudslides on the news these days. They broadcast pictures and videos, but nothing can prepare you for seeing the devastation right in front of your eyes. Half of Ah Fong's hut had collapsed, and a mud-demon had gobbled the other half up. The wind had completely ripped the roof off. Bricks, rubble, trees, planks of wood, furniture and family possessions were all rolled into a big, thick soup of chaos. Villagers, mostly men, were shifting whatever they could, their faces painted with desperation, some with the anticipation of grief.

'Hello? Anyone? Hello? Anyone there? Make a sound if you can hear me,' called one of the men.

All I could do was stare at the carnage the storm had left, motionless. My legs stiffened as my eyes darted everywhere for signs of Ah Fong.

Please, Ah Fong! Where are you? Please be okay. Please be alive!

Someone walked past, shaking his head.

'What a tragedy. So unlucky.' The man's voice was heavy and thick.

'Uncle.' I tugged at his sleeve. 'Is Ah Fong alive? Is she okay? Where is she?' I asked, without letting go.

He said nothing, his eyes avoided my gaze.

'Please, Uncle. She is my friend. Please tell me, where is Ah Fong?' I continued to pull at his sleeve. My voice strained at the thought that something had happened to her. I searched the man's expression for an answer, but I already knew.

'Ah Fong, Ah Fong!' I screeched as my knees hit the mud. My fists beat at the ground in a frenzy. 'My friend! Ah Fong! How could you leave me? How? Ah Fong!' I wailed, pounding the mud harder and harder.

If I hit the earth hard enough, will it feel my pain? Will it bring my friend back?

In the night, the unforgiving heavy rain and winds had caused a mudslide which Ah Fong's little hut could not withstand. The walls gave way as mud and water consumed her entire home. Everything fell onto Ah Fong, her two siblings, father and grandmother. It had crushed everyone to death, everyone except Ah Fong's mother – the sole survivor. A cruel twist of Fate for the mother to wonder for the rest of her life why she was spared. That storm took away Ah Fong – my only friend that I had ever had on that island.

Since that day, I have always hated the rain because of what I know it can take away from me.

VIDEO CALL 4 : 30 JUNE 2020
8pm Hong Kong time

'Eh, Didi! It's you. Have you eaten yet?' my grandmother asks with a mouth full of orange.

'Paupau! I'm not disturbing you, am I?'

'No, no, not at all. I just had dinner. Your cousin bought all this food from the supermarket. He says better to stock up on everything. It's unbelievable. The shelves are practically empty here, even the rice is gone.' She edges closer to the iPhone screen. I can see the segments of orange stuck in the gaps of her teeth.

'Oh no. Have you got enough?'

The second her rice bucket drops below half full, I am certain Paupau would start to panic. Half full is the same as empty to her. One could never have enough rice.

'Yes, yes, I have enough. Your cousin bought me two sacks. And then Auntie Yin bought a lot of canned foods to stock up. They must have had to queue for ages.' She tuts.

'I guess you didn't make any zhong this year then?'

'Ha? Why would I wrap zhong?' She scrunches her face.

'For Dragon Boat Festival, that was a few days ago, wasn't it?' Did I get my dates mixed up again? It's hard to keep track of Hong Kong festivals when no one in my household celebrates.

'Was it? Oh. I didn't know.' Her face is blank as she scratches the top of her hand with her thumbnail. 'You know, every day feels like the same day to me, stuck at home like this. I'm too afraid to go out, even to go to the Hakka pau shop across the street to buy vegetables . . . It makes me more forgetful.'

'I can only imagine how tough that must be . . . Eh, do you remember you used to make the zhong for us?' I ask, hoping to change the subject to a lighter topic – food.

My mind shifts to a much younger Paupau singing to herself in Hakka, peeling lotus seeds with her thumbnail. Her undershirt with the faded peony flower print was practically see-through, damp with sweat, as I watched her squat over baskets and bowls of ingredients that she had laid out on the wooden floor in our living room. Even in the sweltering heat, she wouldn't turn on the air-con. *Waste of money! No need for air-con.* Turning on the fan wasn't an option either, as it would blow all the ingredients away. How I miss the taste of her zhong – the taste of hot and sticky summers.

'You remember? I guess they were pretty good, right? I made good ones, didn't I?' She looks uncertain, as if searching for the memory file in her head. Has she forgotten, or is she trying to recall the past?

'Oh yes, they were the best. You better show me how to make them the next time I am back in Hong Kong.'

But what if she forgets the recipe by the time I can fly back home? I need to write her recipes down, and I need to start doing that now.

Paupau rubs her temples aggressively.

'Are you all right, Paupau?'

'Headache, very bad headache. I'm okay . . . you know I get headaches all the time.'

'Still? Maybe drink some more water or do you need some Panadol? Where's your medicine box? Shall I call cousin?'

'No, no, it's okay. It will pass.' She continues to press and massage her head. 'You know why I get these headaches all the time? All those years being knocked on the head by that Ga Pau of mine and Zeoi Mao!' she exclaims.

'Can I ask you something, Paupau? Um, when you were a san pou chai, why didn't you run away?'

'You think it's that easy? I was merely a child. I had no money, no family . . .'

She pauses. Her eyes glaze over, transfixed, as if lost in a moment in time. Her jaw pulls back and tightens as a tear streaks down her weathered face.

'Paupau? Are you all right? Paupau?'

She answers with her body. Her fists clench as if ready to fight a ghost that had long disappeared.

'Paupau?' I ask, hoping to break her loose from the spell that had engulfed my usually cheerful grandmother. 'Are you okay?'

She shakes her head, freeing herself from her trance.

'Some scars can never heal, Didi.' She exhales heavily, nostrils flaring. 'Your grandmother has suffered a lot.'

I want to know what the image in her head looks like, I want to feel the insides of her skin, but all I can do is picture what it could have been like for her – Ga Pau smacking her around, my grandfather tormenting her every chance he had and Paupau with no one to hug nor comfort her. Then I think of all those times as a child when I had been picky about my food, the times I sulked when I didn't get my favourite stationery pack, the times when I hurt myself and it was always Paupau who was there to comfort me. I can still feel her jade bracelet pressed against my skin.

'Perhaps you could tell me, tell me what it was like for you? Your life?' I ask.

Although she has told me snippets of her life when I was a child and still living with her, I never got to hear all of it. Maybe now that I'm a grown woman, she would tell me.

Paupau clears her throat. I am ready to listen.

Running away

During my years as a san pou chai, time felt broken. Days bled into weeks that became months and soon entire seasons had passed – seasons marked only by the various festivals that Tang House celebrated, which I was never allowed to join but expected to cook for.

As the years passed, I felt something had been taken away from me, something was missing – hope. There was no hole for me to crawl into and disappear from my life and the more I understood there was no escape, the more emptiness ate away at me, but something else had also changed.

In the early years, I so wanted Ga Pau's approval, believing that if I had scrubbed the floors until they sparkled, washed her clothes, cooked enough bowls of rice, that eventually she would be satisfied. But ever since the rotten foot incident, I understood it would never be enough and that I could never be enough because to her, I was and will always be an illiterate stupid Hakka girl.

I cursed Ga Pau in my mind daily and wished for her to die in all kinds of ways until I could taste bitterness in the back of my throat. Whenever Ga Pau or Gong Tau demanded something of me, my lips would utter yes and my head would bow low in submission, but inside, my spirit wanted to squeeze them until they gasped for air.

What have I become? What have they turned me into? I cannot stay here anymore.

My mother and father were gentle and kind people who taught me hatred was like a ghost that once you let it inside, it will swallow you up and leave you with nothing. As the hungry ghost of hatred grew stronger and louder, I knew if I continued to stay in Tang House, it would consume me sooner or later.

I thought about Ah Fong often and wondered what she would tell me to do.

Ah Ping, why don't you run away? Just leave this place and never come back. You can't stay here, Ah Ping.

I heard her voice in the night, beckoning me to escape.

I obsessed over the idea of running away for weeks, playing out how I might do it in my mind, but every time I plucked up enough courage to do it, I changed my mind. This wasn't sneaking out to Ah Fong's for a sleepover, this was different – this was running away.

One late autumnal night, I lay in my sleeping area and waited impatiently until I was certain everyone was asleep. My skin crawled with anxiety as I searched in the darkness for what I could gather to take with me. All I had was a small boiled sweet potato I had stolen earlier and a comb.

Is this all I have in the world? Just this?

I looked upon my humble belongings and frowned as I stuffed them into my pockets before creeping out of the kitchen into the courtyard and straight towards the main door.

You've done this many times with Ah Fong. It's the same thing.

Holding my breath, my hand trembled as I unbolted the door. My heart pounded uncontrollably as sweat dripped down my face.

Don't panic now or they will hear you and kill you on the spot.

The instant my foot stepped outside, I sprinted so quickly that I had forgotten to breathe. I ran and ran until the gentle glow from the huts faded into the background and all there was in front of me was darkness.

My eyes searched frantically for something, anything, to tell me where I was heading, but I couldn't even make out the moon. As I tried to get my bearings, each step became more uncertain than the last.

Where am I? How far had I gone?

Unable to see, the dreaded knotted feeling that I had been running around in circles suddenly overcame me. I stopped abruptly. Uncontrollable thoughts swarmed my mind as I started to cry.

I'm lost. What if I am stuck here? Then I'd be nothing but a stupid Hakka girl with no mother or father lost forever! I barely have enough food . . . what have I done?

Too afraid to care about how cold the soil felt through my thin cotton clothes, I huddled on the ground.

I am an idiot, a useless idiot! Ga Pau was right – I'm a useless san pou chai. I can't even escape properly!

Darkness scares me. It still does but not because of the dark itself, but how alone you realise you truly are.

Somewhere in the middle of the branches, leaves and soil, somewhere amongst my tears, I thought of Kwun Yum and how my mother used to pray to her. I cried out my prayers with all the conviction I could muster and sometime in between my mutterings, I fell asleep.

***

'Eh! You, wake up! What are you doing here?'

I blinked my eyes open. The sky was a bright blue; it was the morning. A middle-aged man was standing in front of me.

'Eh! Wake up! Why are you here all by yourself?'

I shot up from the ground and looked around me. I hadn't dreamt it – I had really run away from Tang House.

'Well, Ah Mui, are you going to answer me or not? What are you doing here on my farm? How did you get here?' he asked with an impatient frown.

I didn't know what to tell him. My tongue felt thick and heavy in my mouth, unable to tell the truth or make up a credible lie.

'Where is your home? Ha? Your parents must be very worried about you.'

Such an innocent little question, but it was a stab to my side that winded me. Home. If only there was such a thing. I thought of my mother and father and wondered if they would have been worried about me had they known I had run away.

A HAKKA WOMAN

They wouldn't know. They have forgotten all about me – their Ah Ping.

Suddenly they felt so incredibly far away, like a forgotten dream I wanted to touch but could never reach. They were the feeling of Despair.

'Don't cry, Ah Mui. Don't cry. Come, let's get you something to eat first. You must be hungry. My wife will make you something to eat.' The man's tone softened.

I followed Uncle to his house at the end of his small plot of land. It turned out I had fallen asleep on the edge of his farm in a bed of his crops. Inside, his wife offered me some congee with flakes of dried salted fish. The warm rice porridge nourished my empty belly, tempting me to gobble it up all at once, but I told myself to take my time to eat. The sooner I finished my food, the sooner I would have to confess where 'home' was. Too bad it was a small bowl.

'So, now that you have finished, you need to tell me where your home is,' said Uncle, folding his arms.

I looked down at my empty bowl and shook my head.

'Hmm. No home? Well, what about your family?'

My shoulders hunched in as I shook my head again, bowing my head even lower.

'No family either? Well, you don't look like a beggar girl, you look much too clean for that. You must have a family or someone you belong to?'

I stayed silent and sat incredibly still, worried that if I so much as flinched, the nice Uncle could tell I belonged to Tang House just by looking at me.

'I see. Well, you cannot stay here. Someone will be looking for you and I don't want any trouble. I'll have to ask around to find out where to send you back. You'll stay here with my wife until I return.'

Every moment of the next few hours stretched with excruciating slowness as I sat wondering if my secret had been discovered and what would happen to me.

When Uncle returned in the late morning, his face was paler than the flesh of a mooli turnip.

'Hey, you! Why didn't you tell me you belong to Tang House? Ha? You know I can get in big, big, trouble for keeping you here. You've got to leave right now!'

The same kind man who a few hours ago had taken me in and fed me was now enraged as he seized me by the arm, shoving me outside.

'You've brought me so much trouble. Don't you know the Tangs can't be crossed? Why did you tell me you're their san pou chai? Mr Tang will be furious with me if he found out I took you in! Ah-yah, you silly girl.'

The man dragged me all the way back to Tang House, his grip so strong on my hand that my skin turned white. Should I have screamed and flung myself free? Would there have been any point? No matter where I went, someone would find and return me – I was property.

***

Ga Pau was sitting at the dining table waiting for me when the man brought me back. I wished I hadn't stopped running. I wished I wasn't such a coward and had kept going until I was far away from that godforsaken place. But like I told you, there is no escape, no hole to crawl into and hide away from my life.

'Lie down,' commanded Ga Pau.

I didn't move.

'Prostrate, now!'

Again, I didn't move. My night of freedom filled me with a stupidly stubborn defiance. If she wanted me to lie down, she would have to force me.

Ga Pau flashed a nod at Zeoi Mao. Suddenly I felt a kick in the back of my knees and my entire body smacked the floor. Before I could crawl back up, Ga Pau grabbed a wooden panel and began striking the soles of my feet over and over whilst Zeoi Mao pinned me to the ground so I couldn't struggle free.

'This is for running away, you stupid Hakka shit. How dare you run away! You belong to us. You cannot run. Wherever you go, you will be found, and they will always bring you back to us. Always!' Ga Pau roared.

When the soles of my feet began to tear and bleed, she went for my ankles until she grew tired of it and threw the blood-stained panel on the floor.

I never ran away again.

Rivalry

Everyone knew Gong Tau was very ham sup and had a big appetite for multiple women, but he never brought home his conquests – not until Ga Pau became severely ill. Sunken cheeks, pasty complexion, and a smaller belly. I watched the signs of her prosperity erode as Ga Pau became a shell of the colossal woman I had met when I first arrived. You'd think in her weakened state she would learn to show some compassion or mercy, but it didn't stop her from instructing Zeoi Mao to beat me on her behalf.

Gong Tau didn't waste any time nor did he bother to wait until Ga Pau had died before acquiring a second wife. In those days, a man's status was measured not only by how many male offspring he produced, but also by how many wives he could afford to keep. As the notorious master of Tang House, it was natural, even expected, for him to take on a second wife.

One day, Gong Tau brought home a fisherwoman, young enough to be his daughter, with small beady eyes, a narrow forehead and the flattest feet I had ever seen. This woman itched her scalp constantly as if driven into a frenzy by the head lice that infested her hair. Tiny translucent eggs threaded her black hair – how they gave me shudders every time I saw her. I never wanted to be anywhere near her in case she passed her lice to me. I knew Ga Pau wouldn't hesitate for a second to find an excuse to shave off my silky waist-length hair.

Head lice or not, Gong Tau didn't seem to care because Second Wife had the biggest watermelons for breasts. It was all you could see when you looked at her – they were enormous, and I always wondered how she didn't fall over from having to carry all that weight around. But like I said, Gong Tau was ham sup.

Second Wife's arrival wasn't as bad as I thought. She never struck me or shouted at me. In fact, she hardly paid any attention to me, and I found comfort in being invisible because if they didn't see me, they couldn't hurt me. There were other advantages too. Even though Second Wife knew Ga Pau was ill, she was still the latest addition to Tang House, which meant her status was uncertain. She had to find ways to make sure everyone knew who was the new mistress of the house. Second Wife used every chance she had to defy Ga Pau, which often involved me. If Ga Pau ordered me to bring her some tea, Second Wife would interrupt and say, 'Ah Ping, bring it to me first and I will give you a dried plum.' If Ga Pau wanted me to massage her shoulders, Second Wife would say, 'Ah Ping, wash my clothes for me and I will give you a tangerine.'

I was punished for it, of course, but I didn't mind – I accepted those delicious treats with such sweet rebellion that I felt it was worth it, especially for tangerines. I kept those precious sun-coloured gems in my pocket and waited to take them out at night when I was alone and could savour every morsel, prolonging every bite to make the taste last longer. In those brief moments, I pretended I was like any other girl enjoying some fruit I had earned for my obedience. My childish mind imagined my father handing me the peeled tangerine, as he smiled, calling me a 'good girl'.

My fingers would still smell of my defiance in the morning. Throughout the day, I would bring my fingers into my nostrils, taking big sniffs to recall the fragrant memory of my sweet and juicy tangerines. It wasn't just the tangerines that were sweet, but the small part I could play in annoying Ga Pau in her power rivalry with Second Wife. I would have never thought it could have escalated any further than that.

'Ah Ping, come here,' said Second Wife one day.

It was late afternoon, before I had to prepare their usual dinner.

'I hear your parents live in a village nearby. Perhaps you'd want to visit them?' She scratched her scalp.

What? Did I hear her correctly?

I had thought about seeing my parents every day since arriving in Tang House, but I never dared to ask, not even whisper it. I had always assumed my parents had never come to visit me because they were forbidden from doing so. If they had written to me, I wouldn't have been able to read their letters – that is, if Ga Pau didn't hide them from me. I had no way of knowing whether my parents were alive or dead. They existed solely in my memory because it was easier to bury the hope of seeing them again than to wish for something I knew I could never have.

This was the first time in five years someone mentioned them aloud.

'So? Do you want to see them or not?' Second Wife raised an eyebrow, her tone sly.

'I . . . I'm not allowed.' I lowered my head, hiding the small spark of hope in my eyes.

'What do you mean "not allowed"? You're a child. Who said this?'

'Ga Pau. She . . . erh . . . she said I will never see my mother and father again,' I muttered.

'Hmm . . . I guess we'll have to see about that.'

Without another word, Second Wife marched off, leaving me to stew in my awkward giddiness. *What now?* It was like receiving a strange gift I didn't know what to do with, but I told myself not to get carried away and get my hopes up.

***

Then during dinner that same evening, Second Wife summoned me.

'Ah Ping, come here.'

They were all there – Gong Tau, Ga Pau, Second Wife, Zeoi Mao and his younger brother – all stuffing their bellies full of food that I had laboured hours to cook. I stood in front of them, listening to them clank their chopsticks and expel loud belches. My mouth watered as I smacked my lips envious of the good white rice they ate whilst I had to eat their leftover burnt and broken rice – the stuff that had stuck to the bottom of the clay pot that no one wanted to eat.

Whilst they picked out the juicy white flesh of fish, they left me with only fish heads, which I had to mix with the burnt rice, shredded turnip, and cook it into a gloopy congee mess. This was what I had to eat for many years because that was all there was.

'So, Second Wife tells me you want to see your parents?' Gong Tau's mouth was still full, the preserved cabbage and meat wedged between his teeth.

I hardly got to eat any meat in those days. If I was lucky, Gong Tau's workers would take pity on me and leave me a piece of meat here and there as I loitered around them during their lunch. But it was never enough food, and I was hungry – always. I would not know what it means to feel full until I was in my mid-forties.

I stepped forward and nodded with my hands folded behind me.

'Well? Are you suddenly mute? Speak!' His deep voice echoed against the walls. Gong Tau was just as intimidating as the first time I had seen him on his sampan.

I glanced over at Second Wife as if asking for permission.

'Ah Ping, answer him,' said Second Wife.

I nodded.

'Ha? No, I won't allow it. She's not going anywhere.' Ga Pau smacked her chopsticks on the table.

'Not allow it? That is not for you to decide. Besides, what harm could it do, anyway?' Second Wife shrugged.

'And what if she doesn't come back? Ha? Then what? No, I forbid it! I am first wife here and I say no,' clucked Ga Pau.

'Enough!' Gong Tau slammed his hand on the table so hard I was surprised it didn't immediately snap in half.

Everyone fell silent. Gong Tau's eyes glared at Ga Pau as she sank into her stool like a timid little girl – so small, so insignificant.

There was a long, uncomfortable pause when no one dared to speak.

'Ah Ping, I will allow you to see your parents. You will have one year with them and when the year is up, you will return. But I warn you,' he said with his icy glare, staring right through me. 'If you do not return to this house, I will personally hunt down your entire family. Understood?'

What? See my parents and for an entire year? Is Gong Tau playing a sick prank on me? It must be a trap or a test.

I couldn't muster a response. I wanted to scream, leaping up and down with joy, but my body remained stiff with fear – Gong Tau's eyes were still glued to me.

'Tell me you understand.'

'I understand.'

To this day, I don't know why Gong Tau had suddenly agreed to Second Wife's suggestion. Perhaps he had wanted to please his new wife, or to show Ga Pau who was really the Boss of his household. Either way, I didn't care because I finally got to see my parents. I scurried off to the kitchen before Gong Tau could change his mind.

***

The night before I was to be taken to see my parents, I couldn't sleep. The excitement kept me wriggling around in my sleeping area, but then my mind begun to weave a thick web of thoughts. So many sticky thoughts that I couldn't untangle.

How will my parents react when they see how skinny I've become? What if they don't recognise me and turn me away? Or worse, what if they refuse to let me in because I belong to someone else?

I imagined every possible scenario and my chest squeezed as if to suffocate me. I think this is what you call anxiety.

PART 2

A STRANGER'S HOME

'Give this to your father,' grunted Gong Tau, as he threw a folded letter at me.

It was dawn, and I was about to set off with one of his workers who would escort me to my mother's house across the island. I took the letter, the paper felt crisp in my hand.

'I know you can't read, so I'll tell you what it says. Your father has explicit instructions – you have one year and after you will return. One year.'

Gong Tau didn't need to raise his voice to warn me what would happen if we did not follow his terms. He was terrifying just by looking at me and I knew he wasn't a man to be crossed, especially with all his firearms at home. Whenever he was drunk, he'd shoot bullets up into the night sky like little fireworks of death, laughing hysterically. Entertainment for him and a reminder to the rest of us in Tai Tong exactly what he was capable of.

With the letter stuffed into my pocket, I nodded and left. The threat of his words pressed against my skin like a tattoo.

One year. I have one year.

I was led to a small stone hut surrounded by trees on the outskirts of a neighbouring village. In between the branches I saw a woman in dark blue squatting over some dried salted fish.

Is that . . . ?

Could it be?

Is that Ma?

As soon as the woman lifted her head, I immediately recognised my mother's unmistakable face. Feet sprinted towards her.

'Ah Ping!' My mother sprung up. 'I can't believe it's you! Oh, Ah Ping I can't believe you're here.'

'Ma, Ma!' I cried out.

As I lunged towards her embrace, she slipped and we both fell onto the ground, her arms still clinging onto me like a protective shield. Suddenly, something in me erupted like a pressure cooker that had exploded. Everything that had happened, everything that I had been put through – it was all real. Those last five years of my life really happened, and I really was a san pou chai.

My mother's jacket was damp with my tears and mucus as I wept uncontrollably. Her bony arms held my shaking body. A part of me thought she might try to stop me from crying like she used to all those years ago, but she didn't. She let me cry until I had no more tears left.

'Ah Ping, let me look at you,' she said when I finally stopped.

Her rough palm wiped the tears and hair away from my face as I felt a rush of warmth surge through me. The feeling of nostalgia. She was speaking in our native Hakka, sounds that I hadn't heard in years except in my dreams or when I talked to myself.

My mother's eyes searched my face as if to find the little seven-year-old girl she had left in the school hall for seventy Hong Kong dollars.

Don't look at me, please, don't look.

I turned away from her gaze. I didn't want her to notice how scrawny I had become and then I caught my reflection in my mother's eyes.

Who is that?

The girl I saw looked like the shell of someone I used to know – a girl who was innocent and happy. I wondered where she went.

Do I still look like the same Ah Ping you remembered? Do I look like your daughter?

I had always wished I could know what was going through my mother's mind that day. I never had the courage to ask her.

'Come, let's go inside. You must be hungry.' My mother wiped my face with her sleeve and helped me up.

My parents' home was much smaller than Tang House, but with only two of them and Second Brother, they didn't need much space.

I naively expected to be stepping back into my childhood home, but the moment I was inside, I knew I was in a stranger's hut. Sights of familiar objects like the half-eaten dried salted fish that hung on the kitchen wall, the dried tangerine peels, my mother's bamboo hat. Yes, this was indeed my mother's home, but it was I who was the trespasser studying their new lives – a life without me.

Ma would later tell me that chief Lam had generously given them their hut to live in rent-free for the first few months and had helped my father set up a small stall in the village market selling cha gou and pulled-sugar sweets. Business must have been good if they had enough money to send Big Brother to Hong Kong after a few years.

'Big Brother is in Hong Kong now as an apprentice dai fu, learning traditional medicine to cure all sorts of diseases and ailments. Remember when two years ago there was that awful spread of measles, and all those children were sick? Your Big Brother tended to all of them. He saved six children and didn't charge the parents a single cent! He only asked that they pay for the herbs. Your Big Brother is very capable, you should be very proud of him,' said Ma.

I nodded as I stood in the middle of her home, not quite sure what to do with myself.

'Ah Ping, you must be hungry. Why don't I steam some cha gou for you as a snack and then after dinner we can make your bed together? Do you still like to sleep right by the stove?' she asked through a pained smile.

'Ma, where is Big Sister?'

'I'm glad you asked. You know, she got married! He's a widower but a very nice man and can read and write, too. They don't live far – in one of the villages nearby.'

'Oh. And Little Sister, where is she?'

My mother paused from steaming her cha gou and let out a forced cough as if her words choked her, words that did not want to come out. She didn't need to tell me what I had already assumed. I remember that cold winter morning like it was yesterday, my little sister standing in that line of children, wide-eyed and clueless, not knowing what was happening around her. Maybe it was better that way – not to know, less painful perhaps.

'Ah Ping, look at you! You've got so tall that you can wear my clothes now. Why don't you have a wash and then put on these clothes?'

She turned around and handed me a dark blue cotton jacket-blouse, matching trousers and some undergarments.

'Thank you, Mother,' I said timidly in the Tung Ping Chau dialect.

'Ah Ping, you are home now. You don't have to speak their dialect. At home we speak Hakka. Never forget you are Hakka.'

I nodded as my toes curled up inside my too-small shoes.

Have I forgotten how to speak Hakka?

All those years of it being literally knocked out of me, it was as though all my Hakka words had fallen out of my head.

'Come on, Ah Ping. Go have a wash before your father and Second Brother get home. The cha gou will be ready soon.'

I pressed her clothes against my nose and took a deep breath. The clothes smelt of her. It was a smell that I had known all my life, and one that I had clung on to for so many nights during the early years as a san pou chai. This was the smell of safety; this was the smell of home.

***

To celebrate my return, Ma had prepared a very special dish – braised pork belly with black fungus, usually served during major festivals like Lunar New Year because the ingredients were very expensive. They must have spent so much money just to welcome me home.

'It's all right, Ah Ping, go sit down,' instructed my mother.

I had been loitering around her kitchen like a character in an opera that had no role. It was the first time in five years I had not prepared dinner and did not know what to do with myself.

'Let me help, Ma.' I inched towards her.

'Maybe tomorrow. Tonight, you are our special guest. Go and sit down.' She waved me away.

The moment I put the chopsticks piled with actual rice in my mouth and felt its warm, chewy texture, I cried. Silly, right, to cry over something so simple? But when you have been hungry for so long, there is no other way to express such gratitude. Not like today where people take things for granted and waste so much food all the time. They don't know the true taste of hunger, the emptiness of it. But I cannot forget, even if I wanted to, my body would not let me.

'Don't cry, Ah Ping,' soothed my father. 'You're home now. There is no need to cry. Here, eat more. You must be hungry,' he said as he heaped my bowl with more pork belly.

'Yes, Ah Ping, eat more. You are still growing. Here, have my portion too,' said Second Brother as he put more meat and rice into my bowl.

'You are home now. You don't have to be shy. Eat as much as you want,' comforted my mother.

This was how I knew they still loved me and that I was still their Ah Ping. We do not need to say 'I love you' because those are mere words that are so easy to say yet so easy to mean nothing. But to show the action of love? That is much harder and more meaningful.

That first meal with my family is still the best meal I had ever eaten in my life. Even now when I close my eyes, I can still remember the taste of my mother's cooking – it is the taste of love.

Video call 5 : 31 August 2020
5:30pm Hong Kong time

'Paupau!'

'Eh, Didi! Have you eaten yet? What time is it over there?' My grandmother sits far too close to my cousin's iPhone and all I can see are her nostrils.

'Yes, Paupau, I've eaten. It's ten-thirty here.'

'Ten-thirty? In the morning? Really?' She scratches the side of her face, trying to work out the different time zones, which have always been an enigma to her.

'Paupau, I have a favour to ask. I'm having some friends over for dinner this weekend and I want to make them your famous braised soya bean duck, but I can't remember the whole recipe. Can you give it to me?' I say as I reach for pen and paper, ready to take notes.

'Ha? What duck? I made duck?' Her eyebrows scrunch up as she tilts her head.

'Erm, yes, Paupau, you did. You know, the Hakka dish where you stuff the duck with fermented soya bean and other things before braising it?'

Did I say the name wrong? I'm sure it's braised soya bean duck.

'I . . . I don't know . . . I don't remember.' She tilts her head.

'Oh, that's okay. Maybe Auntie Yin will remember the recipe, I'll ask her—'

'But Didi,' she interrupts me, 'I made it? I made this dish? How come I don't remember I made it?' Paupau lowers her head, her eyes dart from side to side as she scratches the back of her hand.

Braised soya bean duck was her signature dish and the one that she cooked without fail for every family gathering with special pride. The recipe, the quintessential Hakka dish, had been passed down from her mother, but now poof! It was as though she had never made it, as if it had never happened, and this scares the shit out of me. I feel a swelling, a thick, sticky feeling inside, heavy with worry for my Paupau. How is it possible that she's forgotten this? And not only the recipe, but the memory she had ever made it – the entire existence of this dish? Where did the memory go and how do I help her get it back? How could something so significant disappear like that?

'Oh, well, that's okay.' I push out the best smile I can. 'You're probably having a senior moment – no big deal. Old people forget things all the time. I'm sure it'll come back to you.' I try to brush her forgetfulness off and tell myself that this is what happens when people get old, and Paupau is no exception. She's just out of practice, that's all . . . right? The lack of visitors recently means she's not had anyone to cook for.

I bite the inside of my mouth. Her mother's recipe, now forgotten and lost forever. But it wasn't about the recipe, it was her – I was losing my Paupau. Suddenly, I feel a wave of regret immobilising me. I had not paid close enough attention when she cooked.

'Do you remember any of the other dishes you made? Maybe I could make those for my friends?' I ask.

'Other dishes? I guess . . . erh . . . steamed fish, mince pork with preserved cabbage . . . steamed chicken. You know, the usual stuff. But you know me, I am happy with a cube of fu yu with some steamed rice and a sprinkle of sugar.' Her tone's changed, lighter at the mention of fu yu – her go-to rice topping and comfort food.

'I love fu yu too! Hey, Paupau, have you ever tried using fu yu as a spread on toast?'

'Ha? What? Are you crazy?' She chuckles, half choking on her spit.

'It's pretty tasty, but you can't put a lot, otherwise it's too salty.'

'What a silly, crazy girl.' She is still laughing. 'You can't eat that! At least have some rice with it.'

'Next time I am in Hong Kong, I will show you and you can let me know what you think. And I'll also take you wherever you want to go. How about we feast on your favourite roast goose or raid the hotel buffets like we used to?' I am practically giddy at the prospect of taking my grandmother out.

Expensive four-star hotel buffet dinners were our family's go-to treat on special occasions. Paupau and I would don our smartest-looking outfits an hour before we were due to leave and wait impatiently for everyone else to get ready. As soon as we arrived at our table, Paupau and I would exchange glances before sprinting towards the buffet tables and pile the biggest plate we could find with anything that tickled our fancy. Paupau had always taught me to try everything. *How do you know you don't like it if you've never tried it? Ha? Always try first.* Her eyes glistened and sparkled; her smile was wide like that of a child – it was a smile that had perfectly mirrored mine.

Whilst I loved buffets because I was and still am a glutton, Paupau loved buffets for a very different reason. After enduring a lifetime of hunger, seeing all that fresh, delicious food and being able to eat to her heart's content was pure joy for my grandmother – as a child, I couldn't understand that. She could eat her fill unapologetically and still, there would be more, all for the same price.

'Hotel buffets? What buffet? When did we go?' She scratches her hand.

'When I was little, and we were still living together, we used to go for buffets. Oh, it's okay, it doesn't matter, it was so long ago. Don't worry about it.' I smile. 'When I return, I'll take you and cousin back there and once you enjoy a splendid feast, I am certain it will all come back to you.'

'Oh, that would be wonderful if you could come back.' She inches so close to the screen I can see every pore, liver spot and wrinkle on her face. There are so many, too many. My heart tugs, a sour taste forms in my mouth. I want her to stop ageing, I want her to stay just like this.

'And maybe when I am back, I can watch you cook?'

The image of Paupau in her miniscule kitchen, lifting her cast-iron wok with one hand like it was nothing, is forever emblazoned in my mind. I wonder if she can still do that.

'You want to watch me cook? What for?' She raises an eyebrow.

'So I can keep learning.'

It was through watching her all those years in our cramped kitchen I learnt how to cook and to taste. My first language was neither Hong Kongese nor English, it was the language of food – her food. Whenever I cook her recipes, or I taste her food, I'm not just eating, I am consuming memories – memories of her, of us, of a lineage that traces all the way back to her mother.

There is a taste that I yearn for, the colour of a memory that I seek. I search for it – for her, in foods that I attempt to recreate and dishes I order in Chinatown. But I can never find it, I can never find her. I can never find my taste of home, the taste of Paupau's braised soya bean duck, the saltiness of her mother's sweat and the sweetness of a heritage that had been passed down from generation to generation. Food is the invisible thread that connects all the women in our family, but I find nothing but fragments of tastes – a copy of a copy.

'You know, I learnt how to cook all those recipes from my mother. She tried to teach me everything she knew so I wouldn't forget who I was, that I am Hakka. I hope I'll still be around to teach you next time you're back!' she exclaims.

'Of course, you will, Paupau. You're not going anywhere.' It wasn't a request. It was a statement of fact. She can't go anywhere because I would not know how to be me without knowing she is around.

I miss her, the taste of her cooking. I want to eat my way back home, back to her.

Unsettled

My mother doted on me with all her love and kindness, but it wasn't so easy to accept them. For the first few weeks, any time Ma tried to caress me or place her hand on my shoulder, I flinched. My body would tense up and my shoulders hunched as if to shrink away from invisible blows. Eyes would look back at her but not see that it wasn't Ga Pau, but my mother. She would spring away with her mouth pulled open in shock, not recognising her own daughter. Did she know? Could she tell? If she did, she never spoke of it.

I tried to relish all the small things any mother would do for her daughter, like filling up my rice bowl, washing my garments and plaiting my hair. Tiny acts of love to try to make up for all the things a mother wished she could change or take back. But every time she ran her comb through my long black hair, my neck stiffened. Flashes of being grabbed by the pigtails and dragged around by a tyrant raced through my mind. Cold sweat would bead on my forehead.

It's Ma. You are safe now. It's Ma.

Words I would repeat to myself as I realised, I had forgotten how to accept my mother's affection. It wasn't because I didn't love her, but because I had forgotten how to be somebody's daughter. In my mind, I was always a san pou chai on loan for one year. I was not their Ah Ping.

My mother didn't waste the limited time we had together and took every opportunity she had to teach me how to cook traditional Hakka dishes, spending money on expensive ingredients just so she could pass on her family recipes.

'Ah Ping, you see here – this is how hot the stove needs to be, otherwise the food won't taste good. And when you chop the bitter melon, make sure you don't slice it too thin, or it will become a soggy mess. Finely dice the mushrooms or the texture won't be good. Use more salt! If you sweat a lot, you need more salt for your body.'

A HAKKA WOMAN

I stood next to my mother in the kitchen every evening as she passed on recipe after recipe to me. Food secrets handed down from mother to daughter, generation after generation. The more I cooked, the closer I felt to my mother but also to all the Hakka women who came before us as I traced with invisible footsteps my way back home, to our heritage.

We cooked so many dishes: salt-baked chicken, stuffed bitter melon, chopped pork with cabbage and mushrooms, and of course, your favourite soya bean braised duck. Those exquisite moments with her made me feel like myself again.

But my father, on the other hand, had become a changed man. Before the war, he used to wear a soft smile as he recited Hakka poems, sang mountain songs and teased his children with little jokes and nicknames, like calling me a cheeky water-monkey. But when I saw him, his previously proud stature and confident gait had dissolved into slumped shoulders and shuffled uneasy steps. Although they were well-fed, his cheeks were permanently sunken in, his eyes would dart from object to object as if always on the lookout for danger. He didn't call me his water-monkey once. The war had left a big lesion in his heart, and I don't think he ever recovered from it. Remember, Didi, there are never any winners in war. Everyone loses something.

***

Work is like a scythe that cuts weakness from the body. During the year I spent with my family, I learnt that being a rice farmer is one of the most backbreaking labours there is. It's no wonder rice farmers have earned their reputation as hard workers.

A paddy field isn't very big. Rice doesn't need much space to grow, just water – lots and lots of water. Once the seeds have sprouted, each bunch of rice-grass is planted from the baby field into the main one and of course, everything was done by hand, one bunch at a time. The field would then be flooded with water for the rice to grow and to protect it from the unforgiving sun. And then you had to wait. There is no shortcut to rice.

After about three months, the rice-grass gets to about knee-height and the beautiful golden grain of the rice could be seen sprouting. Insects love to burrow in the grain and eat them, so every stalk had to be combed by hand to prevent the insects from getting in and ruining the harvest. Yes, that's right! Every. Single. Stalk. One by one.

Farmers would then cut the stalks, bunch them together and thrash them against bamboo planks to separate the grain from the stalk. Can you imagine how strong you have to be to do that all day over and over? But wait, it's not over, the rice isn't ready for cooking yet. After the kernels are collected and dried in the sun, they had to be milled. This was the final and perhaps the hardest part of the entire process. You had to rub and rub until your hands became red raw, but if you're lucky, someone in the village might have a rice mill to help, but people rarely had the money for things like that.

Now that you know what goes into putting rice in your bowl, you see it's never as simple as a bowl of rice. A lot of sweat goes into something we take easily for granted. Remember that every time you eat rice, for you are eating the hard work of a dedicated rice farmer.

'Ah Ping, you can help us comb out the stalks for insects,' instructed my mother as she handed me a small bamboo comb. 'Remember to cover your legs when you go into the paddy field. There are many leeches, so be careful!' she warned.

Too occupied with the feelings of self-importance, I tucked the comb into my pocket and with a confident smile I headed out to the paddy fields. You need exceptional eyesight to spot all those tiny insects and it was I who was entrusted with such a big responsibility. I rolled up my trousers and stepped into the field. The water felt cool on my skin as I thought of Ah Fong and how we used to splash around in rain puddles barefoot.

At least I had a friend.

Before I could comb through the first stalk, I felt a slither across my legs. Something was crawling all over them.

What was that? A water snake?

Panicked, I leapt out of the paddy field. Half a dozen leeches had latched onto my scrawny legs. Their black bodies pulsated as they sucked my blood, growing bigger and fatter with each second.

'AHHHH!' I screeched so loudly my mother immediately ran towards me. 'Get them off me! Get them off!' I screamed.

Just as I was about to rip the leeches off with my nails, my mother stopped me.

'No, Ah Ping! Don't pull them off. No!' she shouted and pulled my arm away. 'Sit down and don't move.' She plonked me on a patch of grass next to the paddy field.

'Ma, Ma! Please, get them off. Get them off!' I shuddered.

My mother grabbed a handful of salt that she kept in her pocket and sprinkled it all over the leeches. One by one, the leeches dropped off as if by magic, leaving only red marks on my skin. I watched them wriggle, mesmerised by their dance of death, but then seeing my blood filled me with a violent frenzy. Without warning, I stood up and stomped on every leech over and over – all I could see was Ga Pau's face.

'Die, die, die!' I spat as I squished them beneath my feet until they were nothing more than a crimson, gooey mess.

'Ah Ping, stop. Stop it! They are all dead. They can't hurt you anymore,' said my mother.

We both knew neither of us was talking about leeches.

Lunar New Year

The house was filled with incense and the smell of lo bak go. It was the smell of Lunar New Year.

'Come, Ah Ping. It is time to make offerings to Kwun Yum and thank her for bringing you home to us,' said my father, holding the lit joss sticks ready for me.

I clutched the incense sticks and stared at the statuette of Kwun Yum, wondering why the goddess of mercy hadn't brought me home in previous years, if she could bring me back this time. But out of fear that my thoughts would bring bad luck or worse to my family, I shook them away and joined my parents and Second Brother in prayer.

There was plenty to do. Lunar New Year isn't a time to sit around, relax and do nothing. No, not at all! Those kinds of holidays don't exist for us. My father's cha gou and pulled sweets were such a big hit across the entire island that they were in great demand. We had so many orders for father's delicious treats that every day before New Year was spent busily chopping vegetables, pounding meat, melting sugar and pulling rice dough. On top of that, we had to make sure the hut was sparkling clean. The non-stop work was tiring but I didn't mind. I actually cherished it, because it didn't feel like work. Being able to help my father and then seeing the smile return to his face and the joy that came with it were worth all the hard work in the world.

With Chinese inscriptions stuck outside the entrance, and offerings presented to Kwun Yum, we were finally ready to enjoy our reunion dinner. This is one of the most anticipated meals of the year. People would travel great distances to be reunited with their family members and celebrate with their most cherished loved ones with this hearty feast. This would be my first and only reunion dinner I got to enjoy with my family.

'Ah Ping, come outside quickly. Ah Ping, come and see who has returned!' my mother hollered.

I placed the meat cleaver down onto the kitchen worktop, wiped my hands against my blouse and went outside. A very tall and stylish-looking man walked towards me in wide, confident steps.

Could it be? Is that . . . is that him?

'Big Brother? Big Brother, it's you!' I ran towards him.

Second Brother quickly followed behind me, but his long legs outran mine.

'Big Brother!'

'Ah Ping? Is that really you? Ah Ping!' he said as he dropped his bags onto the ground and welcomed my embrace. 'Oh, my little sister! It has been far too long. What a marvellous surprise to see you.' His arms felt strong around my tiny frame. They were the arms of a man.

'Here, let me help you, Big Brother,' said Second Brother as he quickly grabbed the bags to carry into the hut.

'Come! Come inside, son. You must be exhausted from your long journey. Let me get you some tea,' said Ma as she sat Big Brother down.

I studied my eldest brother, the dai fu. Compared to Second Brother and my father, Big Brother had an air of sophistication about him. He looked nothing like the boy who used to draw characters on the ground and give me piggyback rides. I was elated to be with them but a deep sadness weighed heavily in my heart, knowing my three sisters weren't there with me. As the night sky lit up with dazzling fireworks, and families laughed and chatted over reunion dinner, I wondered if this could really be called reunion dinner without them. I wondered how Big Sister, Second Sister and Little Sister were spending their evening with their so-called-families, and if they too were thinking of me.

'Ah Ping, take these and use them to wash all over your body.' My mother handed me some pomelo leaves. 'It will wash away all your bad fortune and bring you good luck.' She smiled.

Cradling the vibrant green leaves in my hands, I whispered a prayer.

Please don't let me go back to Tang House. Please don't let me go back.

I repeated those words over and over as I washed those miracle leaves all over my body, wondering if eating them would make any difference to my prayers. The harder I prayed, the harder I rubbed those leaves on my skin until they chafed pink, believing this was my single chance to make my wish come true.

***

I awoke early on New Year's Day to the smell of steaming lo bak go and the slurping sounds of my father sipping tea. My brothers were still asleep.

'Mother, Father, kung hee fat choi!' I said, wishing them good fortune for the new year.

'Good girl, Ah Ping. Kung hee fat choi! I have something for you. Here, take this,' said my mother as she handed me a set of new clothes.

'You know, as soon as you arrived, your mother has been staying up every night to make this for you in time for New Year,' said Father.

I studied the neatly folded dark blue cotton jacket and matching trousers. My mother's immaculate handiwork was better than I remembered. This was the first set of new clothes I had received in five years. Any clothes I got from Tang House were over-sized hand-me-downs with rips and moth-eaten holes. I quickly hugged my new garments, squeezing them like a welcomed family member, feeling the textured cotton against my skin.

How many would she have made for me if they had never sold me?

'Why don't you thank your mother? Hmmm? She worked very hard to make those for your,' reminded Father.

'Thank you, Ma.' My lips trembled as I sniffled back my tears.

'Go and try it on, Ah Ping. I want to see if it fits you,' said Ma.

'Wait, Ah Ping. I have something for you, too.'

My father stuffed something that was wrapped in red paper into my hand. I felt the subtle weight of it – it was a coin. It was the first time I had been given any money, the first time I remembered being given any lai see.

My eyes fixated on the lai see and the little coin underneath the paper. I couldn't buy much with it but it didn't matter. My father may as well have placed a piece of jade in my hand because I finally owned something that was entirely mine, something that wasn't just an old comb. I owned something of value and that made me feel like I had some value, too. I knew exactly where to hide it – inside my undergarment pocket.

***

The next three days were like a reverie of feasts. Braised meat, chicken, soup, dumplings, turnip cake, fruits, vegetables. I had never known food like this and whilst my belly filled with abundance, my mind filled with voices.

You don't deserve this food. It is too good for you. You're just a san pou chai! What makes you think you deserve such expensive dishes?

Those voices couldn't be stifled even by the ginger sweets Big Brother had brought back all the way from Hong Kong. They were incredible with their sweet and spicy taste that tickled my tongue. As I felt the warm ooze slide down my throat, I couldn't help but wonder what would happen when it would be time to return to Tang House. It wasn't the fear of being hit, of being ordered around or of the endless chores that I was afraid of. It was the fear of hunger and knowing I would have to go back that ate away at me with every passing moment I spent with my family.

I never want to be hungry again.

I never want to feel that way again, never.

I gorged on everything that was put in front of me, believing the more I ate, the more I could store.

Like the shadow that Gong Tau had cast over me on his sampan all those years ago, every flicker of joy, every smile or crack of laughter was marred by the passage of time. I could hear Gong Tau's threat repeat in my head, and knew the comfort and safety I had felt with my family would soon come to an end.

Holding on to anger is like grasping a hot coal with the intent of throwing it at someone else; you are the one who gets burned.

—Buddha

What if anger is all that you have in this world? What if anger is the only thing that keeps you alive because at least by holding onto it, you can lob it at the people who abused you?

How I bit my mother

A year went by faster than a hungry pig could devour his meal when life was good. My parents and Second Brother doted on me with every chance they had and soon the boulder that used to weigh so heavily on my mind had lightened. I was a daughter and a child again without the shadow of Tang House constantly hovering over me.

'Ah Ping, it will be time to return to Tang House in Tai Tong soon. The year is almost up. In a few weeks, you will have to return,' announced my father during dinner one evening.

I dropped my chopsticks. I looked up at him from my rice bowl and then at my mother.

Has it been a year? But that can't be right . . . I just got here!

I couldn't stomach another morsel. Everything instantly tasted like ash.

No, you must eat, stuff your belly full because soon you will be back to congee and fish heads.

It took me months to sleep through the night, but after my father's announcement that evening, I screamed awake every night. Dreams where Zeoi Mao and Ga Pau were chasing me with distorted faces like hungry ghosts, ready to eat my soul. But no matter how fast or how far I ran in my dreams, they always caught up to me, always. Every memory came back up like vomit and all at once. Some nightmares are real, Didi, and those ones were waiting for me.

***

In the small hours before dawn, I lay awake haunted by a future I could not escape, the weight of it pressed against my racing chest. I thought of my mother's gentle hands as she braided my hair every morning and my father's chopsticks filling up my rice bowl with more fish every evening. For an entire year I had played make-believe as somebody's daughter and now it was all going to be ripped away from me.

I can't go back. I can't! I better think of something, anything, fast.

I was too afraid to run away, especially after what happened the last and only time I had tried to run away. I figured if my parents could not physically reach me, then they couldn't send me back and the one place I could come up with was their tiled roof. Sat up there was my sole act of rebellion. I decided if I had to, I'd live up on the roof for the rest of my life if it meant never having to return to Tang House. No one and nothing was ever going to get me to come down.

On the first day my parents assumed I was simply sulking and that eventually, with no food or water, I would give up and crawl my way back down, but they had forgotten how stubborn their Ah Ping could be. I had been hungry for so many years – what was a day or two without food?

By day two, my mother started to worry, but still, she was happy to leave me up there, occasionally taking a peek to check in on me. It was so hot up on that roof. The sun baked the tiles and roasted my back through my shirt like I was a suckling pig. But still I remained, determined to make the roof my permanent residence. At night I barely slept, dosing off a few moments at a time. The roof was rather narrow, and I was afraid that I would roll off, break my neck and die. I didn't want to die, I just didn't want to go back to Tang House.

'Eh, Ah Ping,' whispered Second Brother from the kitchen window. 'Over here, it's me. I've brought you something, but you need to be quiet. I've brought you some water and some food,' he said as he climbed up to see me on the second night. 'You know you're crazy for doing this. Eventually, you'll have to go back down there. You can't stay up here forever.' He shook his head as he handed me a cha gou.

I stared straight into my brother's eyes.

'I'm not going down there! If I go back down, they will send me back. I can't go back, Brother. I can't.'

Second Brother held my gaze as if he could look through me, as if he could see my thoughts.

'I think . . . I think I understand, Ah Ping.' He nodded. 'It can't be easy for you. I wish there was more I could do. I'm sorry, Ah Ping,' he said and with a sigh, he slid back inside.

By the evening of the third day, I had become a salty preserved cabbage from thirst and hunger. Every time I had a flicker of doubt and wanted to give up, I reminded myself of my life in Tang House – the knuckles, the beatings, the foot pus, the hunger.

No, I cannot give up. I am not going back. I will stay up here forever if I have to.

'Ah Ping, my darling girl, please come down,' my mother hollered out the window at me. 'If you love your mother, you will come down. If you love your father, you will go back,' she called out, as if singing her pleas.

I couldn't bear to listen to her beg, so I stuffed my fingers in my ears.

'Please, Ah Ping. You have to go back, I beg of you, please.'

Why should I go back? Why can't they pay back the seventy Hong Kong dollars they got for me? Don't they want to keep me? Don't they want me?

Hot rage pumped through my body as my mind kept replaying a single thought: I was being sent away for the second time.

'No, I'm not going back! I am never going back, never! You hear me? Never!' I screamed as loudly as I could, pounding my fists on the clay roof tiles.

I had never raised my voice to my mother before. Through my tears, I glanced up at the sky.

Please, lightning, don't strike me for my insolent behaviour.

But it never came. Instead, my mother continued to plead with me in her usual calm, gentle voice.

'Ah Ping, if you come down, I will give you those dried plums you love. Why don't you come down, hmm?'

My mouth salivated thinking of the sour, prickly taste. It was so tempting, but not enough to back down.

'I'm not going anywhere!'

'You've stayed up there long enough,' grumbled my mother impatiently as she clambered up onto the roof.

Suddenly, her arm reached out to grab me.

No, I'm not going.

Without thinking, I sunk my teeth into her flesh and bit her forearm like a rabid dog, refusing to let go. The taste of her blood was on my tongue. My mother shrieked as she swung her arm wildly and threw me off balance. The wet tiles scraped the side of my body like it was skinning a chicken as I skidded all the way down.

'Ah Ping! Ah Ping!'

I lay on the floor, motionless and silent. Everything ached, not because of the fall, but because I knew there was no escape. Nothing I could do or say would change a thing; I was utterly helpless.

THE JADE BRACELET

How many days do you think you could go without speaking to anyone? Two days? Three, maybe? It had been five days since my revolt on the roof and I had since stopped speaking – my final attempt to change what I knew was inevitable.

On the morning that I was due to leave, one of Gong Tau's workers was already waiting for me outside the hut.

'Ah Ping, it's time to go,' he said.

I felt my mother's hand grip my wrist as she led me outside. Her bloodshot eyes were swollen – like a fish that had been left out on land for too long, a fish without life.

Say something. Tell them not to send you away. If you say nothing now, it will be too late!

Suddenly, I broke my silence.

'Ma, please! Please don't make me go back. I beg you, Ma!' I cried, trying to yank myself free, only to slip and crash my knees onto the ground.

'Please, Ma. I am sorry I bit you. I know I am a bad daughter. I'll do anything you want, but please, don't send me away again!'

My mother crouched down onto the soil next to me and with a single tug, she took off her jade bracelet. It was the same bracelet she had worn on her left wrist for as long as I could remember. She gripped my left hand and slid the bracelet onto my wrist and, for the briefest moment, gently placed my palm against her damp cheek.

'Your mother is sorry, Ah Ping.' Her voice quivered, eyes averting mine.

The workman approached.

'Ah Ping, it's time to go. I don't have all day. I have to get back to work,' he said as he lifted me off the floor by my arm. The calluses of his palm felt rough against my skin.

'No, I'm not going!'

With one big motion, I flung myself free and scurried towards my father, grabbing at the hem of his trousers.

'Father, please! Don't make me go back. I promise I'll be good, I'll work hard. Just don't send me back there!' I pounded my head on the ground, kowtowing as if I were a mad girl who had been handed a death sentence.

My father remained silent.

'Ah Ping, you know we don't have a choice. You're a big girl now, so please try to understand,' said Ma. The cries she was holding back garbled her words.

'Come, it's time to go. Mr Tang is expecting you,' said the workman, as he peeled me off the ground.

If you stay, you know Gong Tau will harm them.

Suddenly there was nothing left to say, nothing left to do except to make those unwilling, heavy steps back to Tang House.

***

I expected to see Ga Pau as soon as I arrived back at Tang House. I imagined her waiting impatiently, tapping her rotten feet, ready to bark orders at me. But there was an odd stillness in the house and Ga Pau was nowhere to be seen.

'Where's Ga Pau?' I asked the workman before he left for the docks, cautious to revert to the Tung Ping Chau dialect.

'Didn't anyone tell you? She died a few months ago. I think it was pneumonia or something,' he said nonchalantly.

What? Ga Pau is . . . dead? Really? No, that can't be!

'Are you certain?'

'Why would I lie?'

With a shrug, he left. As I stood in the kitchen alone, I felt my lips curl into a smile as my heart raced. I bit down on my lips, trying to contain the sheer delight that was coursing through me.

That monster had finally coughed herself to death.

The desire to jump, twirl and shout with joy was overwhelming, but then a sudden pang of guilt jabbed at my stomach.

Oh no, I did this! All those nights spent cursing Ga Pau to die of some terrible disease. I said all those prayers and now she's dead. I made this happen.

I chewed on my guilt until the inside of my mouth felt raw. Happiness, I had found out that day, also tasted like blood. I loathed that woman with every fibre of my being and I still do, I can't help it. But what if I had really caused Ga Pau to die? Wouldn't that make me a killer?

You know what I fear the most, Didi? I lie awake every night, scared of what will happen to me when I die. I'm terrified that after I die, I'll be sent to Hell and my punishment would be to relive my life as a san pou chai over and over, for all eternity. That is my Hell. I pray to Mr God every day to forgive me for all the bad things I had thought and done so I won't end up there.

'You must be Ah Ping.' A woman's voice shot across the kitchen.

Strange, that's doesn't sound like Second Wife.

I spun around to find a middle-aged woman with hair the colour of cooked chestnut flesh. It was unlike anything I had ever seen.

'Yes, I am,' I said timidly, trying to steal more glances of her light-coloured hair.

'So, it's true, we do have a Hakka san pou chai. Very well. I am in charge now. From now on, you will listen to me and do exactly as I say. Understood?' She arched an eyebrow.

I nodded.

'Hmm. We'll see,' she said, sizing me up. 'Well, what are you waiting for? Dinner won't cook itself!' she spat and marched out of the kitchen.

No Ga Pau and no Second Wife. But where did Second Wife go? Did she run away? Was she kicked out? Or worse . . .

Whatever had happened to Second Wife didn't seem to matter, and no one had ever mentioned her absence. Gong Tau had replaced her, as if she had never existed. Wife number three was Wong Mo Chai – Little Yellow-Haired Wife. Wong Mo Chai wasn't her real name, but that's what everyone called her because of her light brown hair. Rumours had circulated that she was mixed, but I never asked, nor did I care. She never beat me and that was all I could hope for.

***

'Oh. It's you.' It was Zeoi Mao.

He stood there scowling at me whilst I was crouched next to the crackling wood fire. I had been out of practice for a year but already I couldn't get the stove hot enough to cook dinner. Without bothering to glance up at him, I continued with my chores.

'Oh, I see. You've been away for a year and now you think you're somebody, huh?'

I ignored him and kept my head down.

'Eh! How dare you ignore me?' he said as he shoved me off balance, but I immediately stood back up.

When I had left, we were still the same height, but now he was a whole head taller than me.

'Have you forgotten you're just property? We bought you. You're a stupid, worthless san pou chai and you belong to me. I can do whatever I want to you!'

Suddenly, Zeoi Mao snatched one of the wooden logs by the stove and swung it at me, again and again and again. The force of each strike reverberated through my body as I cowered to protect my head. This was how he chose to remind me that it didn't matter that his mother was dead because his were the hands that would replace hers.

'You're mine to do as I please. I could beat you to death and it wouldn't matter. Even your parents didn't want to keep you. You're nothing, no one wants you!' he shouted as he continued to hammer my body with the log.

Zeoi Mao wasn't wrong about what he said. He was only telling the truth. I had no status, no value – I was nothing. No less than an hour since I returned to Tang House and my cherished moments with my family were beaten out of me. I was never anyone's daughter. I was and always will be nothing but a san pou chai.

I chose to be mute. Silence was the only weapon I had against him as I huddled on the floor, waiting for it to be over.

'Stop. Stop! What are you doing?' roared Wong Mo Chai as she pulled Zeoi Mao away from me. 'You can't kill her, we need her to cook and clean. Who's going to do all that? Ha? You? Stupid boy! Get out of here so she can make dinner.'

'Well then, hurry up, I'm hungry!' Zeoi Mao snarled. His face scrunched up, flashing me a dirty look.

***

It wasn't long before Wong Mo Chai cemented her status as the boss-lady of the house by producing a plump baby boy for Gong Tau. He was so thrilled to have a son in his arms, whom he paraded everywhere like a bar of precious treasure. There was a new Prince of Tang House and that Prince was no longer Zeoi Mao. Gong Tau was so preoccupied with his infant that he paid little attention to his first born whom he had sent to work on the fishing boats like everyone else.

Life in Tang House continued as if I had never left, but the feeling was as if they had released me from prison, only to throw me back in. All those little things I learnt to tolerate as 'normal' started to repulse me, like the charred leftovers of rice and fish heads I had to eat for dinner. Smelling the smoky scent of disappointment, I wanted to scream. With every chore I had to complete, my jaw tightened, and a bitter, metallic taste formed in the back of the throat. I resented every second of my life.

Every day I fantasised about running away, but each time the thought crossed my mind, I remembered the taste of my mother's blood in my mouth and the pain I had caused her. As I fiddled with the jade bracelet she left me, I understood that if I disobeyed, it would be even worse so, I ate my bitterness.

A HAKKA WOMAN

How long do you think it takes for someone to wither away? You don't lose yourself all at once; it happens gradually. You erode little by little until there is nobody left. As time passed, it was as if I had never left and the year I had spent with my family was just like a butterfly-dream – something I could never recapture.

THE ADDRESS

One early morning as I was hanging laundry, I could hear Wong Mou Chai's voice echo against the courtyard walls.

'Ah Ping, your mother and father are here to see you!'

My parents? Why would they suddenly come to see me? Is someone dying, or sick?

It had been three years since my mother threaded her jade bracelet and watched me be dragged away from their hut. Three years since I had seen them. With uncertain steps, I went inside, worried about what was to come.

'Ma! Ba!'

My mother's quiet beauty was exactly as I had remembered. The lines on my father's face had softened, with his sunken cheeks filled out. Next to them stood a tall and stocky man. His face was almost unrecognisable until I noticed the familiar curl of his lips.

Was that . . . Second Brother?

'Ah Ping, look how you've grown. You almost look like a woman now! Doesn't Ah Ping look all grown-up?' Ma smiled.

'Yes, she has. You're all grown up now,' said Father. His words felt strained, unnatural.

Had I grown? What is a sixteen-year-old girl like me supposed to look like?

I had no friends my age, no basis for comparison.

'Is everything all right? Are you ill? Why are you . . . I mean . . . why did you come?' I asked in Hakka. My tongue felt twisted. Words spilled out clumsily and all at once, until my eyes noticed the bags slung across their backs.

'Ah Ping, we need to tell you something,' mumbled Father.

There was an uncomfortable pause.

'We're going back to our village in China. Many Hakka people have returned home and now we've saved enough money to do the same,' said Father.

'Really? Ba, Ma, this is wonderful news! Don't move, I'll go fetch my things. I won't be long. I'll be right back!' I said, ready to dash into the kitchen.

'No, Ah Ping,' he interrupted. 'You cannot come with us. We are going home, but you must stay here,' he blurted out quickly, as if to remove the sting of his announcement.

'But I don't understand. Aren't you here to get me?' The lump in my throat choked me as my ears rung with his words.

'We came to say goodbye,' said Father.

My body tremored as I felt the harsh grinding of my teeth.

This can't be happening. They are here to get me, to take me away. They said they had enough money. Can't they buy me back? Why don't they buy me back? No, not goodbye again. Not again!

I slumped onto the floor. Big, fat, hot tears streamed down my face. Every word that begged my parents to take me with them came out in a garbled mess.

'Ah Ping, you must stop crying. You're practically a woman now. You cannot behave like a little girl anymore,' said my mother.

'We're only going to back China – that's not so far. It's not like we are dying. We'll see each other again,' said Father.

'That's right, Ah Ping. We'll see each other again.'

I said nothing. From the corner of my eye, I could see Wong Mo Chai watching us – my spectacle of grief. She didn't smile. She didn't frown. She stood there, emotionless.

'Here, Ah Ping, take this.' My mother knelt next to me and handed me a dark blue jacket, padded thick with cotton. Small precise stitches, trails of her handiwork.

'Remember to dress warmly in the winter, hmm?' Her eyebrows furrowed.

My mother's arm reached out to me, and just when I thought I could hear a whisper come from her, as if she was about to tell me something, she stopped herself. Her fingers barely brushed my face – my mother's touch that never was. It was easier this way, I guess.

'Take care of yourself, Ah Ping.' Second Brother squeezed me so closely with his now man-sized arms I could smell the sweat on his neck.

'Ah Ping, here, keep this safe,' said Father as he stuffed a folded piece of paper into my clenched fist. 'This is our address in China. Don't lose it. I know you are a dutiful daughter. You were always a good girl.'

With that, the three of them left without me.

But I can't read it. You never taught me! I never got to learn. I can't read this. How am I supposed to find you if I can't read the address? How?

I wanted to scream, but somewhere along the way, my voice had been stolen. I stood there hugging the jacket my mother had sewn me, wailing with an address I could not decipher – the ink had bled through the paper and onto my hands, lost in my tears.

I would not see them again for several decades.

Fried rice

You think I enjoy speaking in the Tung Ping Chau dialect? I had this dialect thrusted upon me and after so many years it became like a habit – another skin that grew all over me. More excruciating than getting hit was feeling like I was losing my Hakka, the language of my mother. To forget it would be to forget who I was; I may as well have been a ghost.

Luckily, I was left alone most days. So long as the chores were done and food was prepared, Wong Mo Chai didn't bother me much. She was too enthralled with caring for her baby that no one else seemed to matter. In my solitude, I would hum Hakka folk songs to myself as I tried to remember my father's poems, but the words often escaped me. Other times, I would narrate my actions in Hakka as if I were telling myself a story. Silly little games I used to play with myself, which to the outsider must have seemed childish, if not crazy. But to me, they were my way to remember where I came from, and the few times after Ah Fong, when the days felt bearable.

'Stop it. You're not allowed to speak that nonsense here!'

I turned around to see Zeoi Mao standing at the entrance to the kitchen.

'Do you need something?' I asked.

Zeoi Mao never came into the kitchen unless he wanted something from me – food, tea, someone to annoy or strike.

'I'm hungry. I want fried rice. Cook it for me.'

If you are hungry, then maybe you should learn how to cook, you stupid, spoilt, lazy shit!

But of course, I didn't say that.

'Dinner will be ready in a few hours,' I said through gritted teeth.

'What? Are you deaf? I said I am hungry. Make it for me now!'

Girls were not supposed to talk back to their future husbands, girls were supposed to obey, so like a good submissive san pou chai, I dutifully did as instructed.

How am I supposed to make fried rice with no pre-cooked rice?

Remember, we didn't have a magic rice cooker that steamed rice at a push of a button or a magic stove that fires up at the turn of a switch. It would take more time than Zeoi Mao had the patience to wait, but I decided it was better to do as I was told than risk getting hit again.

'What took you so damn long? I told you I was hungry!' he snapped at me as I brought out a large platter of gloopy fried rice to the dining table.

I flashed a glare at him over my shoulder.

'Next time, make it yourself,' I barked back at him in Hakka.

Just as I was about to place the platter down, Zeoi Mao leapt off the stool. I felt the heavy thump of his heel against my back, knocking me across the room as I went flying face first. The rice I had spent over an hour preparing scattered everywhere on the floor. What a terrible waste of food.

'How dare you talk back to me? This will teach you to be so slow again!' he shouted as he continued to kick me. 'I ask for one simple thing, and you can't even do it. Useless.'

The hands and legs beating me may have been different, but it was the same feeling. As I clammed up to shield myself from his blows, all I could think about was the wasted rice and how much they looked like maggots speckled across the floor. There was enough there to feed me for three meals.

That night I wondered if there was more to this place called hopelessness and if I would ever be more than the marks he left on me.

This cannot last forever. There must be an end to this one day.

I uttered those reminders to myself every night in Hakka – my Hakka, to keep my mind strong but sometimes there wasn't enough strength because he had beaten it out of me. Sometimes all I could do was cry on the hard floor. My body often throbbed so badly that there wasn't a single position I could lie in without feeling an ache or bruise or a cut. With no medicinal ointment, no painkillers, nor a softer mattress to sleep on, it would take me hours to fall asleep. When I did, I would dream I was in a place far away where no one and nothing could hurt me. It is a place where I could smile, laugh and speak in Hakka, the tongue of my foremothers.

Video Call 6 : 1 October 2020
Mid-Autumn Festival, 5:30pm Hong Kong time

'Eh, Didi, have you eaten yet?'

'Yes, Paupau, I've had some breakfast.'

'Wait there. I want to show you something.' She springs off the sofa and grabs a tin of sweet lotus cakes filled with salted duck yolks. 'Can you see them? Your cousin bought them for me for Mid-Autumn Festival. Looks good right? Have you got any? Can you buy them in . . . you live in England, right?'

'Yes, Paupau. I live in London, England. You know, the one with the Queen. She wears that big crown with the hairstyle that you like.' It's a line that I have got used to repeating.

'Ah, yes, I know. London! Of course, I know.' She places the tin behind her. 'You probably don't have any good food over there, right? Not our kind of food.' She scrunches her face.

'Actually, it's not too bad. The food is getting better here because many Hong Kongers have recently moved over. I can buy plenty of Hong Kong products, even your favourite Vita lemon tea! But I didn't buy any mooncakes. It will be only me that eats them. It would be a waste.'

'Ah-yah, don't eat so many. They are very heavy and fattening. Too many will make you sick. But make sure you get the ones with many yolks, much tastier!'

What were we just talking about? I thought I had said I didn't buy any? It's been happening more frequently when I would say one thing, then Paupau would respond off-topic as if we're talking in parallels. A lack of interaction with others trying to keep her safe from COVID-19 meant she has to stay on her own for long periods of time. It can't be doing her any favours.

'Paupau, do you remember there's a song you used to sing? It's a kid's song about the moon and farming? I was thinking about it for

Mid-Autumn Festival but can't remember how it goes, maybe you do?'

'A moon song? What song?'

I hum the tune off-key but can't remember the lyrics except for the first few words. Paupau stares at me blankly and then, out of nowhere, she starts singing a different song in Hakka, one I have never heard before. A smile beams across her face, and it's unlike the ones I usually see – it's the smile of a child, a child version of my grandmother. There is an innocence to it, a sweet tenderness as she continues to sing. The roughness with which she normally speaks in Hong Kongese or Tung Ping Chau dialect isn't there. This is soft, gentle.

'What song are you singing?' I ask.

'Oh, just some mountain song from my childhood, something my father taught me. I can't believe I still remember them when I can't remember what I ate yesterday!' She sighs.

Why hasn't Paupau ever sung them to me before? Perhaps she had, and I hadn't paid enough attention? There was so much of herself that she gave and shared with me, but I had been too self-absorbed with other stuff – kid, then teen stuff and then it was too late, I had been made to leave Hong Kong. I want to make up for those years. I want to infuse everything about her.

'Teach me some Hakka, Paupau.'

'Why?' she snorts. 'No one speaks it anymore, just old people.'

'Because I want to learn. Because you're Hakka, which makes me Hakka too. And if no one speaks it, then your language will disappear like so many things around us. Soon there will be no Hakka left.'

She nods and then clasps her hands.

'Okay, are you paying attention? Repeat after me: sit faan mao?'

'Sit faan mao? Oh, I know this one. Is it "have you eaten yet?"'

'Yes, good. Okay, next one. Ngi ho, ngai hen Ah Ping.'

'Ngi ho, ngai hen Ah Ping. "Hello, my name is Ah Ping"?'

'Your accent is hilarious!' She chuckles as she stomps her feet. 'It's so funny. How about this one, si kor mor.'

'Si kor mor. . .eh, Paupau, I thought you never swore!' I tease.

'It's not swearing.' She winks. 'Those Hakka women back in my childhood village – they swore worse than construction workers.' She laughs.

'Paupau, what language do you dream in?'

'Ha? What kind of question is that?' She squints.

'Well, you speak three different dialects, and they are all jumbled up—'

'No, not all jumbled up!' she interrupts. 'I only went to school for three nights. Three! And I had no choice but to learn Tung Ping Chau dialect.' She crosses her arms in protest.

'Yes, I know. But because you speak all three, I was wondering which one do you dream in?'

She pauses briefly.

'What a strange question. I never thought of it before. Hmmm, Hakka. I dream in Hakka.' She nods.

'Really? Every night? Even now?'

'Yes, every night. When I was a san pou chai, they forced me to speak their language and I did what I was told, or Ga Pau would beat me. But inside, I thought and dreamt in Hakka, even to this day,' she says, straightening her posture.

Then it occurs to me how sure she is of herself, of her roots, despite having been torn away from them so young.

I gaze back at my grandmother. This Hakka woman had spent most of her life a stranger in another person's land, and yet she never forgot who she is, putting real meaning to what 'Hakka' literally means – guest family. When people ask Paupau where she is from, she never replies with 'I am a Hong Konger' or 'I am Chinese'. She always proudly replies, 'Hakka, I am Hakka,' without a flicker of hesitation.

I wonder when I will start feeling I belong and go back to dreaming in Hong Kongese again.

WIFE – PROPERTY

'No, not ready yet. Not ripe,' said the female elder.

'What? But she's almost eighteen,' said Wong Mo Chai. 'What am I supposed to tell my husband?'

'You can tell Mr Tang the truth. This girl hasn't had her first bleed yet. She won't be producing grandsons anytime soon.'

Gong Tau had sent for the village female elder to come to the house and inspect my body. A pair of old woman's hands, bony and wrinkled, prodded and poked at me only to announce I wasn't 'ripe' as if I were some kind of melon to be opened up and fleshed out by Zeoi Mao. I didn't understand what any of that meant except something was about to change.

'Ah Ping, come here,' called Wong Mo Chai one evening during dinner.

They were all sitting there at the dining table, stuffing their faces as usual with dishes I had prepared but could never savour. Is it strange that I found a twisted satisfaction in seeing them gobble up every morsel of my cooking? I hated myself for it – for constantly seeking their validation and acceptance.

'How old are you this year?' asked Wong Mo Chai.

'Eighteen,' I replied.

'See, I told you. Never mind the old woman, it's time.' She turned to Gong Tau.

'Time for what?' I asked.

Gong Tau's eyes flashed in my direction. I flinched and then lowered my head.

'It's time for the wedding ceremony,' said Wong Mo Chai.

Just like that, my marriage to Zeoi Mao was announced.

***

I knew very well what kind of boy Zeoi Mao was and what kind of man he would become. I had watched him all my life – that spoilt little shit with a wide flat nose, bulgy fisheyes and short stubby legs. He was an ugly boy who could become an uglier man, both inside and out.

Traditional Chinese weddings are not a simple affair, even in those days. Families would splash plenty of money, inviting whole neighbourhoods to the wedding feast to show off their newly acquired daughter, whose main duties were to produce many sons and serve her husband and in-laws.

But I had already been acquired – I was their san pou chai. No point in spending money on something that was theirs. I was no more valuable than a pig or a cow they owned without status or voice. Neither Gong Tau nor Wong Mo Chai cared enough about the wedding charade to choose an auspicious date and simply picked the first one that came to mind. More thought was given to pigs sent for slaughter.

You must run away before it's too late. You can't stay here.

Intricate plans to escape raced through my mind for the next ten nights, but every time I got to the courtyard gate, my legs would stiffen. Flurry of thoughts, of what-ifs and of fear.

Where would I go? I could jump on the ferry to Hong Kong, but how would I pay the fare? And when I got there, where would I stay? That's right... Big Brother is in Hong Kong! But I don't have his address... Perhaps I could run to another village on Tung Ping Chau? No, Gong Tau will find me, sooner or later.

In the end, it was my own cowardice that chopped my legs off at the knees, stopping me from escaping. I was so useless, gutless.

***

On the inevitable day, they handed me a faded red cotton skirt and jacket which hung on me like giant rice sacks. I had to wear my hair in a bun rather than the pigtails I was used to – a sign that from this day I would no longer be considered a child but a woman.

There was no procession or firecrackers, no well-wishes or a female elder to help me dress or comb my hair. I had no pretty headdresses nor gold bangles and necklaces. I told myself it was better this way. Weddings are supposed to be a celebration, but this wasn't one, this was a life sentence.

When it was time for the actual ceremony, a middle-aged woman came into the kitchen and threw a red cloth over my head. It smelt damp, as if it had been dyed recently. What a stupid pretence to cover my face from the same boy who had struck it countless times. But at least I didn't have to look at him.

I felt the woman's hands grip my forearm as she led me outside. There would be many hands that day. Peeking from under the red cloth, I could feel the vibrations on the floor of many pairs of feet shuffling around in the living and dining area.

'The groom and bride will now pay their respects to Heaven and Earth,' a hoarse woman's voice creaked out. That was my queue for the first guk gong. I bowed as instructed.

'Now for the bride and groom to show respect to the parents,' said the same voice.

Hands turned me around so I could face Gong Tau and Wong Mo Chai, and then another hand nudging the back of my head for the second guk gong.

'Now the bride and groom.'

The third guk gong was the hardest. Despite having a stranger's hand pushing my head down, my head barely tilted towards Zeoi Mao, but it was enough to spot he had a pair of brand-new black cotton shoes on his feet when Tang House didn't even bother to get me a bridal jacket that fitted.

'Husband and wife will now perform the tea ceremony.'

Hands escorted me to kneel next to Zeoi Mao in front of Gong Tau and Wong Mo Chai. More hands, this time my own, offered tea to my mother- and father-in-law as they paid lip service to tradition.

'May you be blessed with many sons, prosperity and fortune. May you be blessed with a submissive and obedient wife who will give us many grandsons.'

So many blessings, but none were directed at me. I may as well have not been there. I was a prop in a bad opera.

'Now the bride and groom will offer tea to each other.'

Both hands. It had to be done with both hands – to receive and to offer, as this was a sign of respect. It was the first and only time Zeoi Mao handed me something with both hands. The moment I took a small sip, I thought of the drain water I had to survive on whilst hiding from the Japanese. That water tasted sweeter than the tea Zeoi Mao gave me.

'Take her away,' instructed Wong Mo Chai.

There was a tray of food waiting for me on the floor of Zeoi Mao's bedroom. A large bowl of white rice filled to the top, a plate of meat and vegetables, and a small bowl of soup. It was the most food Tang House had ever given me.

'This is your wedding feast,' said the middle-aged woman as she closed and locked the door.

All that food for me and yet no appetite to eat. I picked at it, listening to the cheerful sounds of Gong Tau's voice and the other villagers celebrating outside. Sounds of chopsticks clinking against china as they feasted without me. I welcomed the solitude and forced myself to eat.

Who knows what they would give me tomorrow? Whatever happens next, I want to be full.

Nothing could have prepared me for that night.

Zeoi Mao's heavy steps storming into his room.

Zeoi Mao's breath that stank of rice wine and sweat reeking of salt and sea.

Zeoi Mao as he ripped through me.

Zeoi Mao's hand covering my mouth, muffling my screams.

This, I learnt, was how sons were conceived.

HARD AS DRIED SALTED FISH

Girls today develop so quickly, so young! In my time, most girls became a woman around fourteen or fifteen, but I was very, very late. I didn't have my first bleed until I was nineteen, which really frustrated Gong Tau, who was eager for grandsons.

I had no clue what mensuration was nor what changes my body was supposed to go through to make me a 'woman'. Every few weeks Wong Mo Chai would approach me, confused why I hadn't got pregnant yet when Zeoi Mao had been planting many seeds in me like I was some plot of land to till.

'Ah Ping, come here. I have something to ask you,' she said as she lowered her voice to just above a whisper. 'Have you had your womanly bleed yet?'

My head quickly jolted up.

What? What womanly bleed? I don't want to bleed. That sounds scary and dangerous!

'Well, have you or not?' she asked impatiently.

I rubbed the back of my neck as I tried to think of a time when I could have cut myself or when I had to push a hard shit out of my ass, but I couldn't think of an answer, so I shook my head.

'Are you sure you haven't had your womanly bleed yet?' Her eyes narrowed as if I was lying.

Again, I shook my head, hoping it was enough to satisfy her.

'Hmmm,' she said with a raised eyebrow.

I was both confused and worried. If I had my womanly bleed, how would I know? I couldn't just ask someone – those were things you could never discuss, things that are too shameful and taboo. But that didn't stop Wong Mo Chai from interrogating me with the same questions and distrusting eyes.

***

I was nineteen years old when it happened. I remember it so well. That morning I woke up especially tired. My whole body felt swollen and sore, my skin pricked at every touch of my clothing. I thought perhaps I was getting sick, but then by the afternoon an agonising ache seeped through my abdomen.

Did I eat something bad? Maybe rotten food?

I continued with my chores, trying to ignore the pain, but still, it would not go away. It was like something was squeezing my insides and shredding everything up. Cold beads of sweat dripped down my back. Unable to do anything else because of the pain, I hunched over on the floor, hugged my knees and hoped the agony would finally ease.

A sudden wetness between my legs. I crawled to the outhouse, thinking I had wet myself because of the pain. I gasped when I saw my blood-stained undergarments had soaked through my trousers and coloured my thighs red.

Where is all this blood coming from? Why am I bleeding? What is happening to me?

I searched everywhere on my body, checking for cuts and wounds, but couldn't find the source of my bleeding. Then a tiny trickle down my leg – it was the blood again, and it was coming from inside me, inside my private parts! Suddenly I thought of Zeoi Mao and the times he forced himself in me. There was blood and pain then, too.

Did he leave a wound inside me? Am I . . . am I dying?

I was convinced I was urinating blood, punished for what Zeoi Mao did to me, and was now struck by some mysterious illness that would cause me to bleed to death. But I didn't have time to think. If I didn't get back to my chores, someone would be looking for me and I would get into trouble.

But what am I going to do about all this bleeding?

Back then there was no toilet paper, not like the stuff you get now, so clean and soft. If you could afford toilet paper, it was more like rough sheets of paper of unknown origin. For us villagers, we had to use leaves, which could get messy.

I used the only thing I could think of – a small cloth I had always kept in my pocket to clean my face, which I folded and stuffed between my legs. With my blood-stained trousers pulled up as high as I could to keep the cloth in place, I got back to work. I dragged my body around, wondering if I was bleeding to death and would collapse on the floor. I doubt anyone would have missed me. It's not like I had anything to show for my life, anyway.

With so many chores to do, I didn't have time to take off and wash my trousers. It's not like I had a magic washing machine and dryer. Everything had to be done by hand, everything took so much longer.

It wasn't until the late afternoon that the sharp pangs finally simmered to a dull ache when I could steal away and wash my trousers and undergarments. The water smelt metallic and stained red from my blood. As I timidly hung my trousers and garments, one of the older women from next door walked past.

'Ah Mui, have you eaten yet?' asked Auntie.

I think she felt bad for me for all those years being hit by Ga Pau and then Zeoi Mao. Every time when she walked past the courtyard, she would always stop and exchange a few words with me. I treasured those small moments of human interaction, those fragments of kindness, from someone asking how I was. It made me feel like I was more than a san pou chai.

'Ah Ping, are you all right? Your face is so pale. What happened? Did he hit you? He hit you again, didn't he?' Ah Sum approached closer to me.

'Ah Sum, my . . . erh, my belly hurts,' I muttered, rubbing my abdomen.

'Your belly hurts? Are you sick? Maybe you ate something bad?'

'Erh, I don't know, erh . . . there was . . . I felt this wetness between my legs . . . so I went to the outhouse. There was a lot of blood.' My face flushed red hot with embarrassment.

'Ha? Has no one told you about this? This can't be your first time?' She gasped, her eyebrows raised.

I nodded nervously.

'Ah Ping,' she whispered as she gestured for me to come closer. 'It means you are a woman now. Your husband's seed can be planted in you, and it will grow into a child. It means you can have sons now,' she said with a deep sigh, knowing this was not a day for celebration.

'Erh, Ah Sum, am I ill?'

'No, of course not!' She laughed. 'Has no one explained this to you and what to do? Not even your mother-in-law?'

My silence told her everything she needed to know.

'Hmm . . . I see.' She looked around her. 'Come with me. I will explain and show you everything.'

***

Ah Sum's bedframe was a simple metal rack with a light sheet of woven bamboo on top that gave off a faint, earthy smell. It was so different from Ga Pau's, now Wong Mo Chai's, imposing wooden bed. I still slept on the kitchen floor.

'Come, Ah Ping. No need to be shy. There's no one else here,' she said, ushering me to her bedroom.

'Ah Sum . . . I . . .'

'Don't worry. I'll be quick. I know you have to get back soon,' she assured me, sensing my anxiety to get back as dinner time was fast approaching and I hadn't cooked the rice yet.

Then Ah Sum took out some old cloths and placed them in front of me on the bamboo mattress.

'You see this? These are rags. You must prepare them every month in advance. You need to remember the day of your first bleed and then count twenty-eight days. On the twenty-eighth day you should expect your next bleed. You must have your rags prepared by then.'

I nodded, but I didn't know what I was nodding for.

Why do I need to count twenty-eight days? Am I to bleed every lunar month? And for how long? Wouldn't I die from all this bleeding?

A HAKKA WOMAN

My eyes zipped around the room and my head spun, as I tried to take in all the knowledge Ah Sum was attempting to teach me.

'Watch, you must tear the rags into strips like this.'

She took a cloth and tore a narrow strip from it, the width of my palm. Then she instructed me to do the same.

'Now fold the strips to make a thick padding. Watch me first.'

I studied her movements carefully and copied Ah Sum as she folded the cloths into a thick pad.

'Now remember, the pad must be no wider than your palm or it will be unbearable. Bind them together with another cloth going the other way, like this.'

I did as Ah Sum showed me and bound the rags together to produce my first sanitary pad, but I still had no idea what it was to be used for.

'Good.' She nodded approvingly after inspecting it. 'Now you cannot just place it between your legs, it will move around, and you will dirty your trousers. You need to use another strip of cloth to wrap it around the gusset of your undergarments. Like this.'

Before I could turn away, Ah Sum had taken a rag-pad and a set of her underwear and slipped it over her trousers. I let out a nervous giggle.

Is this how other woman talk to each other? With such . . . openness?

'Look here, Ah Ping, this is where you put the pad and attach it. When you pull up your undergarments, make sure the pad is against your skin and covering your private parts, otherwise you will bleed everywhere.' Her face was stern, completely matter of fact.

No one had ever spoken to me like that, nor explained things to me with such frankness. Ah Sum's frankness took aback me, but I still wanted to listen to what she had to say. I wanted to know what else this wise woman could teach me.

'Now remember, you must change it often, especially when you wake up and when you go to sleep. Otherwise, it will soak through your clothes.'

'Will there be . . . that much blood?' I fidgeted with my jacket sleeve.

'Sometimes, yes. In the early years, yes, it can be a lot. And when you wash your rags and undergarments, you must wash this separately. Do not mix this with other clothes, certainly not with the Tang House laundry. And when you dry them, you must hide them. Never display and hang them like normal clothes. Understood? It is very shameful.'

I wanted to ask her why it was shameful, but I was more worried about bleeding to death.

'Ah Sum, will I die from this?'

'Die? Of course not,' she chuckled.

I sunk into my shoulders, wanting to hide from my embarrassment, but I still couldn't understand how I wouldn't die or get sick from all this bleeding. *This can't be possible for someone, anyone, to bleed this much and not die, can it?*

'I must warn you, Ah Ping, you will feel pain in your belly like you did today. This is normal. You should try to eat more . . . if you can.' Her eyes lowered as soon as the words slipped out. 'Now, I will show you how to wash it. You must wash the rags in boiling hot water – it will rid the rags of the blood and stench easier. Make sure you scrub the rags well or it will smell. When they dry, they will get very hard.'

Ah Sum then pulls one from under her mattress and taps it against her arm.

'See – very hard, right? You need to rub the cloths together to soften them up before using them, otherwise they won't fold. Understood?'

The rags looked like long, whole dried salted fish.

'Here, take these to use for now.' Ah Sum handed me some clean cloths. 'You should go now, Ah Ping, they will be wondering where you are.'

'Thank you, Ah Sum.' I bowed with gratitude, clutching at my period rags, and hurried back.

***

A HAKKA WOMAN

I muttered Ah Sum's instructions as I carefully prepared my first rag, step by step, following everything I had been told before heading for the outhouse. The blood had completely soaked through my face cloth and the sight of the thick crimson unnerved me. Ah Sum said I won't die from this, that this was normal, and I believed her. I took my pad and put it between my legs and tied it with another strip and pulled my trousers back up. The pad felt so thick between my legs that I walked around like I was on wooden stilts – it'd take me a good few months to get used to it.

That night, I waited until everyone was asleep before I could wash my rags. I tiptoed outside, the darkness thick and heavy, lit by a sliver of moonlight, and I tucked myself into a corner as if I were trying to hide a guilty secret. Worried the boiling water would burn my hands, I used a small branch to stir the stained cloths in the water and watched the water turn red. One by one, I pulled each rag and rubbed them with a small stone, but still the stain would not come out – I guess it never would. I wrung them as much as possible, the skin on my hands felt raw and burned.

Where am I going to dry them?

I looked around the courtyard, trying to make out an area away from view. With no suitable place, I hung them next to my sleeping area in the kitchen, still warm from the stove's fire. In the morning, my rags hadn't dried and were still damp, but I still used them anyway. What choice did I have?

Sure enough, by the next month, the rags had become so hard that it didn't matter how much I rubbed them together, how many times I banged them against a tree, they were still like dried salted fish – harder than cardboard, just as Ah Sum had warned. The edges of my rag-pad were like dull knives that chaffed against my thighs, digging into my skin every time I took a step. Each step broke my skin further until it bled. Each step was the painful reminder of how difficult it is to be a woman, especially a poor woman.

Little lost kitten

Not long after my period began, I was pregnant. I had no desire to bear Zeoi Mao any children but what I desired didn't matter. Zeoi Mao took what he wanted from me whenever he wanted. The more I resisted, the more violent he was. I told myself to accept what was happening, that this is what all wives must endure, that this is the curse for being born a woman. I told myself it was easier this way.

1953. I was twenty-one years old and seven months pregnant. My belly was as big as a winter melon weighing me down, causing an ache deep in my back that never let up. Any energy the leftovers of fish heads, burnt rice, and radish congee gave me drained away faster than the sweat that soaked my clothes. The chores were harder to complete. Some of the workers saw their own daughters in me and feigned fullness, leaving me chunks of meat or chicken with several mouthfuls of rice. I gobbled every morsel, but still, I was always hungry.

Pregnant women have different thoughts – silly thoughts, now that I think back to them. During the day, my mind would drift to a world where I could leave Tang House, never to return. I imagined how giving birth to a boy would finally appease Gong Tau and show him I was worth the seventy dollars he had paid, and he would let me go. I think I even believed this could happen.

The Heavens must have been listening to my secret thoughts because soon after, I got my wish. Friction between stepmother and the first-born son rubbed so hard that it created a fire, burning and changing my life's direction forever.

Wong Mo Chai had always despised Zeoi Mao. He was a spoilt little shit that had grown up to be a cruel and lazy man, often caught napping by the seafront instead of working, but no one dared to speak up. No one dared to challenge him simply because of who his father was. No one except her.

Wong Mo Chai complained to Gong Tau daily about Zeoi Mao. *He's so damn lazy. All he does is eat, drink and sleep. They caught him sleeping by the docks again instead of working. He doesn't listen to me, he never does.* Over time, it worked. Gong Tau only had eyes for his chubby infant and looked at Zeoi Mao with a distasteful disappointment.

'You're a lazy piece of shit!' Wong Mo Chai's voice echoed from the dining room one day.

I had just finished serving breakfast and ran into the dining area to investigate.

'All you know to do is waste money and sleep all day. Even when you're dead, you'll still be useless!' she continued.

'Shut your mouth! You're not my mother. You're just some trash my father picked up. A nobody-third wife. You're no better than a whore!' shouted Zeoi Mao.

I stood there, stunned. Zeoi Mao had done the unthinkable – he had broken with tradition and shouted at his stepmother. Being Gong Tau's wife meant she had assumed the position of 'mother' and had to be treated like Zeoi Mao's own flesh and blood.

'I may be a third wife, but at least I'm not some fat, stinking corpse like your mother. She deserved to die. When she reincarnates, I hope she comes back as a cockroach so I can stomp her to death!' she screamed.

She had cut open an old wound that had never healed. Suddenly Zeoi Mao lost all composure and lunged for Wong Mo Chai. Out of nowhere, Gong Tau grabbed Zeoi Mao by the throat and threw him across the room like a little doll.

At least he now knows what that feels like.

'Out! I want you out!' Gong Tau bellowed. 'Pack your things and take your Hakka wife with you. You are never to step foot in this house again. I don't have you for a son!'

That was it.

Zeoi Mao not only shouted at his father's wife but tried to hit her. Ultimately, he had disrespected his father's house and there was no going back from that.

***

As I gathered my belongings, I let out a deep sigh. I wondered if I had died in that moment, what would I have had to show for my existence? Just some old clothes that didn't fit properly, a bamboo comb, my period rags and the jade bracelet my mother had given me, which I never took off. There was also the fifty-cent coin my father gave me as lai see and my winter blanket.

My thumb ran over the coin that nestled in my palm and told myself that no matter what happened, I could never spend it. If I died, I wanted to at least have something to be buried with, something that had value.

I stuffed my items inside my winter blanket and folded it up. It was something I had quilted over the years from unwanted clothes, sheets and scrap material. The blanket was my only comfort – thick enough to keep me warm in the winter and soft enough to line the floor as a mattress in the summer. Without a calendar, my blanket was a way of marking the years I had spent in Tang House.

'Ah Ping, time to go,' said Zeoi Mao. His tone was softer, almost sheepish, which unnerved me.

I looked at my so-called 'husband' – a man-child standing in front of me with a much bigger bundle of belongings than mine.

Is Fate so harsh to bind me to this person? Why, of all the fishermen on the island, must I leave with him?

There is a saying in Chinese: 'marry a chicken and follow the chicken, marry a dog and follow the dog'. I could have begged Gong Tau to let me stay but I knew he would have refused. Wherever the husband goes, the wife must follow. At that moment, I realised a cage doesn't have to be a physical place, but it can be a person and that person was Zeoi Mao.

I had fantasised about the day I could leave Tang House countless times. I imagined how my spirit would be lighter than goose feathers dancing in the wind as I skipped my way to freedom. But there were no goose feathers, no skipping. Instead, my stomach churned acid and my feet twitched, not knowing what to do with my freedom.

Tang House was the only place I had ever known, the only place I had lived for thirteen years. I had got used to its smells as the seasons changed, the way the moon cast shadows in the kitchen where I slept, the way the hard floor felt on my back. Could I have ever called that place home? No. Living somewhere for a long time doesn't make it home. It would take me many years to understand this.

Zeoi Mao walked slightly ahead as we left for the seafront. My legs felt like someone had cut them off at the knees. I was like a plant that had been pulled out from the roots. Some plants survive, others shrivel and die. I decided I must survive this, I had to.

I paused and glanced over at Zeoi Mao, waiting for him to take charge, to tell us where we were going, to do something. But when I looked at his face, the man-child whom I had feared for so long, he looked so small, so weak. He looked powerless.

'Where will we go?' I asked.

Silence.

He stared at the horizon, his eyes darted from side to side.

'What are we going to do now? Where are we going to sleep?'

Silence.

'Well? We can't stand here forever,' I barked at him, expecting him to strike, but he simply stood there, motionless.

How have I been so terrified of you my whole life? I can't rely on you. You're useless! I have to find somewhere to go, and I have to do that fast.

With the sun baking my face and the weight of my swollen belly suffocating me, I suddenly recalled something my mother had told me. Big Sister had married a widower with his own plot of land in a village somewhere on the island.

I could go there. . . but how could I find her?

The island may be small, but it wasn't straightforward to find someone. There was no such thing as the White Pages or information directory. We certainly didn't have the internet where we can type in a name and see what pops up. So I did what felt natural to do – ask. I started at the seafront at first, asking anyone and everyone the same question.

'Do you know a Hakka woman by the name of Lam Siu Fong? She's married to a widower on this island. Have you heard of her?'

But it was always the same answer: no, never heard of her.

I went to every market stall, every vendor, asking the same question. I searched the faces of anyone who looked vaguely Hakka on the off chance they might know my sister, but no one had heard of her.

Where could she be? Is she still on the island?

Good thing I had my blanket and not much else. It was hard enough lugging a watermelon inside me without having to carry a lifetime of belongings. Of course, Zeoi Mao didn't help. Instead, he followed me like a little lost kitten – the 'man' who was such an expert at giving me orders and battering me was no more than a clueless idiot outside his father's house.

Part 3

Finding her

I was ready to give up. I had spent seven nights sleeping under tree groves and seven days shuffling from place to place, asking everyone I came across if they had heard of my sister. Finding her felt impossible.

'Eh, you there! Are you looking for someone?' said a woman's voice.

We were in one of the villages, stopping at every market stall, asking for Siu Fong. I looked over at the woman who was squatting over her baskets of vegetables for sale.

'Yes, yes, I am. Maybe you know her? Lam Siu Fong? She is Hakka and married a widower. Do you know her? Have you seen her?' I pelted her with my questions.

The woman looked at me up and down and then at Zeoi Mao and raised an eyebrow.

'Are you a relative?'

'Yes, I'm her younger sister. Please, Ah Sim, if you know where I can find her or where she lives, please tell me. I really need to find her.'

The woman rubbed the sweat from the back of her neck.

'She lives in Sha Tau village about an hour's walk from here in that direction,' she said, gesturing.

'Thank you! Thank you so much, Ah Sim.'

I didn't know until that day that pregnant women could run too.

***

I was on my tenth or possibly twelfth door in the village. Nervous sweat drenched my cotton blouse and my knuckles chaffed from all that knocking. The neighbour next door assured me this one was definitely Siu Fong's home. As I stood in front of the wooden door to

Big Sister's house, I wondered if she would recognise me. Big Sister hadn't seen me since the morning in that school when I was sold. That was fourteen years ago.

With a deep breath, I knocked on the door.

No answer.

I knocked again.

The door cracked open to my sister's unmistakable wide forehead and big round eyes.

'Big Sister? It's me, Ah Ping.'

A long pause.

Her eyes squinted, searching my face.

'Ah Ping, it's you! I can't believe it's really you. And you are with child! Come in, please, come in,' she said in Hakka. Our mother tongue soothed the edges of my nerves.

Big Sister lived in a small stone house with her husband and baby daughter on the outskirts of Sha Tau village. Her husband owned a narrow plot of land where they grew radishes, sweet potatoes, tapioca and choi – basic crops. Having your own land is always good because it means you could never starve. It means you will always have food.

'Come in, Ah Ping, don't be shy. Please, come and sit down. You both must be rather tired. Let me get you some tea.' She gestured for us to sit at the table, her newborn baby girl wrapped tightly in a blue sling on her back.

Without saying a word, she handed us both some damp cloths to wipe our hands and faces. What a sight I must have been – like a dirty beggar woman.

'Ah Ping, look at you. My little sister is all grown up and about to have a baby!' She pushed a strained smile as she flashed a glance at Zeoi Mao, who hadn't said a single word since we arrived.

'Ah Jia, I have something to ask of you . . . but I don't know how to—'

'I know what you want to ask, Little Sister,' she interrupted, as if having read my mind. 'But we must first wait for your brother-in-law to return home.'

Once again, my future laid in the hands of someone I had never met. Uncertainty itched like cockroaches on my skin as I wiggled and fidgeted anxiously on a wooden stool, waiting for Jia Fu to return.

My brother-in-law was a tall and slender man with a clean and tidy appearance. His quiet confidence and well-mannered demeanour reminded me a lot of my father. Like most men in the village, Jia Fu worked as a fisherman, but unlike most of them, he could read and write. This rare skill earned him respect as well as extra income, not like Zeoi Mao, who was like a barbarian brute next to this educated man. I felt utterly ashamed to have Zeoi Mao for a husband.

Big Sister led Jia Fu outside the house where they thought I couldn't hear them.

'We have to let them stay. She is my little sister, and the poor thing has nowhere else to go. Besides, she is pregnant and due in a few months. We can't let a pregnant woman stay on the streets. It will be only for a while. I am sure once they get on their feet, they will find their own place. Ah Ping is a hard worker – she can help me around the house and sell crops with me in the market. It would be a relief to have a companion to talk to.' Big Sister's voice was mellow and sweet.

There was a pause and then a sigh.

'Only because she is your littler sister and pregnant,' said Jia Fu reluctantly.

I exhaled, relieved I didn't have to spend another night sleeping outdoors.

***

Big Sister's house was like our childhood home with a mezzanine for the sleeping area. Zeoi Mao and I were given a small space downstairs in the kitchen area and for the first time, I had to share a sleeping space with my husband. It was that or sleep outside and believe me, I had thought about that many times.

Would he try anything with Jia Fu and Big Sister sleeping upstairs? Jia Fu is an entire head and a half taller than him . . . I guess I am safe here?

Sleeping on the floor was normal – I had done it my whole life and was grateful that I had brought my blanket to use as a mattress, but Zeoi Mao wouldn't stop complaining. *It's too cold. It's too hot. It's too hard. It's too uncomfortable. It's too noisy.* What a moany shit. There were moments whilst he snored loudly that I pictured myself taking my blanket and suffocating him with it.

Aside from having to sleep next to him, I didn't see Zeoi Mao much. He left early in the morning and returned in the evening for dinner, drenched in sweat and the stench of alcohol. Apparently, he was 'going to work' or that's what he'd say as he left, and I would feign interest and nod along, but it was a relief not to have him around. Whenever Zeoi Mao stepped out, I felt my body loosen and the knots in my stomach untangle. It was a feeling of looseness, of not having to look over my shoulder, of not having to expect a beating. It was knowing that I was safe and wanted. I knew that as long as Jia Fu was around, Zeoi Mao wouldn't dare to hurt me.

The best part was Big Sister doting on me as if I were a guest of honour, giving me extra portions of rice and soup and the thickest slices of meat.

'Ah Ping, here, have some more. Don't be shy, eat more. You are with child now, so you will need your strength. Here, eat, eat.'

Like our mother, Big Sister showed her love by how high she could pile my rice bowl. Food was the ultimate act of love.

Whilst her hand filled my bowl, her eyes saw what I could not tell her – eyes of concern, eyes that wondered but knew what my years as a san pou chai had done to me. As I shovelled the fragrant white rice into my mouth, I told myself not to get too comfortable.

Remember what happened? That year with your parents and you were sent back? Remember, you're a san pou chai and this is not your home.

I would not let myself forget that easily, not this time, just in case.

The first one is the hardest

Your body can remember a lot of things, but it can also forget many things too.

Something happens to you when you haven't felt kindness for a long time. Your body forgets and blurs tenderness with violence until you can no longer tell the difference.

It was late afternoon and time to prepare dinner. Big Sister tasked me with preparing the fish and vegetables whilst she squatted over the clay stove, blowing and fanning at the flames to get it hot enough.

It was only a touch, a delicate touch, but I immediately spun around, swinging the meat cleaver in my hand. My eyes looked but could not see.

'Ah Ping, what are you doing? It's me!' screamed Big Sister.

With her eyes still filled with fear, she gently lowered my arm.

'It's all right, Ah Ping. It's me.' Her voice was calm and gentle, but her face was still ashen with worry.

How do I begin to tell you? Where would I start?

My body did not feel like my own – perhaps it had never belonged to me. All those years living in Tang House had turned me into something else, someone who was afraid of my own sister's touch.

'Ah Ping. I'm here,' she muttered.

Perhaps it was the tone of her voice or the way her head titled, but, in that moment, I believed her. I knew she understood, and no more words needed to be exchanged.

The warmth of my sister's presence was like a cosy blanket wrapping me on a bitter winter night. So long as I was living with her and Jia Fu, I knew I would be safe and that Zeoi Mao couldn't hurt me. But I still couldn't meet her gaze even when she lavished affection on me, piling up my bowl high with rice and big slathers of meat, knowing that every second I was there, I was living off her and Jia Fu. I was a liability, a burden, useless.

***

There were no hospitals on the island, not even a clinic. The closest hospital was across the sea over in Hong Kong, so if you got sick and it wasn't too serious, you would go to the dai fu, but only if you could afford it. How times have changed! Now when people have a little sniffle or a bit of a temperature, it's doctor this, medicine that. It's no wonder the younger generation has such poor immunity. We only went if we were gravely ill or seriously injured.

But what would have made a big difference to us back then would be female doctors to tend to female affairs. We didn't have nurses or midwives in Tung Ping Chau. Why would we? Childbirth was an expectation, a natural duty, like breathing or walking. Other women in our community, had inherited wisdom from generations of grandmothers, mothers, sisters, aunties on an island that had no running water. If there were complications, if we bled out, got an infection, or got sick, there was little anyone could do.

I had been warned of the risks, of what could go wrong, but when my water broke and the contractions started, Big Sister's words weren't enough to prepare me for what I was about to experience.

'Ah Jia! What is happening? What is this?' I cried out as I clamped my legs shut, terrified of the wetness that trickled down my leg. My body was doing things I could not control.

'It's normal, Ah Ping. Your water just broke – it means you will have your baby soon,' she said as she hurriedly prepared hot water and rags.

The pangs were crippling. I could no longer stand. Hobbling into the kitchen, I dropped onto the floor.

'Ah Ping, don't lie down!' she shrieked. 'Here, squat down and lean over this stool. It will be a lot less painful this way.'

I draped myself over the stool.

'Here, take this.' She handed me a thin piece of bamboo. 'Put it between your teeth and bite down when it's time.'

'Time? Why? What for?'

'Trust me, you will need it.'

I looked down at the piece of bamboo in my hand and took a big gulp.

How bad is this going to be if I needed to bite down on bamboo?

My first child ripped through me as violently as it had been conceived. I caught Big Sister's pained expression when she looked between the legs of the infant, and I knew instantly it was a girl. It's always the same expression anytime it's a girl. We are born to be raised, to be given away – who can love those who cannot stay?

The birth of a girl is met with both disappointment and pity. We are disappointed in ourselves as mothers knowing we cannot give this girl a good future and we pity the girl who will inevitably face a lifetime of challenges. To be born a girl is to be born unlucky.

With no tools or medical equipment to cut the umbilical cord, Big Sister took a string and tied it around the cord and cut it with a small stone that had been sharpened to a knife's edge.

'Tell me I have a son!' It was Zeoi Mao banging on the door outside. 'Tell me now or I will kick down this door!'

'Ah Jia, please, I . . . I cannot tell him. I can't. Please tell him for me,' I pleaded, my face masked with sweat.

Big Sister nodded and went outside to deliver the news for me as I waited. There was no shouting, no throwing things around, no breaking of doors. Silence. I knew what his silence meant – the birth of a girl isn't a cause for celebration. In that moment, I begged the Heavens to show mercy and not to let me bear any more children in case I bring another girl into this world. You see, this world was not made for daughters, it does not welcome them.

PHONE CALL: 21 NOVEMBER 2020
4pm, Hong Kong time

'Paupau, it's me.' I'm unsure if she would want to take my call. There was no time to arrange a video call this week with everything that's happened.

'Eh, Didi. It's you.' Her voice is coarse and thick. 'Your Auntie Lin . . . she . . . passed . . . She's, she's gone.' Paupau coughs. I can hear the mucus in the back of her throat.

I don't tell her that my cousin had texted me the news early this morning.

'Ay! So young, too young. . . I can't believe she's gone. Children aren't supposed to die before their mothers.' Her voice breaks as I imagine silent tears streaming down her face.

She sighs, her breath heavy, uneasy.

'The doctor says she died in her sleep. You know she was in a coma, right? For days she was in that coma – almost a whole week and then . . .' She stops herself from going any further. I know Paupau wants to cry, to wail, but she's holding it all in to the point it almost chokes her.

I don't know what to say or how to console her. I want to snap my fingers and be there next to her so I can hug her, but all I can do is hold the phone to my ear and listen to my grandmother grieve for her firstborn child. How do I fix this? I need to say something, do something. Then I recall what she used to say to me, something Tai Yee Pau, her eldest sister, used to say.

'Don't cry, Paupau, or you will have big eye bags,' I say in the most positive tone I can without sounding patronising.

'Oh, you remember that? Your Tai Yee Pau used to tell me that all the time whenever I cried. I can't believe you remember that.' I can hear her wipe her face as she sniffs.

I exhale. Would it be enough to bandage her pain for a little while? The shock of losing her child – what if Paupau's heart can't take such a loss? What if this is what finally breaks her?

'Tai Yee Pau lived past a hundred. My poor sister was all alone in that sad elderly home with that massive lump in her thyroid – it was so bad she couldn't breathe and had so many tubes . . . even to eat.' She coughs to clear her throat. There is a long, silent pause.

There's no point in asking her if she's eaten yet. I know the answer, and it doesn't feel appropriate. Nothing is well right now. How can she have an appetite when she is full of grief?

'I remember Tai Yee Pau very well. Especially that time when she came to stay in the summer. I think I was around nine or ten. And I remember you took her outside in the communal garden to cut her hair, speaking Hakka.' I don't know why I bring it up. I want to say something that might bring Paupau some consolation, some solace. Tai Yee Pau had always had a comforting effect on her.

I can see my great-aunt in my mind's eye. A soft-spoken woman eleven years older and three inches taller than Paupau who wore her hair cut into a straight bob just below her ears and slicked back – the style of so many Hakka women of her generation. A lifetime spent in Hong Kong, but she only ever spoke Hakka.

'Yes, I remember too. I loved my sister very much. Cutting her hair was the least I could do for her after all she did for me and Ah Lin. You know, it was Tai Yee Pau who named and nursed your Auntie Lin?' She sighs.

'I hope they can both find each other.' Her voice breaks, words muffled.

'I hope so too, Paupau, I hope so too.' I squeeze the phone, wanting to cry too, but I don't dare.

A SISTER'S LOVE

The old women in the village cautioned me, but I didn't listen. They told me that so long as I was nursing a baby, I must not, under any circumstances, cry. They told me that if I cried, I would end up having massive bags under my eyes when I got older. Big Sister warned me, but I didn't listen and now see how big my eye bags are? All puffy and swollen, so ugly! All because I didn't listen to those old women, thinking they were making things up to scare me. How could I have known? But crying was all I could do.

My infant girl could not locate the nipple, which looked more like flattened man tou. There was barely anything there. Pregnancy was supposed to make a mother's breasts plump with milk, but mine were like two tiny mosquito bites. When my baby finally latched on, pain cut through my breast and pierced deep into my spine. All those years of malnourishment had taken its toll on my body. My breasts were dry and empty, now they were punishing my first born.

'Don't worry, Ah Ping. It can take some time until your baby will suckle,' comforted Big Sister.

'Hand me something to bite on,' I said as I nodded to the chopsticks that lay on the kitchen counter.

With one chopstick in my mouth ready for me to bite down, I tried to nurse my daughter again. I felt the sharp slice of pain as the baby sucked on nothing. When I pulled her away from my breast, her lips were stained crimson as she cried out in hunger. I held the tiny girl in my arms and wailed with her.

I am so useless! What kind of mother can't produce milk to feed her own baby? I can't even manage what every mother can do. I am useless.

I had nothing to give her, nothing I could offer her, only my tears, but tears cannot feed anyone except your sorrows.

'Ah Ping, don't cry, or you'll have big eye bags,' lulled Big Sister. 'I have an idea. Why don't I nurse her? I am still nursing my little one.

Let me nurse yours.' She reached over and gently took my baby from my arms and, as if she had done it a thousand times before, she nursed my daughter like her own.

As I watched my baby feed from my sister's milk, a warmth filled my heart as I felt the tears stream down my face. Big Sister did more for me than anyone had done in my brief life and in that moment, I felt it – the unconditional love and bond between sisters. It is the most powerful feeling I had ever known. This is the greatest act of love a woman can show another woman, and I will never forget her selfless kindness.

When she finished, I said to her, 'Ah Jia, please do me the honour of naming my baby.'

'No, I couldn't, really. It should be your husband who names her, or you.' She shook her head.

'I insist, please. I want to name her but I wouldn't know how. You know many more words than me – you have Jia Fu's good influence. Please, it is the least I could offer you for all that you have done for me. It would be my honour for you to name her.'

She paused for a moment and pursed her lips.

'Mei Lin,' she said. 'This was what I was going to call my daughter if I had another one.'

'Mei Lin,' I repeated, sounding it out in my mouth.

This was how my firstborn was named. Her nickname was Ah Lin.

***

A mother's body after childbirth is at its weakest and traditionally new mothers should have a 'sitting month' – thirty days of staying home for the body to fully heal and recover. There are many things you can't do: no crying, no washing or bathing, no lifting or carrying heavy things, no leaving the house, and only bland food and warm drinks. 'Sitting month' is for those who can afford to sit at home and do nothing for thirty days with servants to wait on them; or if you are lucky enough to have an older sister like mine to take care of you.

For thirty days, Big Sister prepared steaming bowls of congee for me and nursed Ah Lin. Whenever she saw my sullen face, she would sing our father's Hakka songs to cheer me up, but my skin itched to leave the house. I wanted to get out, to do something, to work, just so I felt less useless. To be useless is the worst thing a person can be.

I remember the morning when my sitting month was over. Hues of oranges and lemons spread across the sky as I threw myself into the courtyard scrubbing every part of my body, ready to shed my month of doing nothing. I was hungry to get back to work, so I strapped Ah Lin to my chest with a baby sling and piggybacked the basket of vegetables to be sold at the village market. I felt indebted to Big Sister and Jia Fu for their generosity and had to repay them. Now with the baby born, I knew sooner or later Zeoi Mao and I would have to move out and I didn't want to lose my chance to repay them.

Big Sister and Jia Fu never mentioned it but I knew a person's hospitality has its limits. They never went hungry, but they were still poor, and extra mouths to feed meant an added burden and I refused to be a burden to other people. I could not bear to become the unwanted house guest.

One morning before Zeoi Mao left the house, I plucked up the courage to tell him it was time to find our own place.

'We need to move out. It's time. My sister and Jia Fu cannot house us forever.' My words came out in big gulps as my body was ready to duck and cover. Even though he hadn't raised his hand to me since Gong Tau kicked us out of Tang House, I couldn't trust him.

'Fine. We'll go,' he said without so much as a glance.

That was a surprise.

He had been on his best behaviour under Jia Fu's roof and knew if he laid his hands on me, my brother-in-law wouldn't let him off that easily. But behind closed doors . . . Zeoi Mao could do whatever he wanted.

Did I make a big mistake? What's going to happen when we were alone?

In that moment, the all-too-familiar feeling of dread and panic returned as if it had never left. A few weeks later, Zeoi Mao rented a tiny stone hut a few doors down from Big Sister's home.

At least I am close enough to run to hers.

Silence is a source of great strength.

—Lao Tzu

As a girl we are taught to be quiet, to stay silent, to watch as the world in front of us goes by and decisions are made for us. The silence we are taught as a virtue feels like a gag, suffocating and choking us to the point that when we do need to scream, we have forgotten how to use our voice. We have forgotten we have a voice.

TUNG CHAI

I will never forget his face, his short, chubby cheung fun rolls for legs and his thick head of black hair. His name was Tung Chai, and he was my son.

About a year after Ah Lin was born, I was pregnant again – unwillingly, of course. It was an unexpected birth. I was feeding Ah Lin congee one morning when I felt a wetness between my legs as a small trickle of clear fluid ran down them. I had no time to panic as the contractions had already started. Everything was happening so much faster than the first time.

Wait, I'm not ready. Don't come out yet!

No one was at home with me, and I didn't have time to hobble over to Big Sister's home. Alone, I dragged myself around the hut, trying to remember what my sister did the first time.

Rags . . . I need to put something down. Hot water and . . . a stool. I need a stool!

I threw some rags on the floor and slid a wooden bucket of water next to me – *no time to heat it up, it'd just have to be cold.*

'Ah Lin, stay here,' I panted between the contractions as I placed her on our sleeping area. Sweat drenched my agonising body.

My daughter, only two years old at the time, watched me tumble around trying to remove my trousers and undergarments. I hunched over the stool screaming and cursing Zeoi Mao for having done this to me and me being unlucky enough to be born a woman. Ah Lin's eyes filled with confusion and fear, unable to understand what was happening to her mother.

With no one to guide my infant's head or to tell me how hard to push, the baby's head ripped through me. My roar of pain echoed in the walls of the empty hut, bouncing against my loneliness – I had never wanted someone to be with me more than in that moment.

There was so much blood, seemingly endless, much more than the first time. It was everywhere.

Whoever said that after your first child, childbirth afterwards would be a lot easier must have been utterly stupid or a man to promote such a ridiculous lie. It never gets easier, your body merely remembers the pain.

Half dazed, I wrapped the infant in the cleanest cloth I had as I prayed to the Heavens that it wasn't a girl. I looked down between the baby's legs and my eyes widened.

'It's a boy! I have a boy. A boy!' I screamed.

The exhaustion, the excruciating tear he had ripped in me – all were forgiven. None of that mattered because I had produced a boy and Zeoi Mao would finally be satisfied.

I cradled my boy in my arms and a round goop of bright red mess slid out of me.

What is that? A chunk of my insides? An unformed child?

With the first one, I was too out of it to realise that the goop was the afterbirth and Big Sister did the clean-up for me. But alone, I was petrified. Using the old rags, I wrapped the gunk up and threw it aside. I didn't know that some people cooked and ate the afterbirth for its nutritional value, but I don't think I could ever stomach that – not after seeing it expelled out of me.

The umbilical cord was still attached, and I didn't have Big Sister's sharpened stone. I thought about grabbing the meat cleaver.

No, too dangerous.

My eyes scanned the hut for what I could use and saw the many empty tinned food cans with their jagged edged tops that I had collected to sell.

'Ah Lin, close your eyes. Don't look,' I said to her as I took one of the lids and with the sharp edge, severed off the umbilical cord.

***

When Zeoi Mao returned home and saw I had given birth to a baby boy, he stared at the infant, mesmerised as if he were looking at a bar of pure gold. I had never seen him so happy as he laughed, almost giddy, shouting, 'My son, I have a son! You hear his little voice? As strong as his father. A little tiger! I will call you Tung Chai. Yes, Tung Chai, my strong boy!'

It is remarkable how the arrival of a boy can change a man like Zeoi Mao. The man who had never bothered with Ah Lin was suddenly obsessed with his son. He wouldn't leave the baby alone, always cradling him and announcing to an audience of no one how strong and handsome his son was, just like his father. I wanted to throw up in my mouth. But at least Zeoi Mao cared enough to stop drinking and for a period there was relative peace at home. The shouting, the threats of violence, the beatings – all of that stopped, and he was a totally different person. I was wary, feeling as though I was living someone else's life and at any moment, it would end.

A week after Tung Chai was born, he started to cry day and night. Nothing could quieten him. Then when I was changing him one day, I noticed his belly button was enlarged and red like a cherry and his body burned with fever. Without hesitation, I wrapped him up and ran down to Big Sister's home before Zeoi Mao would return from work.

Nothing can happen to this boy. He can't get sick!

'Ah Jia, you have to help me! I don't know what is wrong with Tung Chai. Look at his belly. What is happening to him? Please, you must help me,' I beseeched her.

My sister placed the back of her hand against Tung Chai's head and unwrapped him.

'Ah Ping, Tung Chai is very sick. He has a fever. It's his belly button. Look, it's infected. We have to take him to the dai fu!' she cried as she threw her slippers on and dashed outside.

'But I don't have any money.'

'Don't worry. I will pay for it.'

The dai fu gave us a packet of herbs which Big Sister helped me boil down into a dark green paste that I plastered across Tung Chai's belly. But after two days of applying the medicinal paste and praying desperately to Kwun Yum, the infection would not subside.

'Tung Chai, please get better. You have to get better – for your mother's sake,' I uttered as I smothered the herbal paste on him. Zeoi Mao stood over me, watching, waiting, calculating. 'I don't know what else to do. What else can I do?'

The worry-acid that had boiled in my stomach was burning a hole through me. There is nothing worse than a mother feeling completely powerless in helping her child.

'If you have killed my son, I will kill you,' Zeoi Mao warned. He didn't shout, he didn't raise his voice. He didn't need to – it was a promise.

With those words, he snatched Tung Chai out of my arms and rushed him to a hospital in Hong Kong.

My boy was admitted to Kwong Wah Hospital in Yau Ma Tei on the Kowloon side. He was barely two weeks old when he went in and I, still on my 'sitting month', was banned from leaving the house where I had to stay and wait.

'How is he? How is Tung Chai?' I ran to Zeoi Mao as soon as he returned, impatiently desperate for some news.

'How do you think he is? Ha? My son is very sick, and the doctor said he has to stay in the hospital for two weeks. Two weeks!'

My eyes searched for an invisible calendar in my head.

'Two weeks? For that long? Is it serious? He won't die, will he? Can I see him? I want to see him!'

Zeoi Mao said nothing and glared at me. His jaw clenched tight, eyes wide with warning.

If anything happens to Tung Chai, I will have to pay with my body, possibly my life.

I gulped and prayed that my son would get better fast.

***

A HAKKA WOMAN

The two weeks were an agonising wait of half-eaten rice bowls and sleepless nights. Zeoi Mao barely spoke to me during that time as if he was waiting on a jury to decide what my sentence would be. There was nothing I could do but wait. When it was time to collect Tung Chai, I left Ah Lin with Big Sister and defied tradition by leaving the house before my sitting month was up and went to the hospital with Zeoi Mao.

The morning we left on the ferry for Hong Kong was especially humid. I remember how my clothes stuck to my skin as I sat on the wooden bench that had been nailed down to the floor. I had seen the ferry so many times over the years, but that was my first time on it. Had it been under different circumstances, I may have enjoyed the ride, which felt so much more stable than a rocky sampan.

A wall of noise hit me the moment I stepped off the ferry at Tai Po Pier in the New Territories. Everything buzzed and hummed with a frantic business. We had to get on a bus to Kowloon and until then I had no idea what a bus was.

'Eh, excuse me, do you know which number bus goes to Kwong Wah Hospital?' Zeoi Mao asked a man at the bus stop.

We had been walking up and down the same road for over fifteen minutes as I watched Zeoi Mao try to figure out which bus we were supposed to get on.

Hadn't he been here before? Why doesn't he know the way?

'Two seven one, over there, where it says Yau Ma Tei,' said the man.

'Two seven one,' repeated Zeoi Mao as his neck craned to look for the bus sign. 'Where? Which one?'

'Over there, it's right in front of you. Can't you read?' grumbled the man.

I observed Zeoi Mao's face, still painted with confusion, and then it dawned on me.

He can't read . . . He can't read!

All those years of schooling and still he was simply an illiterate island-man-child.

Why was I so afraid of him? He is just as uneducated as me.

I would never forget my first bus ride. The bus zoomed down lanes and roads as my heart raced. Fingers gripped the seat in front of me, as I feared I would be flung out the window. Through squinted eyes, I saw the landscape change to a labyrinth of buildings stacked next to each other, some three, even four storeys high! Women in their colourful, tightly fitted cheong saam looked more like goddesses from Heaven walking next to men in strange outfits. Apparently, they were Western-style suits, but they looked more like pyjamas to me. My eyes didn't know where to look or how to take in everything I was seeing.

All around me was a cacophony, and a thousand living things, vibrant and alive. Surely, Hong Kong was a beautiful place – a place of dreams, as everyone had said. Seeing this shiny, busy place when I got off the bus made me realise the shabbiness of my own dreams and just how small my world was as a stupid, uneducated Hakka woman from the countryside. As I looked around the many buildings and people around me, my damp clothes felt tighter, and a heat rose from the back of my neck.

Tung Chai, you must get better so your mother can take you to this glorious place when you are older. There is such a big world outside of Tung Ping Chau, such a big world to see. You must get better so you can see it.

When we arrived, the nurse waved us away to go and wait for the doctor. We sat there for hours. Zeoi Mao, who would normally kick up a fuss about being made to wait, was unusually sheepish. Being surrounded by so many educated people, people with money, he looked like a small little man and I even smaller. I was an insignificant woman next to him.

Finally, a skinny man in a white coat and black thick-rimmed glasses came out. This is who they called doctor.

'I am very sorry, but unfortunately your son has passed away.' The doctor spoke with no emotion.

What? No, it can't be. It must be a mistake. The doctor must have got us mixed up with someone else. It can't be right!

'What do you mean, passed away? How is this possible? I was here a few days ago and even gave him some water to drink. I held him in my arms. What are you saying? You must be mistaken!' shouted Zeoi Mao.

'I am very sorry.'

Sorry? What am I supposed to do with your sorry?

'Where is my son? Where is he? Bring me my son! Bring me my son!' The recent memories of Zeoi Mao beating me flashed before me as I shrieked.

'Please, calm down. You must calm down. As I have told you, your son passed away a few days ago,' said the doctor.

'No, you're lying. It's a mistake. It can't be possible. He was fine a few days ago and didn't have a fever anymore!' barked Zeoi Mao.

'I am very sorry, but these things happen sometimes.'

'If he is dead, then where is his body? I want to see his body. I want to see my baby!' My voice trembled, holding back my tears.

Don't cry, you cannot cry, not yet.

'Well, we had to cremate him straight away. There isn't a body. I am sorry.' The doctor showed no remorse, no empathy.

'What? You cremated him without telling us first? How could you? I am his father. You owe me a body!' Hearing Zeoi Mao's rage suddenly threw me into a frenzy.

'I don't believe you! Where is my baby? Where is my son? Give me back my son! Tung Chai! Give me back my son. Tung Chai!' My arms swung wildly as I lunged at the doctor, claws scratching at him. I wanted to hurt him. I wanted him to feel just a grain of what I knew was waiting for me after this.

Many pairs of arms grabbed me and yanked me back as I continued to scream uncontrollably like a feral animal.

'If you don't calm down, I will have security throw you out and I'll call the police. Now get out of my sight!' shouted the doctor.

With that, he shoved me away, dusted off the front of his pristine white coat as if my touch had dirtied him, and marched away. I sank onto the hospital floor and thumped at it with my fists, willing the ground to crack open and swallow me whole. My Tung Chai – one day he was my baby boy in my arms with his fat rolls for legs and chubby cheeks and the next some man in a white coat tells me he is dead without a corpse. I remember little after that, because little else mattered.

***

It was in the choking, drowning silence of the ferry ride back to Tung Ping Chau that I realised what had happened.

I did this. I cut the umbilical cord with the dirty edge of the can. I caused the infection. No one else can be blamed but me.

I looked down at the water and I wondered if it would have been easier to jump off and drown than face Zeoi Mao.

No, I deserve whatever punishment that awaits me. I did this to my Tung Chai.

'You stupid Hakka bitch! This is your doing. You killed my son!' Animated by rice wine, Zeoi Mao threw me across the small hut.

In the past, I might try to run, hide or push him away, but not this time. This time I ate every strike and blow he gave me – I took it all. The physical pain he inflicted was nothing compared to the pain that ripped through my heart.

'You stupid fucking bitch. My son is gone because of you!'

Hit after hit. Knuckles broke my skin, but it didn't matter because I was already broken inside and deserved the punishment for losing our son.

'One way or another, you will give me back my son!' Zeoi Mao grabbed me and pinned me against the floor as I lay there, a motionless, bloodied shell.

This was how I became pregnant again.

***

'You better pray to the Heavens this one will be a boy. Stupid bitch, you owe me a son!'

Zeoi Mao repeated this threat over and over during my third pregnancy as if I had any control over the matter. If a woman gave birth to a girl, it was her failure. If she gave birth to a son, it was her husband's glory.

Less than eight months later, I gave birth to my third child, with Big Sister next to me as my midwife. When I saw her strained expression, I knew my prayers to Kwun Yum for a boy had not been answered. This scraggly little thing came screaming into the world, protesting Fate for making her a girl. Second Daughter weighed practically nothing in my arms, her scrawny body scratching at the air like a helpless little kitten. Cradling her, I cried knowing what kind of life of hardship lay before her.

Out of all his children, Zeoi Mao beat Second Daughter the most. He despised her because she was not a boy – the one to replace Tung Chai. But it would be Second Daughter who would come and save me decades later.

Be content with what you have; rejoice in the way things are. When you realise there is nothing lacking, the whole world belongs to you.

—Lao Tzu

When your rice bowl is empty and has been for days, weeks, even months, the only thing you can realise is how much you truly lack. When you have nothing, is there anything to rejoice? When you are hungry, can you really believe the whole world belongs to you?

1957

'Ah Ping, I have something I have to tell you, but I don't know how to,' said Big Sister, her eyes averting mine. 'We are leaving Tung Ping Chau.'

It was late afternoon, and the hut swelled with the day's humidity. Big Sister had come over to hand me some extra swaddling cloths, and rice. We were squatting in my kitchen area as I diced turnips to add to the rice for dinner later, padding out our meals with anything that was available. Money was a problem, and that problem was we didn't have any. Two young children to take care of, little work available for someone like me on the island and a 'husband' who drank everything he earned made every meal preparation seem almost impossible.

'I see.' I paused my chopping and put the cleaver down. 'When?' I asked without looking up from my rice substitute.

'Next month,' she muttered.

'Oh. That soon.' It was not a question, it was a matter of fact – I had one month left with my sister.

'You know there's no work left here on the island and so many people have left for Hong Kong,' she said, as if her explanation would make the news easier to digest.

I pursed my lips and nodded as I continued to chop my turnips.

'Maybe you could come with us? You could bring Ah Lin and the baby, and we could all go to Hong Kong together.' She inched close to me, her faced animated by the suggestion.

I turned around and looked up at her. As soon as the reality of what she had suggested sunk in, her face fell. We both knew it was impossible.

'Don't worry about me, Ah Jia,' I said with a forced smile. 'You'll be much happier in Hong Kong. It will be good for you and your family. You know, I don't think I could have survived without you taking care of me these past few years. I don't know how I could ever thank you.'

I continued to chop, cutting and slicing those turnip pieces so finely, pretending I wasn't gasping for air, wondering what would happen to me now without my Big Sister.

The thought of my sister leaving looped in my mind.

She was my only relative, my only companion and friend. I have no one else. What will I do without her?

She never asked but she saw, and she knew what it meant to be Zeoi Mao's wife – she knew everything.

'Ah Ping, I'll get the ointment,' she would say every time she saw the marks Zeoi Mao left on me.

With the tit da jau, she would gently massage the bruises in silence, as if she could somehow rub the memories off my body. She would never ask what happened, why I was so badly bruised. You see, if our husbands hit us, it was our fault and ours alone.

Anything could be the reason:

- the soup was too salty
- we asked too many questions
- we nagged too much
- we caused our husbands to lose face in public
- we didn't produce sons.

There was always a reason, and it was never because our husbands were wife-beaters.

***

I stuffed all those little pockets of time that I had remaining with Big Sister into my heart so that on the harder days to come, I could take them out and revisit them. I wanted to collect as many memories of her as I could whilst she did her best in passing on our mother's Hakka recipes. Together we cooked the dishes we could afford, which wasn't much, and shared them, giggling in the kitchen like two young girls. The reminder that those moments wouldn't last tainted the tenderness of us sharing our mother's recipes, and after twenty-eight days, it was time for her to leave me.

There was a time when the sight of the pier would fill me with hope – that there was a world beyond Tung Ping Chau and Zeoi Mao. Sometimes I caught myself staring at the pier just to watch the ferry arrive, telling myself that one day I would get on and finally leave the island, never to return. But after what happened to my Tung Chai and then knowing it would take my sister away to a place I couldn't reach, the sight of the pier filled me with dread.

I didn't allow myself to believe Big Sister was really leaving until I took Ah Lin and Second Daughter to the pier to see them off.

'Ah Ping, take good care of yourself. Your Big Sister cannot look out for you anymore. Try to eat more, hmm? Wear more clothes when it is cold.' Her voice trembled as she spoke.

Then she turned to my eldest, who was barely four years old at the time.

'Ah Lin, be a good girl and look after your mother. She will need you now more than before. If aren't a good girl, your Tai Yee will be very upset with you.'

Ah Lin looked up at her Tai Yee through her fringe with her big, round eyes and nodded.

'Ah Jia, I . . .' But I couldn't speak. My words were stuck in my throat and suddenly I was seven years old again, standing at the front of the school watching my mother say goodbye to me. My sobs choked me as mumbled half syllables came out in a garbled mess.

'Ah Ping, remember, if you cry you will have big bulgy eye bags when you grow old. No need to cry, hmm?' she uttered as she wiped my face and then hers, our tears mixed. 'It's not like I am dying, right? I'm only moving to Hong Kong. We will see each other very soon. I am sure of it. No more crying.' She forced a smile to comfort me.

'Here, take this.' She took my hand in hers and stuffed a small silk purse into it. 'Take it and hide it.' With those words, she pulled me close for our last embrace.

Ah Jia, please don't go. Don't leave me here, don't leave me here all alone with him, not again! Take me with you, take me far away from him, from this place. Ah Jia, please. If I let you go, I could lose you forever, like I lost Ma.

But I couldn't say those words. I couldn't say anything. I just held onto her as tightly as I could, hoping she could hear what was in my heart.

'It's time,' said Jia Fu.

I watched the image of my sister shrink as she was being carried further and further away from me.

'Ah Jia, come back! Please don't leave me. Don't leave me all alone!' I screamed louder than I had ever screamed before.

Why didn't I say something before? Why did I stay quiet?

But it was no use calling out to the sea. The sound of the waves and wind muffled my voice, and I might as well have been calling out to nobody. I collapsed onto my knees as if to beseech the Heavens for mercy. I was, once again, alone. Goodbyes are always hardest on those left behind, not the ones who leave.

Before returning home, I found a secluded place and opened the silk purse. I couldn't believe what was inside! Enough money for at least three months' worth of food and a familiar pair of gold hoop earrings – the same ones Big Sister had worn for as long as I could remember. There was something else, too. A small, folded piece of paper with some writing on it – an address, perhaps? A sour reminder that I could not read as I thought back to when my father had also done the same. I clutched the silk purse in my hand, feeling the smoothness of it against my skin, and the stillness in her voice echoed in my heart as I wept. She needed all the money she had to resettle in Hong Kong and yet still she gave it to me.

Ah Jia, what would I do without you now?

Grief tastes of ash, leaving a metallic dryness in your mouth from crying for so long.

She really has gone.

'Mama, Mama,' babbled Ah Lin as she tugged on my sleeve.

Zeoi Mao would be home soon. Quickly, I jammed the contents back into the silk purse and tucked it in my undergarments where I had sewn a secret buttoned pocket.

There is no way he is getting his drunken hands on this. No way!

That was the last time I would see Big Sister for many years. Her name was Siu Fong.

Video call 8 : 21 December 2020
Winter Solstice Festival, 4:30pm Hong Kong time

'Eh, Didi, it's you! Have you eaten yet?' Paupau is still chewing on tong yuen. I can hear my cousin tell her to put the bowl down so she can focus on talking to me.

'Yes, Paupau. Happy Winter Solstice!'

'Ah, good girl. You remembered. Have you had some tong yuen? Your Auntie Yin bought some for me, otherwise I wouldn't get to eat any this year. Ah-yah, so many places have shut, closed down. And I'm afraid to go out by myself,' she says as she wipes her mouth with the back of her hand.

The last time I had any tong yuen was the last time I was in Hong Kong, sat in Paupau's dining room. Certain foods just don't taste right without her, so I don't bother. At least she's getting her appetite back, but I can't help but notice the jade bracelet that usually fits so snuggly around her wrist is still loose. Some things take time, I guess.

'Have you got enough food? Enough warm clothing?' I ask. I worry all she's eating is fu yu with steamed rice and nothing else.

'Yes, yes. Plenty. It's only me. Besides, how much can an old woman eat and wear, anyway? I'm getting so old, it doesn't really matter.'

Is she that old? For the first time, Paupau actually looks like an old woman. The grey-and-white hair that she used to dye black and perm is the longest I have ever seen it – it's down past her ears. Her hair looks limp and greasy, with big patches of white. Ever since Auntie Lin passed away, Paupau has stopped bothering with her hair. It worries me what else she will stop caring about, if she'll ever bounce back from this. She has to, she always does.

I'm halfway curating Paupau's stories, but I'm stuck. The timeline surrounding her children, who she had and when is a bundled mess. So much of what she has told me was when we were still living together, and I was a little girl. I find myself writing a memory of memory. I can't seem to place a specific one – an image of a black-and-white portrait of a little girl who looks so much like Auntie Lin. What was her name? I want to ask Paupau about it, but I'm worried it's too soon, too sensitive to talk about her children, but my cousin thinks she'll be all right with it.

'Didi, you okay? Why so quiet? Something wrong?' She furrows her brows.

I haven't told her I'm writing her story, her life, yet. Should I tell her now? I definitely need to, I have to – I need her permission, her blessing, but what if she says no?

'Oh, it's nothing, Paupau. I was just wondering if one day when you have time and feeling better, maybe you could tell me more about your life? About what happened to you?'

She jerks her head back.

'You want to know? Why?'

'Of course I do! You're the one who raised me. Who else's story should I know better other than yours? I already know about the Japanese and being a san pou chai and your life on Tung Ping Chau, but not about what happened after. Will you tell me one day?'

'Hmm . . .' She pauses. 'They are such sad stories . . . Why would you want to know and remember them?' She scratches the back of her hand.

I look straight at her.

'Because I want to remember them for you.' I hold her gaze as long as I can to show her that I am being serious. As I stare at her, Paupau's black sesame eyes look grey. She looks so small, so old. *Please don't fade away, please don't go anywhere. I won't know how to be me without you.*

She nods and then shuffles back to the dining table to bring back her bowl of tong yuen.

'See, look – they look so good, right? They taste pretty good too.'
She slurps a tong yuen into her mouth loudly and smiles.

I want to cry and hug her, but I can't, so I caress the screen and try to smile.

TAI PO

When you are poor, you dream of being some place else because you want to believe anywhere must be better than where you are right now. But a new place doesn't always mean having a better life because bad luck can follow you wherever you go – like a ghost that sticks by your side forever.

There were so many rumours and talk amongst the villagers, all banking on a dream, and that dream was Hong Kong.

Hong Kong has plenty of work. Lots of opportunities and it is rich! So much money. Anyone can make it in Hong Kong.

Eh, did you hear? My sister-in-law's cousin's neighbour made big money in Hong Kong! Now he lives in a big, fancy house.

Eh, did you hear? In Hong Kong, people drive automobiles and wear gwai lo clothes – they have plenty of money. Better to go to Hong Kong than stay here on Tung Ping Chau!

The villagers spoke about Hong Kong with such a frenzy that it sounded like a place of unlimited bags of rice so long as you were prepared to work for them. At first, I brushed off their rumours – surely a place like that doesn't exist and everyone was exaggerating. But as time passed, I couldn't help but wonder if there was a place for someone like me in Hong Kong. The more I fantasised about it, the more my heart filled with great impatience, wanting to go and see this Hong Kong for myself.

The timing could not have been better. Zeoi Mao had exhausted all the favours he had managed to squeeze by simply being Gong Tau's son. No one would hire him anymore. Any time he got a job, he would show up late for work and slack off whenever he had the chance. Other times, he would cause trouble by starting fights like he had something to prove – he always had something to prove. He had to be the 'tough guy' when really, he was a lazy, useless drunk. Whenever he came back beaten up from picking a fight with the wrong guy, he was sure to prove his 'manliness' on my body. My futile attempts at fighting back simply made things worse.

Somehow, I believed that if we moved to Hong Kong, if Zeoi Mao could get work, things could change and that he would be too busy and tired to hit me.

***

It was after Lunar New Year 1959. I was pregnant again, this time with child number four, and once again, it was time to pack up my entire life. A familiar ritual of surveying my belongings before wrapping them up in old clothes and donated bags.

Is this all that I have to show for? If I died tonight, is this all that I'd leave behind? Maybe it's better this way, at least I won't have too much to carry to Hong Kong.

The chilly breeze felt sharp against my face as the very same ferry that had taken Big Sister away from me only two years before was now sailing me to Tai Po in the New Territories. With the gentle rocking of the sea, my mind drifted, imagining what life would be like in Hong Kong.

We could get a bigger hut that doesn't smell of damp rot. I could find work and buy buckets of rice. I will make my daughters' faces plump with satisfied full-belly smiles. Yes! And a dining table packed with many dishes of meat, fish and vegetables. And rice, lots and lots of rice!

I giggled, lost in my fantasy.

'What are you so happy about, laughing like that? You look retarded,' Zeoi Mao spat out.

'Nothing . . . it's nothing. Nothing at all,' I muttered as I shook myself out of my silly ideas. Dreaming is dangerous for people like me, inflating my hopes until they are so big, they burst, and when they do, I am left with deflated, empty nothingness.

With Ah Lin sat quietly next to me and Second Daughter strapped to my chest, I watched the horizon slowly swallow up

Tung Ping Chau and my jaw clenched so tightly to suppress my screams I thought my teeth would break.

That pok gai island and that pok gai Tang House!

I glared at that island. It is the place that robbed me of my innocence, my childhood, my life and I swore to myself that I would never, ever return. There is nothing anyone could say, do or give that would make me even think about going back to that damn island. I would rather eat shit than go back there!

***

Tai Po at the time was still a rural fishing town right by the sea and the single place on the Hong Kong mainland that was accessible by ferry from Tung Ping Chau unless you had your own sampan. Most Tung Ping Chau immigrants used Tai Po as their first stomping ground before eventually moving out to Kowloon or to the more affluent Hong Kong Island, but many would live out their entire lives in Tai Po.

We moved to a squatter's village called Wan Tau Tong, not far from Tai Po River. All sorts of people lived there – islanders from Tung Ping Chau, refugees from China, social outcasts and people who simply couldn't afford to live anywhere else. Nowadays, if you were to look around Wan Tau Tong with its high-rise residential blocks and shiny shopping centres, it would be hard to imagine what a dump it used to be.

The squatter's village was a cluster of huts and makeshift houses that suffocated each other, jammed side by side with no regard for housing regulations. Health and safety? Ha! There was no such thing. So long as the hut didn't collapse, it was good enough, and no one seemed to care, anyway. All the huts and houses were built by the same people whose hands were just trying to carve out a tiny place of their own, a place they could call home.

The families who had a bit more money or who had been there the longest lived in stone houses, much like the ones on

Tung Ping Chau, with a mezzanine or extension. The poorest families lived in wooden huts, and this is what I had to call home.

The hut we rented was originally designed as a pigpen and smaller than the one I lived in on Tung Ping Chau. It was a single room which we separated for different functions, one side was the sleeping area (on the floor, of course) and the other side for cooking and eating. A small, narrow platform with a bit of space under it was meant to be the kitchen. No stove, no electricity, no running water. Our windows were two small squares that had been cut out of the wood, which made the hut especially hot and stuffy in the summer. For months it stank of pig faeces and whatever the previous occupants had left to fester and later it smelt of us – our damp, our sweat, our tears.

Our toilet was a hole outside that led directly to the sewage system, poorly covered by a few branches and trees. At least in the last hut we had a shared outhouse which, although reeked of piss and shit, had four walls for modesty and I never had to worry about falling into raw sewage. I was terrified of going to the toilet, having to tread each step with such caution in case I slipped and literally fell into human waste. Fumbling around in the dark for the toilet was the worst; I could only see a faint glimmer from the moon or the huts around me. If I ever woke up in the middle of the night needing the toilet, I would hold it until the morning.

Showering was more or less the same. We had a sliver of a space outside which we curtained off with an old large cloth. There's no space for modesty when you're poor. My hair had grown down to my waist by then and it was such a pain to wash, having to squat over a bucket and use a ladle as a hose. Sometimes when I hunched over for too long, my back would seize, sending pins and needles down my legs.

By the first week, I wondered how something that could sparkle so much from afar could be just as grey and grotty as everywhere else. This was not the Hong Kong I had seen on the bus nor the place I had so foolishly fantasied about. I hadn't factored in the extortionate rent that was triple what we were paying on Tung Ping Chau. With no work and little money, I didn't know how we'd survive.

The very next day, I found a barbershop in the village and chopped off my wall of silky black hair in exchange for two dollars. It was barely enough to keep us going for the first few weeks.

Did I make a mistake?

SAAM MUI

It started so subtly, so gently – the dull throbbing ache in my belly that woke me up in the middle of the damp, humid night. As soon as I sat up and felt the familiar dampness between my legs, I knew my water had broken.

'Eh! Wake up. Wake up, it's time!' I shook Zeoi Mao. 'Turn on the lamp and get me some hot water, rags and a clean knife. Make sure it's clean. Come on, get up!' I pushed and nudged him.

Relying on a stone was better than on Zeoi Mao, but with no one else to help me, I didn't want to take any chances.

In the choking darkness, baby number four slid out of me almost silently.

'Huh, another girl,' Zeoi Mao spat as he cut the umbilical cord and bundled her up. 'Here, take your daughter,' he said as he handed her to me and went back to sleep.

'What should we call her?'

'Call her whatever you want. She's a girl, so why would it matter?' mumbled Zeoi Mao, half asleep.

As if on cue to protest her father's indifference, the baby girl began to cry. I looked down at my child and shook my head, pitying this innocent baby.

You poor thing. Fate hasn't been kind to you, has it, for you to be born into this family?

Remember when I told you, names in our culture are supposed to have a special meaning? Well, that is if you're lucky enough to have an educated family to give you one. This time, I didn't have Big Sister to name my child and with nothing coming to mind, I simply gave the baby the only name I could come up with.

'Saam Mui. I'm going to call her Saam Mui,' I said.

Saam Mui was a plump, gentle little thing who quickly learnt to sleep through the night and barely cried. She was the easiest baby I had ever had.

***

Useless. Totally useless mother.

Every time I heard Ah Lin's rumbling tummy or saw how gaunt Second Daughter's face had become, I thumped my chest, blaming no one but myself for my daughters' hunger. I did not have the means to feed them.

By the time Saam Mui was six months old, money became a problem – and the problem was we had none. The high rent and cost of rice had quickly drained the money Big Sister had left me, including her gold earrings, which I reluctantly pawned. You can't eat gold, anyway. Zeoi Mao picked up some odd jobs here and there, sometimes as a road sweeper, other times as a coolie, but it wasn't enough. It was never enough. Anything he did earn, he drank away, leaving almost nothing to feed us.

As a san pou chai, I became accustomed to the sound of my own hunger. It is the sound of emptiness growling to be full. It is a sound I had learnt to live with, but hearing the same sound coming from my daughters was shattering. I crumbled inside. I will never forget how Ah Lin pleaded with her eyes – those big round eyes, after finishing her half bowl of rice, yearning for more. There was never more. My rice grain bucket was always empty as we lived hand to mouth, one meal at a time.

With each night that passed, Saam Mui felt lighter in my arms. I could barely produce any milk to nurse her.

What am I going to do? If you get any lighter, you will disappear into nothing. I have got to do something or you, me, the others – we will all starve.

It was in that very moment I decided upon the unthinkable.

There is a saying: it is better to raise a goose than it is to raise a daughter. A goose can be slaughtered and fed to your family, but girls are raised and then given away to someone else. Years spent raising a daughter for her to become someone else's property. This was what happened to me. This was what happened to my sisters.

For a long time, I had never really understood how my parents could sell me. I knew their reasons and I have even accepted them. But for years I could never understand, really understand, why . . . until that moment. Life had squeezed and pushed me so far that it felt like my only option was to throw myself off the moral cliff and hope for the best.

She's only a baby, she won't remember this, she won't know what happened to her. If she stays, she'll starve. It's too late for Ah Lin and Second Daughter. They are too old but it's not too late for Saam Mui.

It's not the same as what Mother and Father did. That was different.

Look at her, with those pudgy cheeks and dimpled smile. I am certain someone would want her. Someone else can give her the life I never can.

It's better this way. At least she'll have a chance, a better chance.

Saam Mui, please forgive me.

***

'It's time,' said Zeoi Mao impatiently.

'Let me bathe her once more,' I muttered. 'Her new parents would want a clean baby.'

Bathing Saam Mui, I sang Hakka songs as I tried to commit every part of her to memory. Every fold of her skin, every eyelash, every toe. I wrapped her in the best swaddling clothes I had and repeated all the blessings I could think of, over and over. I wanted to believe that if I had said them enough times, they would come true.

'I wish upon you rich parents who will buy you all the food you could ever eat, so you will never go hungry. Plenty of toys and beautiful dresses to wear. For you to go to school to learn how to read and write so you can have power over your own Fate. I wish for you to grow up into a useful person in society, that you honour your new parents and look after them until they are old. I wish for you to find a good husband who will protect and take care of you and make you happy. May you never go wanting for anything in life, my Saam Mui.'

I held Saam Mui in my arms and took one last look at her.

'I hope you will find it in your heart to forgive me, like I forgave my parents. Please know I did not want this for you, but if you stay, you will starve to death. Heaven forgive me for being so poor and useless that I cannot give you a good life with me. I will cherish you always, my dearest Saam Mui,' I said in short, soft whispers.

'Take her,' I said as I handed her over to Zeoi Mao. 'Just go.' I turned my back to them, believing it would be easier if I didn't see her leave.

I held my breath until I heard the door slam shut.

I did the right thing. It was for the best. She would have starved otherwise. She would have a better life with someone else, a family that could buy her all the food she could eat. It was for the best.

I muttered to myself as I wiped my face, surrounded by grief.

Girls' lives are cheap. Saam Mui was sold to a couple in Yau Ma Tei for fifty Hong Kong dollars, which was less than what I was worth all those years ago. How we came to know the couple was through a barber in our village who had heard about our trouble since arriving in Hong Kong. Perhaps he knew of Zeoi Mao's drinking problem, perhaps he took pity on us. Whatever it was, it was enough to get him to talk about our situation with his wife, who put poor couples in touch with wealthier infertile ones. This was how it was back then in Hong Kong. The poorest of us, unable to feed our own, sold our children in hopes they'd be given a better chance with families that had more money. Can you imagine an entire generation of boys and girls raised by strangers they grow up to call Mother and Father? The players and the scenery may have changed since they sold me, but the opera tune stays the same.

'Where have you been? You've been out the whole day,' I said as Zeoi Mao walked through the door, but the moment the waft of alcohol hit my nostrils, I knew.

'None of your damn business where I've been!' he barked, one hand still clutching a bottle of rice wine.

The heat in the back of my neck rose as I watched him plonk himself onto the floor, chugging his booze.

'Where is the money from Saam Mui? I need it to buy rice for us.'

No response, but did I need one? Wasn't it so obvious where the money had gone?

No, he wouldn't do something like that. Would he?

'I ask you again, where is the money? Ha? Where is it?' I stood over him, my body tensed, ready.

'Stop pestering me about money. Who is the head of the house here? Ha? Me and I say what happens. Now fuck off!'

'You spent it, didn't you? You spent the money. That wasn't just money, that was her! That was Saam Mui!' I screamed.

Without warning, Zeoi Mao sprung up, instantly animated by alcoholic-fuelled rage as he glared at me with his bloodshot eyes. I knew what would happen if I spoke again, but I didn't care.

'You spent our daughter, you disgusting mongrel beast! You heartless piece of shit. Damn you, Tang Tin Yeung. Damn you straight to Hell!'

Everything he had put me through, everything I had to endure – it all came exploding out of me as I clawed at Zeoi Mao in a frenzy, hungry for violence. I wanted to gouge his eyes out, I wanted to taste blood. I no longer cared if I lived or died. He could beat me, he could even kill me, it no longer mattered.

With a single shove, he threw me against the table, my back smacked against the hard wooden corner, and I dropped onto my knees. I could barely stumble back up before Zeoi Mao spat on me as he left the hut, shouting and cursing.

I don't remember how long I sat on the floor of the hut, saturated in my rage and grief. And it was grief. I had sold Saam Mui and Zeoi

A HAKKA WOMAN

Mao had drank her. It was all for nothing. My sole consolation was knowing that wherever Saam Mui ended up, it would have to be better than staying with us – a drunken, violent monster for a father and a useless mother that can't feed nor protect her daughters.

There were no tears that night. The emptiness that was left from selling Saam Mui had sunk deep into my bones. It was an emptiness I had to learn to swallow – it is still there, and I have to live with it every day knowing I am the mother who sold her own daughter.

***

Some years later, a neighbour from the squatters' village handed me an envelope telling me it was addressed to me.

Strange, I don't know anyone who'd send me anything and everyone knows I can't read.

I opened the envelope to a letter and a black-and-white photograph.

Who is this? She looks . . . no, it can't be! Is it . . . Saam Mui?

'Please, could you read the letter out to me?' I asked my neighbour.

Streams of tears poured out of me as I listened to the letter being read aloud.

We hope this letter finds the right person. We are looking for a woman called Lam Ping Mui, and the man called Tang Tin Yeung living in Tai Po who sold us their daughter seven years ago in Yau Ma Tei. We have been trying to search for the parents for some time. Our daughter has grown up healthy, happy and safe. We couldn't bear not letting you know so your heart could be at ease.

I studied the photograph again and there was no doubt it was indeed Saam Mui who looked so much like Ah Lin and Ah Yin. The resemblance was uncanny, with her round, flat face, almond eyes and jet-black hair braided in two thick pigtails. Sat on a big wicker chair in a pretty floral dress, she looked like a young princess on a throne. Her face was as plump as a suckling pig, cheeks augmented by her demure smile.

You look happy and full, Saam Mui.

I clutched the photograph close to my heart and then that knot which had been sitting in my stomach for years, wondering how Saam Mui was doing, started to release.

It's okay, she's okay. She is safe.

This is the same photograph you had asked me about. It is the only record I have of my daughter.

Talk does not cook rice.

—*Chinese proverb*

Mr Jesus

I had never seen a gwai lo before, most people in my village hadn't either. Why would we? Most of us were too poor to even make the bus fare out to Kowloon, let alone Hong Kong Island, where most of the white people lived. They had their area spread out in airy, clean and comfortable white colonial buildings and we had ours – crammed side by side and on top of each other in sweat, dirt and squalor.

But I didn't know about any of that back then. All I knew was that gwai lo were rich and powerful – so powerful that they could put a Queen with a fancy jewelled crown on our money. I always did like her hairstyle.

Rumours of a gwai lo priest handing out clothing, food and money had spread across our village. Apparently, it was easy to get those handouts. All we had to do was show up to his miu on Sunday morning, listen to him talk about some famous gwai lo called Jesus, and wait until the end to get some handouts.

I was more than intrigued, I was confused.

A white man coming to help us? Sure! Why would he come all this way from his country to help poor Hong Kong people? What nonsense.

No one ever came to the slum village to help us. We had to fend for ourselves, and that was how it had always been. I would forgo food for days so my daughters had something to eat whilst Zeoi Mao spent almost all his wages on booze, leaving me very little for food and rent. Hunger torments and twists. It left me contemplating eating the rats that scurried across our cockroach-infested hut. As much as I hated living in Tang House, there was at least fish heads and broken rice to eat. But now, living on a cleaver's edge with the constant worry that the landlord would kick us out, I was desperate. When someone is desperate, they will believe anything, even if it's something as ridiculous as a gwai lo coming to help.

***

One Sunday morning there was a lot of commotion outside my hut as neighbours called for us to come out.

'It's the gwai lo priest! He's here again, and he's giving handouts. Come out and see for yourself!'

I didn't want to believe it. Why would anyone, let alone a white man, come and help us? But I had enough of seeing my rice grain bucket always being empty, so I went outside and followed the others towards the small courtyard at the centre of our dilapidated village.

Everyone was wide-eyed, eagerly craning their necks to get a better look at the gwai lo. For most of us, it would be the very first time we would see someone that didn't look like us. A crowd had already gathered, but I couldn't see anything except the backs of my neighbours, their familiar black hair and tattered blue and black clothing. Then a man's voice filled the air, speaking in Cantonese with a funny and unfamiliar accent.

Could it be? Is it possible? That white man is speaking our language, and fluently!

My jaw dropped.

I need to see him. I need to see what he looks like.

I tiptoed and hopped about, even for a Hong Konger I had always been on the short side. And that's when I spotted him.

So, this is what a gwai lo looks like... he is so... so beautiful!

I was filled with both nervousness and awe. His hair was the colour of smooth golden sand in the midday sun and his piercing eyes were bluer than the clearest water. No doubt he was taller than anyone I had ever seen, with his slender frame and long arms and legs. He didn't wear those silly Western suits but had a Western-style black shirt with a strange white square in the middle of the collar.

This beautiful man said he was a priest, looking after a miu called a 'church' and worked for a very special man called Jesus.

This Mr Jesus must be very a big deal if he can send a Cantonese-speaking gwai lo all the way to Hong Kong.

I stayed so I could find out more about Mr Jesus and how he could help me and my family.

The priest talked about so many complicated ideas that day, things I had never even considered, let alone understood. Things like forgiveness, love and God and the afterlife. Who had time to think about this stuff?

'This is from Jesus. He knows of your suffering, and he wants to help you. I want to help you,' announced the priest as he passed sacks of food and clothing to each of us.

Did it matter that I didn't understand any of it? Would that have changed anything? I don't think so. I knew I had to eat first and think later.

'Here, this is for you,' he said, a sack of rice and two cans of luncheon meat in his hand.

I reached out for the bag of rice, feeling the cloth's rough texture against my fingertips as I stared, captivated by the vibrant colour of the priest's eyes.

This man must be from the Heavens if his eyes look like them and this Jesus is a very generous man.

'Thank you,' I muttered, embarrassed at how dirty I looked and felt next to him.

I loitered outside my hut, unsure how to make sense of my encounter with this gwai lo priest.

Is it possible for someone to help me but ask for nothing in return? Could this priest and Jesus truly understand my suffering? But how could they? Don't they have all the money and power? Maybe I should follow Mr Jesus, he seems to be the only one who can help me.

***

Tai Po Catholic Church was unlike any *miu* I had ever seen or visited. Chinese temples are often stuffed with too many joss sticks in a small space with little ventilation, and cluttered with all kinds of statues and plaques. This church was so different. The hall was spacious and lined with rows of polished wooden benches, filled with a beautiful musky fragrance that I would later learn was called frankincense. That smell would become one of the most comforting smells to me.

I walked down the aisle and looked up at the altar. That was when I saw *him*. A figure of a man with pale white skin on a wooden cross at the front of the church behind the large white altar.

Who is this man? What is he doing up there?

I inched closer and saw his wrists and ankles had been nailed to the cross as he hung there with a crown of thorns around his bleeding head.

This is awful! Why would anyone do such a thing? And why would a miu put this statue up to worship?

I studied the cross, thinking back to all the pain and sorrow I had endured and wondered, if this Westerner had suffered through such a torturous death, perhaps I could bear my own anguish. Perhaps I wasn't alone, perhaps someone out there could understand.

'Hello, can I help you?' It was the same man – the priest who had come to my village.

'Yes, erh, I . . . I want to . . . erh . . . I want to . . .' I stuttered, feeling my face flush with embarrassment at how dishevelled I looked in my tattered, rat-gnawed clothes.

'It's all right, take your time. Erm, I think I remember you. Aren't you from the squatter's village? Please, come, sit.' He gestured towards a bench.

But it's so clean, if I sit on it, I will dirty it.

'Yes, yes, I am.' I hesitated, barely perching on the edge of the bench. 'I can't stay for long. My family . . . my children . . .' I didn't know what to say. My cheeks burned as I mumbled.

The sun shined through the stained-glass windows, illuminating the space. I felt so small in the presence of a white man.

Don't be so ridiculous, he isn't going to help you. Look at you – you are nothing but a stupid illiterate Hakka woman. Why would anyone want to help you?

'It's all right. You are safe here. This is a house of God. And I think I know why you are here. You have come to the right place. Jesus wants to help you and I want to help you.' The priest smiled.

Wah! His teeth are so white and straight.

'You must have many questions like why would a gwai lo come all this way to help people like you? What's the catch, right?'

I froze.

How does he know what I am thinking? Is he a magician?

'That's okay. If you didn't have those questions, I'd be worried. You see that man over there nailed on the cross?' He pointed towards the altar. 'That is Jesus. He is God's only son. God loves us so much that He gave Jesus to us, to wash us of all our sins so that when we die, we may have everlasting life in Heaven with Him.'

God? Which one? There are so many Chinese gods, most wanted offerings like bribes. Who is this one then? And Heaven? With the Jade Emperor? But then who is greater – this god or the Jade Emperor? Or Buddha?

My head drowned in questions that I had never thought about before.

'Don't worry, I can see it's a lot to take in. You should come to Mass on Sunday so you can learn more about Jesus and God,' offered Mr Father Priest.

'Mass? What is Mass?'

'It is when we worship together here in this church. You should bring your children. They are always welcome. Everyone is welcome.'

His eyes were a crystal blue, the colour of Heaven, and they shined as brightly as the sun that beamed through the windows.

As I hurried back home, I felt a warm, tingling feeling inside that rippled and radiated through me. It was the feeling of hope, something I thought I had lost long ago.

Wah, this Mr God must be powerful if he can bring back my feelings of hope.

***

Every Sunday I gathered my children and together we walked down the mud and gravel path from our squatters' village and across Tai Po Market to the Immaculate Heart of Mary Church where we attended Mass.

At first, I was more motivated by the handouts at the end of the service, eagerly waiting for small sacks of rice and canned foods. But the more Mr Father Priest spoke about Mr Jesus and his teachings, the more I longed to go. Mass was like school, a place where I could make up for all the things I had never learnt and what was better, it was free! Imagine, all that knowledge was suddenly available to me, and all I had to do was show up. Mr Father Priest had an answer for everything from how the world was created, why bad things always seem to happen to good people, why there is pain and suffering, what to do and not to do and how to pray. After each explanation, he made sure to inform us that what he was saying were the words of Mr God.

With the passing of time, I discovered that my suffering was not meaningless because I was loved by the All-Powerful Mr God and his beloved Mr Jesus and Mrs Mary – the Mother of all mothers. They were watching over me and my children. Can you believe that? *Loved.* No one had ever told me they loved me before. We don't say such things aloud to others because we speak our love through our actions. And Mr God showed me His love by His actions, giving the world His only son for us. A son!

This may seem foolish to you, but all those teachings and hours spent at church made me feel like my little life had some meaning and that I finally had some purpose. There was more to my existence that surviving an alcoholic and abusive husband, putting food on the table and feeding my children. I felt that my life was worth living. Isn't this the best lesson you could learn?

***

'Ah Ping, would you like to be baptised?' Mr Father Priest asked me one day after Mass.

'Baptised? What is "baptised"?'

'To be baptised is to formally welcome God and become one of God's children. You will be making a commitment to God, in accepting His love.'

'Yes, yes! I want to accept. Yes!' I said, even though I wasn't entirely clear on what baptism was, but the invitation to be formally part of Mr God's family was more than good enough.

'Wonderful. This is most joyous news.'

'Eh, Mr Father Priest, can my children join and become Mr God's children too?'

'Yes, of course! We can baptise all your children.'

'Thank you, Mr Father Priest. Thank you for accepting us. Thank you, thank you!' I beamed, knowing soon Mr God's love will also protect my children.

I will never forget the cool trickle of holy water on top of my head, nor the feeling of being reborn. Everything bad in my life that had happened before that moment felt washed away by a simple gesture – Mr Father Priest pouring the holy water on me. I was bestowed with a great honour as Mr God's daughter and felt as though my past could not hurt me anymore.

No matter how shabby our clothes were, no matter how skinny our legs, nor how many bruises were on our bodies, Mr Father Priest never turned us away. It was the one place that never judged us and welcomed us like we were family.

'Here, Ah Ping, take this. This is for you and your children,' Mr Father Priest would say as he loaded our arms with food, clothing and sometimes stuffed a banknote into my hand.

I was hesitant to accept his charity at first, but when you are poor, hungry, on the brink of getting evicted with so many mouths to feed, there is no room for pride. Pride you must eat and keep inside for the sake of your family.

Mr God was an ever-present source of hope during those dark years in Tai Po. From that day of my baptism, I made a promise. So long as I am able, I will attend Mass every week come rain or shine and offer my most solemn prayers of gratitude to Mr God, Mr Jesus and Mrs Mary for saving my children. I have kept my promise to this day and every week at church, I empty my purse to repay all the church had given me.

It is better to raise geese than it is to raise daughters.

—Chinese proverb

Video call 9 : 27 December 2020
4:30pm Hong Kong time

'Eh, Didi! Have you eaten yet? It must be cold in . . . where are you?' Paupau tilts her head.

She is wearing her black wool cardigan with the bright red peonies, a pattern from my childhood, over thirty years ago.

'Hi, Paupau! Yes, I've eaten. London – I live in London and it's pretty chilly.'

'London? Have I been there? I think I have . . .' She squints as if trying to squeeze the memory out of her brain.

'Yes, you came to visit in 2006 when I graduated. You know all those photographs of my graduation on your wardrobe door? They were taken in London. We went to Chinatown, and you had cha siu rice. I remember you complained it was so expensive,' I laughed.

Does she still have her collage of photos taped on her wardrobe doors? Snippets of her favourite memories: my 2006 bachelor's graduation, snapshots of us when I was barely eight or nine, portraits of Auntie Yin at every graduation, the only photos she has of her brothers.

She scrunches her face and then bursts into laughter.

'Yes, yes, I remember now! Good thing you have such a good memory.'

'What have you been up to in the last few days?'

I feel a pang of guilt that I had barely managed to speak to her on Christmas Eve.

'Oh, it was terrible. I can't go to church because they closed it. I haven't been to Mass for . . . I don't remember how long. What a disaster! There is no Mass and all the churches are closed, so no one can go in. What would Mr God think? Ha?' She sighs, shaking her head.

'I'm sure God will understand and forgive you, Paupau. He can see what's happening in the world right now. If you continue to pray at home like you always do I'm sure it will be fine.'

'But it's not the same. How can that be enough? We are Mr God's children. He did so much for me, for us. I must repay this debt to Mr God, otherwise . . . Ah-yah, I hope He can forgive me for not being to attend Mass.' She scratches the back of her hand.

'Do you know they have Mass online? You know, like with a computer? Maybe Auntie Yin can help you set it up and you can watch it?'

'Computers? Ha! Me using a computer? Don't be silly, Didi. I'm too old and too stupid to use one. You know I can't read. Besides, what if I play around with it and it blows up like the TV?' Her shoulders narrow.

There are very few things Paupau is afraid of, exploding electronics is one of them. Apparently, back in the day, TVs would explode. I think she meant the fuse.

'Don't worry. I'm sure church will reopen soon and then you can go to all three services back-to-back to make up for it,' I tease her.

'You're still such a cheeky girl,' she giggles.

Suddenly, her face changes and her lips pull back.

'What's the matter, Paupau? You okay?'

'Ah-yah, you know, I am all by myself every day, all day. I get so bored by myself. I can't read and I forget which buttons are which on the TV remote, so I keep myself busy by looking outside my balcony and popping bubble wrap. Sometimes I'll listen to the radio but every day is the same. I get so bored and so lonely.'

Her words punch my gut. In all the years I have known my grandmother, she has never expressed her own feelings so directly, at least not to me.

'Sitting by myself all day, I'm rotting away. This is why I forget so many things. Nowhere to go, no one to talk to, I feel myself becoming stupid, totally useless! One moment you say something, the next minute I forget. What is happening to me?' Her voice breaks.

A HAKKA WOMAN

All I can see is Paupau sat by herself, engulfed in loneliness and the constant reminder that she is losing her memory. I need to cheer her up.

'Paupau, do you remember when I was a little girl? You used to take me to church every Sunday.'

I can almost feel her hand tickle the soles of my feet to wake me up hours before Mass, so we would be the first people there. For her, proximity to the altar was the same as proximity to God. If church was a rock concert, Paupau would be the ultimate groupie, glow sticks and all.

'Oh yes, I remember. I took you every Sunday without fail. It was in Tai Koo Shing, right? Every Sunday, the ten o'clock service, front row seats.' Her lips form a crescent. I knew talking about church memories would cheer her up.

'We must have looked so funny to the others – an old Hakka woman next to her chubby little gwai mui granddaughter pretending to be able to read the order of service!' She laughs.

'Well, it never stopped you from making sure we were always on the right page. That's very impressive.'

'You know, after so many decades, you learn to pick up a word or two.'

There were so many moments in the middle of a Bible reading that I would turn and watch Paupau as she held the page so close to her nose so she could see all those tiny character strokes – she was studying. Church wasn't soley a place of worship to her, it was a source of her hope and sense of self-worth, a place that reminded her that given the chance, she too could read.

'But you know what my favourite part of church was? It was after Mass when we would go to CityPlaza for lunch,' I smirk.

'Ah-yah, always thinking about food!' She sniggers.

How I loved those late mornings when we marched, arms linked, straight to the chaa lau, ready to munch on delicious steamed dim sum from bamboo baskets. Sometimes we headed to the food court where we were spoiled for choice – Hainan chicken rice, BBQ pork and duck rice, deep-pan pizza with extra anchovies and KFC. Each week after we nourished our souls, we nourished our bodies with our food adventures, always trying out new things.

'But it's true – that was my favourite part. we had so much fun eating together, didn't we?'

She smiles, all teeth.

'My favourite was going to the supermarket after. You know, the Japanese one with all those giant apples and eel rice. So much food and so clean!' She is practically giddy recalling those pristine aisles.

'You're thinking of Uny. I hear it's still there. Next time I'm in Hong Kong, let's go there together with cousin and I'll buy you all the eel you can eat. What do you think?'

'I hope there will be a next time. I hope I'll still be here when you come back.' She fumbles with her hands.

'What? Of course you will. You're not going anywhere, Paupau! We still have so many things to do together.'

I speak with a thick ball of mucus forming in my back of my throat. *Don't go anywhere, Paupau, I need to come back home first.*

FOUR IS THE UNLUCKIEST NUMBER

To be a mother doesn't stop at giving birth to a child. To be a mother, you must also be able to raise her.

When I found out I was pregnant again in mid-1960, I was filled with apprehension.

What if it's another girl? What kind of life will she have staying in this family? I can barely provide for my two girls now.

But survival is never about doing things you like. Survival is about having to do whatever it takes, no matter how you feel about it. As much as I hated the idea, I decided that if this baby was a girl, I would have to sell her.

The months passed and my belly grew heavy, as if it too was carrying the weight of my dread.

Please be a boy, please, Mr God, give me a boy. I cannot bear to have another daughter, one that I will have to give away. Please, don't be a girl, anything but a girl.

***

It was the first time I gave birth in a hospital. Tai Po Hospital was all white. White walls, white floors, white nurses' gowns, white doctor coats, white sheets. White. How strange, especially for us, because white is used for death and funerals. But at least everything looked and felt incredibly clean. There were no flies, no cockroaches and there was a distinct smell which I later learnt was bleach. I found it comforting.

They put me on a bed in a long room lined with many other beds occupied with other expectant mothers. I didn't know why I had to lie down and initially thought the bed was for me to rest, but no, I was expected to give birth like that – lying down. Can you believe it? Ah-yah, what a crazy idea to give birth that way!

But I was so intimidated by the doctor, I listened and did what I was told.

There was a reason Big Sister and all the female elders told us never to lie down. The pain was a thousand times worse as the baby pushed against my spine when it came out. I thought my whole body was going to be crushed into the thin mattress as the baby ripped through me. It was the hardest birth I had ever experienced.

Daughter number four was born in 1961. You see, for us, the number four is a bad sign because when pronounced, it sounds like the character for 'death'. Anything with the number four is unlucky: four, fourteen, forty-four, seventy-four. And this baby was doubly unlucky because she was born both a girl and the fourth one.

Maybe your luck will change after you leave this family, I thought, holding Fourth Daughter in my arms at the hospital. Having made up my mind that I would sell her, I decided not to give her a name and simply called her Sei Mui – Fourth Daughter.

Your new parents can give you a proper name, a good one that has a lucky meaning for you.

***

Sei Mui was about a month old when we found a young couple to buy her. They had no children and as they weren't wealthy enough, they couldn't afford the high price for a son. But at least they had more money than us and could provide Sei Mui a better life – I don't know how many times I had repeated that to myself, as if it were a spell to numb myself from my decision.

As I had done with Saam Mui, I bathed Sei Mui one last time so she would be clean and ready for her new parents, but this time, I couldn't bring myself to sing to her. The emptiness from selling Saam Mui left me so hollow, I no longer had any more well-wishes for this daughter who never cried and barely made a sound. She just lay against my hands in the water.

A HAKKA WOMAN

The young couple arrived at my hut to collect Sei Mui. A snooty-looking young woman in a fancy Western-style dress and dark red leather shoes, she looked ridiculous coming to a squatters' village dressed like that. Her husband was a small man with a thin frame and a vulnerability that made it seem like a gust of wind could take him away.

'Is that her?' she asked. Her voice had a high-pitched, squeaky tone.

'Yes, this is her. I haven't named her yet, so please give her a good name,' I said as I handed Sei Mui over to the woman with both hands, as if she was an offering.

'Don't dirty my dress!' she squealed as she flinched away from the baby. Her face scrunched up as if Sei Mui was diseased.

'She is clean. I bathed her earlier,' I snapped, still holding my daughter.

'You take her.' The woman waved at her husband.

I had never seen a man listen to a woman before. I wondered what that felt like. The man gently took Sei Mei off me and cradled her.

'Here, take it.' The woman handed me forty-five Hong Kong dollars as agreed.

I fumbled to stuff the clammy notes into my undergarment pocket. My stomach twisted inside me, seeing Sei Mui in her new father's arms. Something didn't feel right.

How can this snooty woman take care of Sei Mui if she doesn't even want to hold her? What happens if the baby needs her nappy changed or vomits, gets sick? What then?

'Time to go. I don't want to stay in this place,' she spat out with her nose held up.

My stomach continued to knot.

Am I making a mistake? Look at this woman. How could she be a mother? Were the forty-five dollars worth it? No, Sei Mui will be better off – at least she won't go hungry. If she stays with you, she will be hungry all her life.

'Eh, wait! Don't forget to take this,' I said as they were leaving and handed the woman Sei Mui's one possession – her swaddling cloth.

'This dirty rag? I'm not taking that with me,' said the woman as she left.

'You better take good care of her and give her a good life!' I chased after her down the mud road, but as I warned her, my threats felt empty.

Even if she doesn't take good care of Sei Mui, what power do I have to do change things? It's done.

***

For weeks after I had sold Sei Mui, my tummy was all gee-li-gu-loo, bloated and unsettled. I couldn't shift the image of that snooty woman and how her face twisted with disgust when she saw Sei Mui. My worry turned into a headache that wouldn't go away. Something didn't feel right.

'Ah Ping! You better go see your daughter, she is very sick!' one of the villagers shouted as she ran towards me.

I was returning home from the communal well with two large metal tins of water weighing heavily on my shoulders.

'What happened? Is it Second Daughter? What is it?'

'It's your daughter, the one you sold. That fancy woman is back with the baby. Poor thing looks like a sick cat!'

Before my neighbour could finish speaking, my hands had let go of the two tins, which crashed to the floor. Water spilled everywhere. Legs, faster than I could imagine, carried me back home quicker than ever before.

'Where is she? Where is she?' I screamed as soon as I reached the hut and flung the door open. 'Where is she?'

The snooty woman was there waiting for me. This time she didn't come in her ridiculous Western-style dress but was in a pristine blue blouse and trousers, but she still looked out of place.

'Here, take your baby,' she shrieked, picking up the wicker basket from off the floor and handing it to me. 'I don't want this baby anymore. Give me back my forty-five dollars!'

'Are you crazy? You can't keep a baby in a wicker basket. She's not fruit!' I grabbed the basket off her and placed it on the table.

'The baby you sold me is sick. There is something wrong with her. I don't want a sick baby!' the snooty woman complained in her high-pitched squeak.

The second I picked Sei Mui up, my nostrils filled with a rotting stench – the smell of urine, faeces and damp.

Where was it coming from? It's Sei Mui!

The poor girl didn't cry, she didn't even make a single sound. Immediately, I laid her gently on the table and unwrapped her.

'What?' I gasped. Sei Mei's nappy was soaked in urine and faeces. Who knows how many days she has had to soak in her own waste? 'You didn't change her? Are you crazy?' I barked at the woman.

An awful rash covered Sei Mui's body. Her red skin reeked with the pus and infection.

'What did you do to her? Why is she covered in a rash? What is this pus?' I screamed as I tried to wipe Sei Mui clean as carefully as I could.

'Well, I told you she is sick. Look at her. Now give me back my money. I don't want this baby. There's something wrong with her.'

My whole body shook as my jaw pulled back.

Sei Mui, I have done this to you. It was my fault for selling you to her in the first place.

Without hesitation, I lunged at the woman, ready to squeeze her throat until her eyeballs popped out of the sockets.

'What is the matter with you, you pok gai fun gee khan!' I roared with my fists clenched. I had never hit a woman before and I never will, but in that instant, I had come closer to it than I had ever been.

'Are you so heartless that you let a baby sit in her own filth? Why did you not clean her or change her?' I poked at her.

'I tried to, but . . . but I didn't know how,' the snooty woman stuttered, shuffling backwards.

'Are you that stupid that you don't know you need to change and clean a baby? Are you even human?' My heart pounded ferociously as I pictured throwing the faeces-covered nappy at her.

'She was dirty, and I didn't want to get her filth on me.' She was sheepish, her eyes averting my gaze.

'But you are her mother now. You bought her from me. You were supposed to take care of her!'

'She is so dirty and smelly and has this rash all over. What if she gave it to me?'

'She has a rash because you didn't change or clean her, you idiot!' My face was right up in hers. It was the first time I had ever stood up to anyone like that in my life.

'I . . . I . . . didn't want to . . . in case she infected me. I don't know what disease she could have.' The snooty woman started to cry like the little spoilt child she revealed herself to be – a little girl wanting to play house with no idea of the sacrifice and responsibilities involved.

'I sold you my daughter so she can have a chance at a better life, and this is the life I sold her for? I sold her to some spoilt shit like you wanting to play mummy? Here, take your money!' I reached into my undergarment pocket and counted forty-five Hong Kong dollars before throwing it in her face. 'Now get out of my house!' I roared.

The snooty woman squatted on the floor to pick up the notes. As I looked down at her, I realised that in the end, it didn't matter how much money you have because money cannot buy human decency and compassion.

Sei Mui was so poorly when I took her back that no one thought she would make it. Every few hours, I had to wash her body and pat her dry to make sure her skin could heal. A neighbour gave me some medicinal leaves for Sei Mui to bathe in and that worked miracles. After almost a month of my stomach bloated with worry, I had nursed Sei Mui hack to full health.

Thank Mr God that she did survive because Sei Mui would grow up to be your mother.

Naai Gong

A woman's worth is measured by how many sons she can produce and the amount of hard work she can withstand. But if you're a poor woman like me who can only produce girls with no education or skills, what worth could I possibly have? Women like me are fit soley for manual labour. Luckily, or unluckily, I had the strong, sturdy frame of a Hakka woman, otherwise I doubt I could have endured almost a decade of naai gong.

Many Hakka women at the time worked in construction. It felt like a natural transition from the laborious grind of the rice paddy fields to the fields of concrete and brick – the same hard work we were used to. Remember, Hakka women never had bound feet so we could work in the sun, baking our backs and tanning our skins into dark leather. We were made for this.

A few of the women I knew in the squatters' village made a reasonable enough wage to feed their families working in naai gong.

'Hong Go the foreman likes people who work hard and complain little. It's pretty tough work. You'll have to carry the cement, stone and tools for his builders, but I'm sure you'll manage. Why don't you come with me tomorrow morning and see if he'll hire you?' said one of the Hakka women who had been working in naai gong for some time. We all called her Lai Jie – Big Sister Lai – because she was one of the eldest amongst us and had been doing naai gong the longest.

As the sky lit up with the first rays of dawn, the village bustled nosily with people getting ready for work, people forced out of necessity to become early risers whilst others slept. Nervous about going for my first job and whether the foreman would hire me, I was up before daybreak.

'Ah Lin, make sure before you go to school that everyone eats some breakfast. If you don't eat breakfast, you don't have energy for your studies. There's rice and some salty eggs here,' I instructed. 'Don't forget to tell everyone to brush their teeth, no stinky breath. Second Sister will stay at home today to take care of the others and...'

'Ma, don't worry. I will tell her. It's okay.' Ah Lin's voice sounded so mature, yet her face still had the softness of a child – a child who had to grow up too quickly.

As I scanned around the hut and saw Zeoi Mao was still snoring after a night of drinking, my feet were hesitant to leave. My mouth felt dry and stomach queasy with anxiety. This would be the first time I would leave my children alone with their father, and I didn't want to leave them. Who knows when Zeoi Mao's violent, intoxicated fits would erupt and which of my girls would have to endure his rage?

This is the right thing to do. At least the girls won't go hungry. At least they will have something to eat. It's all up to you.

With a deep breath and one last look at the girls, I left the hut.

'Good morning, Ah Ping,' said Lai Jie.

We waited for the other women and then we walked down the mud path out of our squatters' village together. After about half an hour, we arrived at a building site.

'Ah Ping, get in line. The foreman is coming,' instructed Lai Jie, so I copied and lined up next to the other women.

A stocky and very tanned middle-aged man with a cigarette dangling between his lips walked towards us. I would later learn this was his signature style – everywhere he went, he always had a cigarette in his mouth.

The foreman stopped in front of me, his gaze sizing me up, scrutinising me. I didn't dare move as I lowered my head. I needed this job, but I hated the feeling of being gawked at like I was cattle in a market.

'Hong Go, this is Ah Ping, my neighbour. She's the Hakka woman I told you about yesterday. She's a very hard worker and very strong,' said Lai Jie straight away.

'A Hakka woman, eh? Okay. What did you say your name was?'

'Ah Ping,' I said timidly.

'Okay, Ah Ping. You can come work for me, but if you slack around, I will fire you on the spot. You can collect your wages at the end of the shift in the evening. Lunch is at noon – you eat when we eat. Don't let me down.'

'Yes, mister.' I bowed.

'Listen, let's not pretend I'm some kind of mister. Call me Hong Go.'

'Yes, Hong Go.' The loudness of my voice surprised me. I had never spoken so confidently like that in my life to a stranger, let alone a man.

He hired me, someone hired me. I have my first job!

My body buzzed with renewed energy, ready to work.

***

6pm. The end of my first day. I queued like everyone else to collect my wages from Hong Go, wondering how much I was going to get. It had never occurred to me to ask before.

'Ah Ping, this is yours,' said Hong Go as he handed me five one-dollar coins.

My eyes fixated on them as I thumbed the coins, feeling the silhouette of the Queen's profile against my skin. My first ever wage and yet I didn't know what to feel. I had been carrying baskets of cement and stone up and down ladders all day. It was as Lai Jie said, hard, physical labour. *Was this how much a woman's labour was worth?* The sweat on our sun-scorched faces and hunched backs only got us five dollars.

'I know it's not a lot, but you're new. Stay working for me and you can get a bit more,' assured Hong Go, as if he had read my mind.

Hong Go made good on his promise. The more days I worked for him, the more money he handed me in the evening, but it was Lai Jie who taught me the ins and outs of working in naai gong.

'Carry more to get more. Hong Go calculates your wage based on how many baskets you carry to and from the site. The maximum you can get is ten dollars. Someone will be there to check, so don't even think about getting tricky,' explained Lai Jie.

'Tricky? How?'

'Like splitting one load into baskets, so it looks like you're carrying more. A woman did that and got caught. Hong Go fired her straight away! Oh, and the wages depend on how many women show up for work. The more of us there are, the less we get.'

'Oh, I see.' I bit my lip. I didn't know when Hong Go hired me it would mean the other women would be earning less. They had made a collective sacrifice so I could get some work.

'Don't worry, I had asked the others. They didn't mind. We all know what you have to deal with at home.' Lai Jie's voice felt like the warm comfort of congee in an empty stomach.

***

Five Hong Kong dollars – that was my average daily wage. Sometimes I got six or even ten dollars, but never more than that. So little right? I couldn't and didn't care too much because no matter how little I had earned, it was still more than nothing. Anything was better than nothing. Nothing is the feeling of hunger, the bitter metallic taste in your mouth. Nothing is the feeling of dread that there would be no food to put on the table for your children and knowing you are responsible.

Hunger is the greatest motivator for work. Every morning I left for work after dawn and every evening I sprinted home with basic groceries in hand to cook and feed my children. I always had the same pangs of pre-emptive dread and guilt, fearful of what carnage Zeoi Mao would leave behind. Every time I was about to step through the door to my hut, my legs were like cement blocks, not wanting to move.

'Ma, you're home!' My children would welcome me as I scurried into the kitchen area to cook dinner. It was usually Ah Lin or Second

Daughter who would help me whilst the younger ones did their homework or played under our only lamp. Dinner was very simple – rice, some vegetables and a few salted eggs. If it was a good day, we had some luncheon meat – one can could last a week. There weren't many good days.

Human scales – that was what us naai gong women looked like. Our bamboo baskets were loaded heavy with cement powder, stone, bricks or tools – whatever was needed. Using a bamboo pole, I had to loop it through the handles of the two baskets and balance the pole on my shoulder. It wasn't as easy as it seemed and involved a delicate balance of weight. If the baskets weren't of equal weight, one would slide down and all the materials would spill out, which meant a wage cut.

The baskets were so heavy that they left a permanent dent of chaffed and scabbed skin on my shoulders. There were days when I felt like I couldn't take a single step further, days when my lips cracked from dehydration and sunburn. The bamboo pole pressed against the bruises Zeoi Mao had left on me the night before. In those moments, drained of all energy, I would think of my children and their hunger, and the steps would come.

What do you think the hardest part of doing naai gong was? It was going to the toilet. Construction sites varied from place to place and there was never a guarantee of a toilet. Men are lucky, they could go anywhere they wanted, but for us we had to rely on outhouses. These were filthy, reeking of shit and piss, with no lock on the door, so any man could burst in. Some women took their chances and braved the outhouses, others went around the corner and squatted near some bushes.

I remembered Big Sister's warning about the women who ended up with bladder problems because they held their pee in whilst working on the rice paddy fields. But I was too embarrassed to pee in public and too afraid to use the outhouse, only going when I was desperate. My solution was to drink less so I wouldn't need the toilet until I got home and after a few years, the feeling of being a little thirsty, a little dehydrated became normal. Today, your Auntie Yin always tells me off for not drinking enough water.

Naai gong was dangerous work at the best of times, with no harnesses, safety hats or proper footwear. Most of us wore slippers or cotton shoes with bamboo soles. But being six months pregnant with daughter number five, naai gong g was especially tough.

***

The morning air was heavy from the night's heavy rain, and the ground felt slick beneath my feet. Everything was slippery and swollen. As usual, I looped the bamboo pole through the two baskets and stepped up onto the wooden plank that travelled from the ground to the first storey of a half-constructed building. My back throbbed but I didn't want Hong Go to think I was slacking off because I was pregnant. I filled each basket to the brim.

'Ah Ping, be careful! The plank is very slippery,' one of the builders shouted from the top.

Just as I was about to reach the top of the plank, *BAM*! In my fog of clumsiness and exhaustion, my foot skidded across the plank, missing my step, and I went plummeting to the ground.

'Ah Ping! Ah Ping fell. Help! Ah Ping's dead, help!' the women workers shrieked.

Am I dead? Did I die?

It would have been easier. I didn't and couldn't move as I opened my eyes. Everything above me spun lopsidedly. Silhouettes of familiar faces with concerned brows hovered over me.

'Ah Ping? Are you alive? Ah Ping? Don't die!' said one of them.

Someone's arms gripped at me as I sat up sluggishly and touched between my legs, half expecting my hand to return wet and red. No blood, but the pain spread all over – an agonising, crushing pain.

'Ah Ping, are you okay?'

Someone helped retrieve my baskets as more arms came to help me up. Hong Go, with his cigarette dangling between his lips, walked over.

'Are you hurt, Ah Ping?' he asked, not breaking from his usual stoic expression.

'I am fine. I'm okay.' I nodded, trying to hide the pain and worry.

'Good. Didn't I tell you not to fill the baskets that full? But you're okay. Good, so get back to work,' he instructed, and everyone else did the same.

'Don't worry, Ah Ping. Let me help you,' said one of the women as I grabbed my baskets. I would have to reload them and return to the same plank.

There was no time for fear when you're poor; you did everything you could to survive. Thank Mr God I came away with only a badly bruised hip and back – nothing I hadn't had before, and the baby came out fine. See, Mr God watches out for us.

***

After a few months when I had become more experienced, Hong Go had a builder show me how to mix cement. In principle, it was the same as mixing flour and water for dumpling skins, but it was so much harder than I expected. Instead of chopsticks, I had a large metal shovel. Instead of a bowl, I had a huge tin bucket. The cement dough would get so thick and heavy that even with both arms, I could barely swirl it around. My weak arms shook at first and it took me months to build up the strength to mix cement correctly.

One day as I was mixing the cement, I heard the dreaded voice of Zeoi Mao bellowing across the construction site.

'Ah Ping! Where are you? Come out here. Ah Ping!'

My stomach lurched, seeing him charge towards me. His face twisted with menace – he was drunk.

What did he want from me now? Why can't he leave me alone when I'm at work?

'What do you want? Can't you see I am working?' I uttered as I scanned around to check if the other workers had seen him. It was worse than embarrassing being seen with him in public, especially when he was drunk.

'I need money. Give me some money.' His eyes were the familiar bloodshot red and his breath was hot with alcohol.

I pretended I didn't hear him as I continued to mix the cement, hoping he would go away, hoping he wouldn't want to lose face in front of others and leave me alone.

'Eh, Ah Ping. Are you fucking deaf? I'm talking to you. I need money. Give me two-hundred dollars.'

'Ha?' I laughed and placed the shovel down. 'Are you so drunk that you lost your mind? How would I have that kind of money? You know how much I earn.'

'I know you have it. Give it to me. Give it to me now! I know you have it on you!' he barked as he thrusted his face in front of mine, hands grabbing at me, searching for pockets.

'I don't have any money. Stop it! You're drunk again. Go home! I need to work.' I flung his arms off me as I scampered away.

'You useless bitch!'

A rush of air and then Zeoi Mao came sprinting towards me, shovel in hand.

BAM!

With a swing of the shovel at my ass, I went flying face-first towards the ground.

'Hogging all the money! I am your husband, so if I tell you to give me money, you give me your money. Stupid bitch!'

Cowered on the ground, I screamed for Zeoi Mao to stop striking me with the metal shovel. Women shrieked for help in the background, but it was too late. Zeoi Mao had already ripped my blouse and tore open my undergarment pocket – my secret pocket I had sewn to safeguard my wages from him. When he saw it was empty, he stood up.

'You better have money for me tonight,' he spat and he walked away.

I remained huddled on the floor, motionless until I was sure he had gone. Zeoi Mao had beaten me so many times that I almost expected it, but this time felt different. He had come to my place of work – the one place where I had gained a tiny ounce of respect. In an instant, he had stripped me of any self-esteem that I had. I had never been so humiliated. That's when I realised no matter where I went, no matter who I was with, Zeoi Mao would always find me. He would always be stronger than me and he would always win. Being beaten by a shovel was merely a reminder.

'Ah Ping, are you all right?' It was Hong Go. 'Are you hurt? Lai Jie rushed over and told me what happened.'

I nodded, too ashamed to speak, too debased to look at him.

'If I had been there, I would have beaten the shit out of him! How dare he come to my territory causing trouble and hitting one of my workers. Ah Ping, if he ever comes here again, you must tell me straight away.' Hong Go's jaw clenched as his face reddened with fury, breaking from his usual detached demeanour.

His words triggered something in me, something I can't explain. Instantly, I shot up from the ground and ran, weeping as I raced away.

Everyone had seen what a useless, weak woman I am. They all saw I couldn't even stand up for myself! How can I ever show my face again?

As I ran, one of the naai gong women, also with the Lam family name, came chasing after me.

'You're pathetic! So pathetic. How can you let him hit you like that and not try to fight back?' she screamed, following me. 'Ha? Don't you dare say we share the same surname. I don't want to be called a Lam. We are not the same!'

She is right. I am nothing but a weak woman who can't stand up to my abuser.

Her words felt like a hungry meat cleaver that cut deeper than any strike Zeoi Mao could give me. I wanted to escape, to hide from everyone, even myself, as I ran towards a building we had been contracting and shot all the way up six storeys.

A HAKKA WOMAN

How can I show my face at work now when everyone saw what happened? They must all think I am utterly pathetic and useless. Because I am!

I stepped out onto the narrow scaffolding that framed the building and looked down. Sweat and tears drenched my blouse, my eyes swelled up.

How can I call myself a person? I am no more than an animal carrying cement every day, forced upon every night, beaten over and over. No, I am worse than that. At least an animal would know to run away. There must be an end to this because I can't take it anymore.

'NO! Ah Ping, don't jump! You can't jump!'

I turned my head around. It was the same woman who had shouted at me earlier for not defending myself against Zeoi Mao.

'You can't jump, Ah Ping! Think of your children. What would become of them? Ha? Who will take care of them? They need you,' she said as she inched closer. 'If you jump, he wins.'

'But he has won, hasn't he? I have had nothing but suffering in my life. Sold at seven as a san pou chai, abused by his mother, forced to conceive his children, beaten over and over . . . Can't you see? This is my life.'

'Ah Ping, if you jump, your children may as well be orphans. They are innocent in all this. You cannot leave them. Please, come down,' she urged.

The image of my girls' faces, the sound of their voices and their laughter shot through my mind as I clenched onto the scaffolding.

What would happen to my girls? I am the only one who stands between them and Zeoi Mao, the only one to take care of them. Their lives are already so tough. If I die, what then? They would have no one. No, he can't win, not after everything he has put me through.

Cautiously, I stepped off the scaffolding and back into the building.

'I am sorry, Ah Ping, for what I said before,' said the woman. 'I didn't mean it. . . you need to stand up for yourself. You can't let him do that to you.'

I looked up at her through my swollen eyes.

It isn't so easy. I wish it was.

'Next time when he sleeps, you should snip off his dick with a pair of scissors. That will teach him never to hit you again!'

I didn't know if I should laugh or cry when she said that.

***

I continued doing naai gong for as long as I lived in Tai Po. Over time, my body got used to it and became stronger. The full baskets that once ached my shoulders no longer felt as heavy and the cement I had to mix swirled smoothly. It was strenuous work, but it was mine and I had sweated for every single cent I earned. This was how I supported all my children for all those years as the single wage-earner in the family.

I will never forget my lunch as a naai gong worker: three bowls of white rice and two salty eggs every day. Even to this day at lunchtimes, I would get little cravings for this meal.

Tough times

I had left Tung Ping Chau clinging onto the dream-ends of others and believed Hong Kong would bring me and my children a better life, but those years in Tai Po were especially hard.

In the late summer of 1962, Hong Kong endured one of its worst typhoons. Wanda ripped through our city, showing no mercy as she caused chaos and havoc. Have you noticed that they used to name all the typhoons after women? All women. How I wished I had a fraction of Wanda's power and ferocity.

Like every other Hongkonger, typhoons were nothing to us. In the late summer when the Heavens would crack open and empty buckets of water across the village, Hong Kong continued. But for the poor living in squatters' villages like ours, our homes were delicate structures made of thin sheets of metal and splintered wood, vulnerable to the slightest wind.

That morning before the typhoon, the air felt thick with the smell of rain. At dawn, I braved the wall of rain and headed for work as I watched villagers stabilising their huts by boarding up whatever they could. I have always hated the rain for what it took from me, and for what I know it could take from me again. I wanted to turn back with each step so I could be with my girls, but I knew I couldn't. Failing to show up for work meant not getting paid, which was the same as going hungry.

Please, Mr God and Mr Jesus, protect my hut. Mrs Mary, please look after my girls, so they are safe.

When I arrived at the construction site, I was surprised to see only a few of us had showed up. Hong Go was there, as always, standing with his cigarette dangling between his lips, drenched from the rain.

'Go home, everyone. The radio says there's a big typhoon coming. We can't do any work today,' said Hong Go.

'But what about our wages?' asked one of the builders.

'What wages? You don't work, I can't pay you. Just go home. Come back when the storm is over.' Hong Go waved us away.

The rain pelted my face, and the wind whipped against my body as I ran home. I ran so fast that I didn't care if I slipped or fell. All I cared about was getting home to my girls.

I have to get home, I have to get home.

'Ma! Ma!' Second Daughter called out.

They were all waiting for me, their eyes wide with fear.

'Ah Lin, where is your father?' I asked.

'On the roof. What's happening?'

'Here, put Sei Mui on your back,' I said as I handed Fourth Daughter to Ah Lin. 'All of you must stay together. Don't go outside, or you'll be blown away.'

I snatched up our clothes, food and blankets and crammed them into the tin buckets we used to collect water before perching them on the highest shelf in the hut. Luckily for us, we only had a small sliver for a window, so didn't have to worry too much about boarding it up, but the wooden door left us exposed to the storm.

We huddled together in the stinking damp heat, waiting for Wanda to finish pounding on our walls as she ripped through the village. My skin tingled with fear. I don't think anyone in the village slept that night – I certainly didn't.

In the early hours of the morning, when we thought it was all over, Wanda's furious winds raged stronger and louder than ever, shaking our hut like it had been made of paper.

This was it. This was how we were all doing to die.

'Ma, that water is coming in!' cried Ah Lin.

Water seeped in slowly at first, finding every crack and hole, then faster and faster until it gushed through the door.

'Ma!' screeched Second Daughter.

'Get on the table!' Zeoi Mao instructed the girls.

The girls clambered onto the dining table whilst Zeoi Mao and I held it down, watching the dirty water rise higher and higher, brown from mud and human waste.

'Hang on, stay in the middle!' I shouted as the table wobbled from side to side.

Loud crashing and banging sounds – sounds of objects, trees, people being swept away or crushed. Sounds of screams and cries that sliced through the howls of the wind. All of us, the whole village, were at Wanda's mercy.

'I'm so scared.' My usually brave Ah Lin started to cry.

I'm scared too.

I clung to the table, my knuckles turned white as I struggled to control my terror.

The girls can't see me afraid.

'It'll be all right. Don't be afraid, it will pass. Don't be afraid,' I tried to assure her, but I was never good at lying.

A loud crash. Part of our roof blew off as we shrieked. Even Zeoi Mao looked petrified.

'Ma! Ma!' screamed Second Daughter.

We're going to be blown away. We're all going to die here!

In our utter helplessness, I did the one thing I knew I could do: I prayed.

'What are you doing? You really think your god will help you?' mocked Zeoi Ma.

I ignored him, defiant that Mr God would surely hear me. With my hands still clenched on the table, I bowed my head and prayed with every ounce of faith I had.

'Mr God, Mr Jesus, Mrs Mary, please protect us. Almighty God Most High, please watch over your lowly servant and my family so we don't come to any harm. I beg you, Mr God. Please keep us safe,' I repeated over and over.

By late morning, the winds had quieted to a gentle whisper and Wanda's anger had finally dissipated.

'Is it over?' asked Second Daughter.

'I don't know. It sounds like it. Wait here, don't move, and don't go outside,' I instructed.

Zeoi Mao and I stepped outside to survey the carnage that Wanda had left. Familiar scenes of mud, debris, stone and wood all piled up and scrambled into a soupy mess – my mind shot to memories of Ah Fong and her tragic death. All the huts on the edge of the village had collapsed either from the wind or mudslide. A few others were completely flattened by trees that had been ripped off from their roots.

All those homes, what will those families do? Where will they go?

I looked back at our hut – the wooden pigpen home that somehow remained standing. Thankfully, we were right in the middle of the village, wedged between other people's huts, so we didn't have to take the brunt of the wind. Only half of our roof had been blown away, that was all.

A miracle! It's a miracle. Thank you, Mr God, Mr Jesus and Mrs Mary. Thank you for protecting us. Thank you!

'I guess that god of yours was listening after all,' smirked Zeoi Mao. 'Next time pray for money instead,' he barked and headed back inside.

I gritted my teeth and forced myself to tune out his voice.

At least we are all safe.

By the next evening, I developed a terrible cough. In the panic before the typhoon, I had forgotten my clothes were still wet, and stayed in them all night and all day. The damp had sunk into my chest like it did when I had to flee the Japanese. The familiar ailment from my childhood had returned as I coughed and wheezed uncontrollably.

We had barely enough money to feed the girls so going to the doctor or dai fu would be the same as taking food out of my daughter's mouths. I couldn't bear to do it. I had always kept a small tin of Tiger Balm with me and used it for everything from mosquito bites to belly aches. Tiger Balm was always the solution to everything that physically bothered me.

I figured if it worked for everything else, it also would work for my cough. Who had money for cough syrup or lozenges? It was too expensive. So, I scraped a tiny amount of Tiger Balm with my fingernail and stuck it down my throat, reaching as far as I could without making myself gag. The menthol burned and my eyes watered, but at least my cough subsided for a few hours so I could continue doing naai gong. There was no such thing as a sick day.

Don't forget to wash your hands after using Tiger Balm! One time I forgot and rubbed my eyes. Ah-yah! It was worse than chilli. I still carry a tin of Tiger Balm with me wherever I go. It can cure everything when you have no other option.

***

Too much water one year and then too little the next.

Our village of over fifty households had only one water pipe in the middle of the village courtyard. One water source that supplied everyone. There was nothing else – we all had to share. Every morning and evening, water had to be collected and then stored at home in buckets. This was before plastic, so we reused tin cans and buckets that previously contained cooking oil. So many things were reused back then: tin cans, glass bottles, buckets, baskets. Everything! Not like now where you use something once and then throw it away. So wasteful.

Summer 1963. I remember it was the dusk, right before dinnertime. I returned home from naai gong and was queuing to collect water for cooking and washing.

'Something's wrong with the pipe,' shouted one of the villagers. 'Nothing's coming out.'

'Is it broken? Check if it's broken,' called another woman.

'Let me see,' said the village plumber as he tried to work the pipe. 'No, it doesn't look broken. Nothing seems wrong with it.'

'Maybe the pipe's blocked? Why don't you open it to see?' asked a villager.

'I can't just open the pipe! What if I damage it? Or if it bursts and floods everything? I won't be able to fix that,' replied the plumber.

'Ah, yes, I remember now! The radio said something about water restrictions,' a woman blurted out.

'What? What water restrictions?'

'But that's only during the day. They said nothing about turning the water off in the evening!' replied the plumber.

'The government has turned off our water? What? We have no more water. They've turned off our water!' butted in another.

'What are we doing to do? How are we going to cook rice? How will we survive?' yelled someone else.

What are we going to do now? How am I going to feed everyone?

I stood there with my two tin buckets and watched an opera of panic spread as villagers shouted and cursed at the government for switching off our water. When you are the poorest in society, it is so easy for those in power to forget about you, to even remember you exist.

Our water pipe that had previously flowed freely gave us water only once a day, usually in the evening. Every able-bodied person – man, woman and child – queued for hours with every bucket and bottle they had. We all feared that even our once-a-day water supply would suddenly end so we hoarded water in any way we could. I remembered all too well how vital water is from the eight days I hid in the mountains from the Japanese all those years ago. Water is everything. Without it, you die.

With so little water, we had to adapt. Clothes that could be 'sun cleaned' outside were left to air out, our hair went without washing for weeks and our 'showers' were a small damp cloth that we rubbed all over our bodies so we could save as much water as possible for drinking and cooking.

***

A year passed, and this way of living started to feel normal.

'The water is back! We have water. The water is back!' A young mother's voice echoed across the village one morning.

'She's right. Come, everyone and see for yourself. The water is back!' shouted another woman.

The entire village was swept up in a frenzy. As if on cue, buckets of all sizes appeared, mothers strapped with their infants, young girls with their long, greasy hair – all swarmed the courtyard.

'Ah Lin, I have to go to work so take all our buckets and fill them with water right away. Grab your sisters to help you and wash every item of clothing. Don't forget to wash yourself and the others too,' I instructed.

As I walked through the village, I watched children throw buckets of water at each other as they ran up and down the small alleys, playing and laughing. Their laughter captured how I felt, how we all felt – a sense of pure joy. But joy doesn't last long. They are fleeting moments you try to store in the memory box inside your heart. In 1967, we faced another water shortage and yet again, we went through the same routine of long bucket-lined queues, dirty clothes and hair.

When you have lived through two major droughts, when you have lived most of your life at the mercy of a well or a main water pipe, you cannot bring yourself to waste any water. It feels like a crime, a sin. Every part of you cannot bear the sight of it. Your body aches when water is wasted, your mouth turns dry and scalp itches, because you remember the feeling of drought, of thirst, of being filthy. When you have lived this way, you always think twice before turning on the washing machine or having a longer shower. And a bath? Ha! Totally out of the question. Well, unless you can wash all your clothes in it afterwards.

Zeoi Mao Gong

Zeoi Mao was a man of two extremes: the sober Tin Yeung and the drunk Zeoi Mao. Sober, the man I had known all my life quietly kept to himself and was almost docile, like a meek kitten. But drunk, Zeoi Mao's wild and violent fits were worse than any typhoon or draught I had to endure.

But I didn't fear Zeoi Mao because he would beat me – there was nothing new in that. No, my fear was far worse. It was in never knowing which Zeoi Mao was at home and that uncertainly felt like I was living on a cleaver's edge, constantly trying not to fall.

A loud thump and crash jolted me awake. Darkness cloaked the hut.

What was that? What time is it?

'Ma, Ah Ba's outside again,' mumbled Second Daughter, half asleep.

'It's all right. Go back to sleep.'

Pok gai, you can't even let us sleep in peace. Some people have to wake up early for work.

The commotion outside continued as I peered through our only window. It was him, it was always him.

'Don't you know who I am? Ha? I practised gung fu under Bruce Lee. I can beat anyone up. Anyone!' barked Zeoi Mao as he swayed side to side with a bottle of cheap rice wine in his hand.

'Diu lei lo mo! We're trying to sleep. Some of us have work tomorrow!' shouted a neighbour.

'Yeah sure! Of course, you trained with Bruce Lee. Of course, you are the toughest guy out there! Fuck off back to sleep!' yelled another.

'Come and make me if you dare. I'll beat all you fuckers up. I can beat anyone!' roared Zeoi Mao.

A HAKKA WOMAN

Why can't you go away and drink somewhere else? Why do you have to be here? As if it's not shameful enough to be your wife, you have to make things worse.

I could see every pair of eyes peering through windows, watching their personal TV sitcom, my spectacle of cringe, outside their homes as Zeoi Mao imitated what he thought were gung fu moves, showing off how 'strong' a fighter he was. In his mind, he was as slick as Bruce Lee.

'Zeoi Mao Gong is performing again. The show is on! Come and see, he's drunk again!' I could hear villagers call out.

Zeoi Mao Gong – drunken cat man – this is what they called him because that was how he behaved, like an unpredictable, violent drunken cat that would start on anyone in the village unprovoked.

'Eh, you! What the fuck are you looking at? You wanna fight me? Ha? I could beat you to a pulp! Don't believe me? Come and try. I'm the toughest there is!' Zeoi Mao would say with a wild energy fuelled by the alcohol in his veins.

Villagers would shake their heads and snigger as they walked away, turning their heads to see what he would do next, but no one bothered to answer him. He wasn't worth it, and everyone in the village knew that.

***

One night Zeoi Mao, in his usual intoxicated state, kicked some baskets outside a neighbour's hut but he had picked the wrong home. A tall and stocky naai gong man marched out.

'Eh, you, Zeoi Mao Gong. You kicked my stuff and woke up my son!' the neighbour snapped, shoving himself in front of Zeoi Mao. He stood over a head taller than him.

'Yeah, and what? Ha? What are you going to do about it? I'll kick what I want!' Zeoi Mao squared up to the naai gong man and jabbed his finger at his chest.

'Oh, really?' The man raised an eyebrow, puffing out his chest.

With a single kick, the man sent Zeoi Mao flying across the floor. Before Zeoi Mao could stand up, the man lunged at him.

'You want to kick my stuff? Ha? Go on, kick my stuff again! Try. Try and kick again!' said the naai gong man as he pounded Zeoi Mao over and over.

I couldn't stop watching. My eyes widened, wanting to take every moment in, relishing in the revenge.

That's it! Kick him! Kick him harder! Go on! Keep kicking him! That's for all those years of beating me, you fucking pok gai!

Zeoi Mao huddled on the floor like a helpless, tame animal. He didn't stand a chance against the naai gong man. How I wished I had the courage to join in and kick him in the throat as he lay there, begging for the man to stop, crying for mercy.

Mercy? What about when I begged you for mercy? Now you know what it tastes like.

The naai gong man finally tired himself.

'You kick my stuff again, I'll chop off both your legs!' he said as he spat on Zeoi Mao's bloodied face.

I felt my lips curl, forming a contented smile.

Zeoi Mao rolled onto all fours and flashed a look at me.

Oh, no! He's seen me standing there watching.

But it was too late, he had caught my smile and seen how I revelled in his pain. Dread wiped off my smile, knowing I would have to pay for this later but you know what? It was worth it, just to see him beaten up like that. Retribution tasted good.

***

As Zeoi Mao's drinking got worse, my children and I would often find him passed out outside our hut. Sometimes without clothes, other times he had wet himself – his patch of disgrace for the whole village to see.

'Hahaha! Zeoi Mao Gong's wet himself again! Look, look!' The villagers would point and sneer.

Everyone in the village had stopped calling him by his real name. He was simply Zeoi Mao Gong. The neighbourhood children would tease and bully mine, calling them disgusting Zeoi Mao children, and would throw rocks at them. The adults were no better. Some would lower their gaze whenever they saw me as if their pity weighed too heavily for them but most sniggered with disgust.

Is there a word stronger than humiliation? Stronger than shame? Whatever face I had, whatever smidgen of self-esteem I had left in me was wiped away. All gone.

At some point during those years, I stopped calling my husband by his name because only people deserve names. I was too afraid to call him Zeoi Mao to his face but he knew and after a while we all seemed to have forgotten the name Tang Tin Yeung. By the end of the first drought, Zeoi Mao had stopped looking for work altogether and became a full time alcoholic, and wife- and daughter-beater.

Do you know what it means to be afraid of tomorrow? Tomorrow didn't bring new opportunities and the promise of another day. It brought new and more problems, ones I couldn't solve like empty stomachs, frightened faces, bruised bodies and the feeling of hopelessness. No, I didn't like tomorrows. I feared it, but time felt slippery. It's like fish, difficult to hold as it slipped and slid between my fingers. The days bled into each other, that became months and then years. All the time, repeating the same routine each day.

When does it end?

Finally

Late spring 1966, Tai Po Hospital. The labour was intense and abrupt and I knew from how it felt that I had given birth to a boy, one who couldn't wait to enter the world and enjoy all that it could offer as a male. He was truly a fire horse.

Thank you, Mr Jesus. Thank you for giving me a boy, finally!

'No, stop. What are you doing? Where are you taking him? You can't take him!' I shrieked at the nurse as she wrapped up my boy.

'We need to cut the umbilical cord and clean him.'

'But he's my son. Please don't take him away from me, please. He's mine.'

'Don't worry, he will be right back.'

'My son! Don't take him from me. I only have one son now. Please, don't take him from me.' I tried to scream, but my throat was rough like sandpaper. My arms wanted to reach out for him, but they were as limp as overboiled choi sum.

You see, some things, once damaged, can never heal. The pain of losing Tung Chai and the fear of what Zeoi Mao would do had never left me. I couldn't trust anyone at the hospital, and it seemed Zeoi Mao felt the same.

My face twisted at the mere sight of him as my skin curled. It was as though my entire being wanted to recoil inwards so I wouldn't have to see him or be near him. He was and is always the last person I would ever want to see.

'What are you doing here?' I snapped.

Zeoi Mao's clothes were surprisingly clean and there was no putrid hint of alcohol on his breath. He almost looked passable as a human being, which I had never thought possible.

Are you sober? Actually, sober? What do you want from me? Why are you here?

'Ah Ping, I came to see my son,' he said.

The instant he approached my bed, my body jerked, bracing itself for him to strike me. After so many years of his abuse, it had become a natural response – my body was programmed in such a way that it would take another lifetime to undo.

'Hmm. Well, as you can see, he's not here, so why are you?' I raised an eyebrow.

You wouldn't dare hit me now that I've given you a baby boy, not with all these people watching.

'I've been standing outside the baby ward for hours, watching him. He looks so strong, so healthy.'

My eyes darted, sizing up his every word and move, wondering why he was pretending to be civil, to be nice. I didn't like it because this version of him wouldn't last – it never does.

'Ah Ping, I brought you something to eat, to help you recover,' he said, placing a red food thermos on my hospital bed table.

'What's this? Poison? Since when did you bring me anything?' I crossed my arms and turned away from him.

Zeoi Mao said nothing and opened the thermos. The vapours wafted into my nostrils, and I instantly knew what was inside: jyu geuk geung – ginger vinegar soup with pig trotters. It is a speciality for new mothers, very nutritional.

Am I dreaming? I must have died giving birth, and this is my Hell. Yes, I am in Hell and my punishment is to spend an eternity with Zeoi Mao.

It was the first time Zeoi Mao cooked me anything, the first time he had done anything nice for me and the first time he brought me something that didn't come with trouble or pain.

'Ah Ping, eat it whilst it's still hot,' he said.

Watching Zeoi Mao scoop out some of the vinegar soup into the thermos cup was both ridiculous and unsettling.

How do you even know how to make this?

'What do you want from me?' I asked, clutching at the sheets underneath the hospital blanket.

'What do you mean?'

'You have never been nice to me. And now you bring me food? Jyu geuk geung no less?'

'Well, you just gave birth to my son,' he replied with his dark-yellow-stained-teeth smile. I don't remember when I had seen him smile like that before.

A son. That was the answer. That was the way a woman could have power – by giving birth to a boy. I had been an object of abuse and shame for so long, but finally my body and my existence were seen simply because I had finally produced a son.

By dusk, the hospital discharged me and before I could protest, Zeoi Mao had strapped my son to his chest. As we headed back to the village, I watched Zeoi Mao parade my son like a trophy, grinning all the way home. Every few minutes, he would stop and ask me how I was feeling.

This must be Hell. I did die, and this is my Hell.

My poor daughters who were obedient, hardworking and dutiful, they meant nothing to Zeoi Mao simply because they were not sons. Those girls didn't matter to him, but at least for a time, they and I would be safe.

***

We were now eight mouths to feed. This included me and Zeoi Mao who, after a few odd jobs as a road sweeper, no longer worked. Making sure no one starved and had a roof over their heads was a suffocating responsibility, one that weighed so heavily on my chest I often felt like I couldn't breathe.

The stinging tear between my legs had barely healed when I returned to naai gong work after only three days with my son strapped to me. Sitting-month was a long and forgotten memory because the poor and desperate like me cannot afford to do nothing. No one was going to work for me or help feed my children. I had to do it myself. Through dull pangs and sharp stabs, I worked through the pain as I had done before.

A HAKKA WOMAN

'Ah Ping, make sure you eat more. You are one of my hardest workers. I need you at full strength,' said Hong Go.

His words of encouragement soothed me like a cold, wet cloth on a hot summer's day. Over the years, Hong Go had become like a big brother to me – to all the women who worked for him. Despite never showing any emotion, Hong Go always made an effort to check on me after childbirth. This was more than what any man had done for me.

I had often wondered what my life would have been like if Zeoi Mao had been a little bit like Hong Go, someone hard working and considerate. To my surprise, Zeoi Mao offered to take care of my son whilst I was at work. He had stopped drinking, but the years of damage to his body left side effects that frightened the girls. His hand trembled and sometimes it was so bad he could barely hold a pair of chopsticks. At night, his whole body shook as he scratched at his skin. I was ready for him to give up his sobriety, but it did not deter Zeoi Mao. Such was the power of having a son – the drunken cat man stayed sober for almost an entire year.

It didn't matter to me because I didn't and couldn't trust him, especially not with my son. This man had never looked after anything in his life, not even himself, and now I was supposed to trust him with my boy? But a construction site was no place for an infant. On the couple of days when I did take my son to work, I couldn't concentrate, too afraid I would fall or crush him. I had previously lost one boy and could not bear to lose another. Reluctantly, I handed my son to Zeoi Mao before dawn each day. At around lunchtime, he would bring my son to the construction site so I could breastfeed him. Nursing him wasn't easy – my breasts felt dry and empty.

***

'Ah Ping, this is for you,' said Mr Father Priest as he handed me a tin of baby milk powder. It was something I could never afford, even if I worked my hands to stubs.

'But Mr Father Priest, this is . . . this is too much. . . I can't accept. It's too expensive.'

I handed the can of baby milk back to him.

'Please take it. You have so many children to look after and feed. You can give it to your girls as well as your infant son. They should drink it so they can be healthier.' He placed the tin in my hands.

It wasn't a secret how poor we were. Anyone with eyes could see how scrawny my daughters' legs were, their shorter-than-average height, their gaunt faces and rat-gnawed clothes. There were poor people, and then there were us. I knew Mr Father Priest meant well, and I knew the milk powder would give the nutrients my girls desperately needed, so I accepted.

As soon as I arrived home with the tin, I yelled out to my daughters to come and enjoy the milk formula.

'What are you doing?' said Zeoi Mao, scratching his ass. He had just woken up from his afternoon nap.

'Mr Father Priest was so generous. He gave me this can of milk powder and not only for the baby, but for the girls too,' I said, as I started to boil some water. I couldn't wait for the girls to have some.

'No, it's not for them!' he shouted.

'What do you mean, no?' I put the spoon back in the tin and closed the lid.

'I said no! This milk is for my son and my son only. The girls don't get any. Are they babies? Ha? No, so they can't have any.'

Zeoi Mao snatched the tin away from me.

'Who are you to decide? You didn't buy this. I got it from the church – Mr Father Priest gave it to me for the children, so I will decide who gets some,' I said, grabbing the tin back from him.

'I said no!'

With a single shove, Zeoi Mao sent me skidding across the floor. I hit my back against the table and the precious tin of milk slipped out of my hand. The granules scattered on the ground.

'The milk!' I shrieked.

'Now look at what you have done, you stupid bitch!'

No, don't say anything. Don't wake the monster up inside him.

We had been living in relative peace that year because he didn't hit me and had stopped hitting his daughters and life was almost tolerable. I didn't want that to change.

I picked up the tin and saw there was barely enough left inside for one portion of milk.

'What are you doing?'

'Making milk for the boy,' I said as I prepared the drink for the boy who was never hit, ever.

VIDEO CALL 10 : 12 FEBRUARY 2021
Lunar New Year, 4:30pm Hong Kong time

'Paupau! Gong hei fat choi!' I exclaim at the iPhone screen. Another new year.

'Eh, Didi! Gong hei fat choi! Have you eaten yet? What time is it over there?' Paupau is wearing her dark red wool jumper again like she does every year. This year the sleeves and shoulders look so much looser than last time.

'How was reunion dinner last night?' I ask.

'What reunion? Only your cousin and Auntie Yin were there. Not much of a reunion.' She exhales and shakes her head.

'That's okay, at least you weren't alone, right? And I'm sure you're going to have some visitors today?'

'Maybe. Some of your aunties said they will come and drop off some food. And your uncle too . . . but I don't . . . I can't remember what time . . . later, I think. Later tonight.' She nods.

'Will you be cooking tonight?'

'Cook? Auntie Yin said not to bother. Too much work for me apparently, so she asked your uncle to buy poon choi for us instead.' She purses her lips in disapproval.

Lunar New Year dinner used to be the main annual event when Paupau would show off her culinary skills cooking nine delicious dishes which we spent all evening feasting on. And as always, her famous braised soya bean duck was the highlight – now a memory that but a few people still recall.

'But it'd be nice for you to have someone treat you? Right?'

'Hmm. Yes, maybe. Cooking is all I know. It's what I do. And again, this year I don't have to do it . . . I know they mean well, they don't want an old woman to work so hard but what else am I supposed to do? I sit at home all day doing nothing, being useless, rotting away.' She slaps her hands together as her jaw clenches.

'They just don't want you to stress and overload yourself,' I assure her.

'Yes, I know. My son is filial, bringing me poon choi . . .' She pauses. 'I wonder if the other one is still alive.'

'What? What other one?'

I remember Paupau telling me about her first son – Tung Chai whom they had initially been told had died in hospital. Many decades later, there was a big scandal that uncovered how many infants, especially boys, would disappear from the hospitals, sold to wealthy infertile couples who paid big money for the hospital staff's cooperation and silence. Nurses and doctors teamed up to scout for poor illiterate parents who brought their baby boys in for treatment only to be told they had died. Some cases were worse – new mothers were lied to that it was a still birth as midwives took the babies away. A whole generation of children living in strangers' homes, brought up by people who weren't their real parents.

'My first son – he came after Ah Lin. Fat chubby boy, oh, he was so cute! I wonder if he is okay if he is healthy.' She stares into the distance, eyes widened.

'How old would he be now?'

'Oh, he'd be a grown man by now. At least sixty-something.' I watch her try to do the maths.

'Have you ever thought about looking for him? There are ways to do that now,' I suggest.

'What for? He wouldn't know who I am. And how would I even start the search? We didn't even have a birth certificate for him.' She shakes her head. 'No, some things when they are lost, can never be found and some things are better to simply leave alone.'

PART 4

Turn me to stone

When I was a san pou chai, I loved to sleep, as it was the only time I could momentarily press pause on my life and to escape all that was happening to me. In my dreams, I could see my parents, my siblings and my childhood home, where I could feel safe. But the moment my eyes peeled open, reality would come crashing in with the morning sun. I hated those mornings – they were blaring reminders that my life did happen, it was real.

Sometimes I would have bad dreams, terrible ones where Ga Pau or Zeoi Mao were chasing to beat me, but those nightmares could never be worse than reality. Still, I loved to sleep.

Things were very different by the time I became a grown woman. I slept solely out of necessity as I learnt there was no escape from my life, no pause button to press. I also had to accept that dreams were dangerous because they filled my heart with a longing for a life I knew I could never have.

The price of food and rent skyrocketed amid droughts and typhoons, as the burden of the cost of living became heavier than the baskets of cement I had to carry each day. My wages didn't come close. We were living head barely above water, always on the brink of drowning. Ah Lin had moved out by 1967 but I still had six other children to feed. My older daughters did their part, taking on odd jobs weaving wicker baskets or painting dolls' faces before and after school, but we still struggled. Second Daughter would come to work with me, but that poor girl was as scrawny as a matchstick and barely able to carry one basket-load of cement. I didn't want her there, watching her struggle as the others looked upon her with pity-eyes. I wanted her at school getting an education, so she won't end up like me, but Zeoi Mao had grown tired of his brief period of sobriety. Bringing my daughter to work was the only way I could protect her.

'Ah Ping, don't worry about it. We know what responsibilities you have,' the naai gong women would say as they gently patted my shoulder before loading Second Daughter's lunch box with extra rice and luncheon meat.

I felt indebted to these women who had been working with me, side by side, for so many years, with hands just as rough as mine. They knew all too well what kind of life I had at home.

'You should have castrated that pok gai hum ga chaan years ago! Wait until he is sound asleep and then snip, snip! Any time you need a pair of sharp scissors, Ah Ping, you let me know,' laughed one of my colleagues. It was the same woman who had stopped me from jumping off the sixth floor a few years back. We had become good friends.

'Shh! Her daughter's right there. You can't talk like that in front of a child,' hushed another.

Everyone laughed to lighten the mood. I wanted to laugh with them, to brush off how much of a joke my life had become like a stupid prank someone was playing on me. But all I could do was stay silent.

I won't lie. There were times when I wished I had the guts to castrate Zeoi Mao. Times when he had passed out after a night of rice wine and carnage. But who would that have helped? It wouldn't have fixed our financial situation.

I stared down at my hands – the only things I could rely on to feed myself and my children. If hard work was a marker for good fortune, my girls and I would be millionaires. But no matter how hard we worked, how many wicker baskets we made or how many dolls' faces we painted, it didn't matter. Everything we made, Zeoi Mao stole or took by force.

'Hide your money. Make sure your father doesn't find it! If he does, he will take it and spend it. If he asks you for money, tell him you don't have any. Tell him you gave it all to me. If he asks where I hid it, tell him you don't know. Understood? Let me deal with him,' I warned my daughters.

A HAKKA WOMAN

I could not allow Zeoi Mao to drink what my girls had worked so hard for. But they were clever, so much more clever than I had ever been at their age. They hid their meagre coins in food cans, slid them into the small cracks of wood next to their sleeping areas, in places where only tiny hands could reach.

Zeoi Mao was a drunk, but he wasn't an idiot. He knew the girls went to work and had money stashed somewhere, and he knew how to get it.

***

It was dusk. The end of another long day of knotted shoulders and a sore back as I trudged home. My arms hung heavily with basic groceries for dinner.

What was that scream?

I had never heard a sound like it, a shrieking cry that echoed through the air like an animal begging for help.

It's coming from the hut! Second Daughter!

I ran so quickly that I didn't even feel the baskets of food slip from my hands and onto the ground.

'I'm going to chop you into tiny pieces and feed the pigs next door!'

It was Zeoi Mao waving the meat cleaver in his hand, chasing a squealing Second Daughter around the tiny hut. Without hesitation, I lunged at him, mustering all my force to pin him against the wall.

'Don't you dare touch her!' I roared.

Startled by my sudden rage, he dropped the cleaver with a loud clatter.

'She's your child, leave her alone. If you're going to chop anyone, chop me! She's your daughter! How could you? Are you totally insane?'

'Let go of me, stupid bitch! Yes, she's my child so I can do what I want with her. I can do anything I want with you too!'

He shoved me off so hard I stumbled and fell back and hit the ground.

'Who told you that you can get involved? Ha? Stupid Hakka bitch!' He hovered over me.

'No, please, don't. Please!' I begged.

I scrambled to get up when I suddenly felt something very hard strike my back.

BAM!

It was the wooden stool, followed by a barrage of fists and kicks that landed all over my body. Someone in the background screamed, someone cried. I remember little else.

I was unconscious.

I would later learn that my children huddled around me, my clueless two-year-old son lay on my body and immediately Zeoi Mao stopped. He didn't dare lay a hand on his precious son, and I was spared. Second Daughter dashed out to a neighbour who called the ambulance. We didn't have a phone.

How it all started was because Zeoi Mao had caught Second Daughter trying to 'steal' her money back from him and, in his intoxicated rage, demanded she return it. When she refused, he slapped her around, but she wasn't a weakling like me and fought him with everything she had. It only made things worse. What if I had got home a moment later? What if I wasn't there to stop him? What then?

I could not open both eyes when I woke up in the hospital. My left eye was swollen shut and when I went to touch it, I felt mesh had been tapped over it.

Did I lose my eye? Am I blind? If I lost my sight, I won't be able to work, I won't be able to feed my children. What am I going to do?

As I tried to take in big, deep breaths, I felt a tugging sensation at my ribs – one broken, several bruised. I pursed my lips. The taste of dried blood still lingered on them.

My children! I have to get back to them. They must still be at home. Mrs Mary, please take care of them and protect them until I can return. Please, I beg of you, don't let anything happen to them.

'It's time for your injection,' said a junior nurse as she approached my bed.

'An injection?'

'Yes, an injection. Stay still and don't move,' she said as she rolled me onto my side.

A sudden prick of the needle into my spine. Half dazed, I screamed awake.

What kind of injection is this? Stop! What are you doing to me?

'Stay still,' she snapped.

I wriggled on the bed, desperate to roll off to make the nurse stop.

'Stay still!' She pinned me against the bed so I couldn't resist. The pain seared through my spine and spread through every nerve in my body.

'Stop, please, stop!' I screamed.

The nurse ignored me as she continued to hold me down. Her body was like a crushing force against mine. When she was done, she rolled me onto my back and that's when I saw it – a bag filled with red liquid, lighter than blood, a bag of something that she had taken from me.

'What is that? What did you take from me? Give that back to me! What did you take from me?'

I tried to get up and grab the bag off her, but my body felt totally broken. I had lost all my strength.

'Don't bother trying to argue with them. They won't listen,' said a middle-aged woman in the bed next to me. 'She did the same to me, too.'

'What? What do you mean?'

'That nurse – she did the same thing to me. That was bone marrow she took from you. Precious stuff. Too bad, we are poor and uneducated. They can do anything they want to us. But don't worry, you'll feel better in a couple of days,' said the woman. Her words rung in my ears as I closed my eyes and drifted somewhere else.

Take me somewhere, anywhere but here.

Apparently, it happened. Apparently, it was common. Nurses and doctors took advantage of us: the poor, the vulnerable – we are society's forgotten people. Bone marrow was in great demand and wealthy sick patients needed it, so they bribed the nurses and doctors to find 'donors' – people like me, people like that woman. They knew we didn't have the means to stop them or to kick up a fuss. We were expendable.

***

Here are some of the stupid things I have heard over the years:

- when a man hits a woman, it is to discipline her, so she deserves it.
- when a husband hits his wife, it's to show how much he cares for her.

What utter dog shit. They find ways, fancy ways, to dress it up, but you can call it gold, call it whatever you want – abuse is still abuse.

So many women in my generation have been hit, so many women still get hit. We learn from a young age what being 'disciplined' means first from our fathers and then from our in-laws and husbands. We are sold, exchanged, married off and the same thing repeats. Generations of women who measure their worth by the lack of bruises or scars on their bodies.

It was both common and shameful: common because this was what the men in our lives did and shameful because it was always our fault. If they hit us, it was because we must have done something or said something wrong. The cuts and bruises we wear on our faces showed the world what a worthless daughter, wife or daughter-in-law we were.

As for the man? The world can degrade him, and society can despise him, but still there would always be someone lower than him. There will always be someone at home he could pound out all his frustrations on – his daughters and his wife. Zeoi Mao did exactly that. Any injustice he felt life had handed him, however bruised his ego, he took it out on me and my daughters.

A HAKKA WOMAN

My body remembers everything, even if this feeble mind cannot. Every strike, every blow. And now, in my old age, my body reminds me of everything that had been forced upon it, upon me. Why, if women hold up half the sky, do the men who share it with us insist on beating us?

As I lay on that hospital bed, I wondered, if I turned myself to stone, would I still bleed?

If you realise that all things change, there is nothing you will try to hold on to. If you are not afraid of dying, there is nothing you cannot achieve.

—*Lao Tzu*

It is not dying that I am afraid of, it is the fear that after I die, nothing changes.

The day I don't talk about

My body did not feel like my own. Was it ever mine? I had nothing to show for my existence except for being a bag of meat to thump or a pair of hands to make money. The growling bellies, the sullen eyes, the beatings day in, day out. Rinse and repeat. There had to be an end to this. I could no longer withstand the scraping sound of hopelessness against a hollow spirit.

I had failed as a mother. Unable to protect my daughters from their father and his violence, unable to give them a safe home where they can eat dinner in peace. I was empty. Life had sucked everything out of me except for a single driving thought: this all had to end, now.

'Ma, are you ill? Why aren't you at work?' asked Second Daughter.

I had never missed a single day of work except for childbirth or when Zeoi Mao sent me to the hospital.

'Put your clothes on. We're going on an outing,' I said to my children.

The sun was still low in the sky. It was just before dawn.

'But where are we going? Don't you have to go to work today?'

'We're going out. Get your sisters ready.'

The sky was a dull grey, and the clouds weighed heavy with the promise of rain as we reached the bridge that crossed Tai Po River. It was a bridge I had crossed so many times to and from work each day. The thick, humid air choked the usual smell of the sea. A storm was coming.

'Go and play,' I said and waved my children off.

I watched my four girls and little boy. They looked so happy playing their games, racing each other up and down the bridge, and competing in jacks. Their delightful laughter were tiny abrasions scratching my heart, chaffing me inside. When there wasn't enough food, they never complained. Whenever the other kids called them

'Zeoi Mao children' and threw stones at them, they never threw tantrums. When their father beat them, my daughters only ever whimpered.

My poor children. How can they still laugh? They deserve so much more, but I have nothing to give.

Guilt wove thick webs, tangling my mind as my children played.

Mothers are supposed to care, protect, and provide for their children, but what have I done for them? I have doomed them to a life of poverty and can't even give them the most basic thing: safety.

My children are being punished because of me, because I was so unlucky to be bound to Zeoi Mao and too chicken shit to leave him. What could I give these girls? All I can teach them is how a man can throw them around, beat and use them. I have nothing to teach them. I am useless, just as I have always been told. How can anyone live like this?

With those thoughts banging on the walls of my mind, I stepped onto the edge of the bridge. I felt myself crumpling, ready to let it all go, to give up. As I looked down at the water, my legs stiffened. I was and still am afraid of the water. My blouse was soaked in sweat as I took a deep breath, ready to slip off over the edge.

I am so sorry, my children. Your mother cannot do anything more for you. I have nothing to teach you, nothing to give you except pain and poverty.

'Ah Ma, can we go home now?' Second Daughter's voice trembled.

I steadied myself on the railing.

'Ma, what are you doing up there? Ma?' asked Second Daughter as she made timid, hesitant steps towards me.

The instant I saw how her eyes filled with worry, I was certain she knew what was happening.

What am I doing? My daughter!

I was jolted out of my trance and slid off the bridge.

'Ma! Ma!' cried Second Daughter.

I embraced her and fell onto the floor, wailing harder than I had ever done in my life.

'Your mother is sorry, your mother is sorry,' I repeated through garbled sounds in between my sobs.

I was bathed in sorrow, completely embalmed by it as heavy tears fell onto the ground, disguised by the rain that had started to pour.

'Don't leave us, Ma!' cried Second Daughter. 'Please don't leave us.'

Her words were like a knife that had cut my spirit free.

How could I ever think of leaving my children? My poor, innocent children!

'I want to live. I want to live. I want to live!' I screamed as Second Daughter clung onto me.

'Ma!' Sei Mui tugged at my sleeve with her other siblings behind her and my son on her back.

I looked down at their faces painted with a fear they couldn't understand, faces that I could not bear to part. They mirrored my own – they were my flesh and blood. If I jumped, they would have no one. They didn't choose this life. The least I could do was endure their suffering with them. I must live for them.

In that very moment, crouched on the wet floor, drenched in rain and tears, I vowed to myself that I will outlive Zeoi Mao, no matter what it takes. If I gave up, he would have won and all my suffering, all my children's suffering, would be for nothing. No, that cannot be. He can take every part of my body, he can bruise and break whatever he wanted, but he will not take my mind or my spirit. I refused. My will to survive was stronger than it had ever been.

I must live.

The last two

I was ready to welcome the end of the 1960s, but then in 1968, a flu pandemic hit Hong Kong. Much like the one we recently had, it was society's poorest and most vulnerable who suffered the most. People who could never in their lifetime afford the space to quarantine, nor the food and medicines to make them feel better because social distancing is the privilege of the rich.

We didn't know there was a pandemic, no one in the village did. It wasn't until it had spread across Hong Kong that we realised a flu had crippled the city. None of us in the village had a TV and only a couple of households could afford a radio, which we eavesdropped for the news. The news we heard came to us in morsels – chunks of half stories of this and that happening somewhere we had never heard of. Who had time to sit around listening about the world outside when all anyone could think about was filling their own rice bowls? I felt like I was sleepwalking through my life.

'I hear there is a flu, a really bad one! Apparently, it's pretty serious and many people have got really sick,' said Lai Jie as we loaded our naai gong baskets.

'Did you hear? The hospitals are jammed with sick people, all with this flu!' said one of the naai gong women.

'That's awful. Imagine going to the hospital for help and not getting any?'

'I hope I don't get sick,' I muttered quietly.

'Me too. I've got too many mouths to feed,' said another.

'We all do,' said Lai Jie.

We chatted about the pandemic like we were discussing the weather – no big deal, not because we didn't care, of course we did. None of us wanted to get sick or die, none of us wanted anyone else to either, but we simply didn't have the mental space to care.

Worrying about the flu or other diseases was for the rich who had the means and time to concern themselves about getting ill. We didn't have that luxury. We had to work, or our children would starve.

Please, Mr God and Mr Jesus, keep my family healthy. Don't let anyone get sick with this awful flu.

As Hong Kong battled its first pandemic, miraculously, none of us got ill, not even a sniffle. Was it the dirty living conditions that had made our immune systems impenetrable? Or the daily prayers of petition I offered up each day and night to Mr God and Mr Jesus? I'll leave that for you to decide.

What I knew for sure was that as the pandemic's grip loosened, Mr God brought a woman called Lee Kah Wing into my life.

It was right after Mass. My children and I were standing outside, the wind rustling our ill-fitting clothes, while we waited for Mr Father Priest and the church donations.

'Children, here, don't be shy. Take an orange. They are very sweet,' said an immaculately dressed woman in a crisp white cotton jacket and black trousers. Her pitch-black hair was braided in the customary way of the ma jie. She looked so clean, so tidy.

'Eh, stay here. Don't bother this nice woman,' I instructed.

'It's all right. I bought too many oranges and now I can't finish them all. Please, take one,' said the woman.

As she pulled an orange from her bag, her sleeve exposed the woman's forearm. Light skin – much lighter than mine. It was a clear sign she didn't have to work outdoors.

'Oh, thank you. That is very generous of you,' I said.

I looked at this woman up and down. She was my age, or possibly a few years younger, but next to her pristine clothes, I looked like a dishevelled beggar.

'You have very well-behaved children.' She smiled. 'Here, girls, take some more oranges and put them in your pockets for later.'

'No, no, no! We can't accept this. We don't have any money to pay you back for these. And now you have nothing left. I don't know how to call you erh, Mrs . . . ?' I said, unsure of her generosity.

'I'm called Lee. Lee Kah Wing.'

'Nice to meet you, Mrs Lee. I'm Ah Ping.'

'Oh, there's no need to be so formal, Ah Ping. Please call me Ah Wing.'

This was how I met Mrs Lee.

Like so many girls from poor rural families, Mrs Lee was married off to be a san pou chai at a young age and had quickly gained favour with her in-laws by producing a son. But as soon as her life seemed destined for prosperity, the sudden death of her husband left her feeling desolate and alone. Her in-laws shunned Mrs Lee and blamed her for their son's death and kicked her out of the house. Empty-handed, Mrs Lee had to return to her mother's home with nothing to her name, not even her son. Sons belong to the husband's family, not hers.

Luck would have it that Mrs Lee ended up as a ma jie working for a wealthy gwai lo family in a big fancy house on Hong Kong Island. Ma jie were often young illiterate women from poor families employed as a live-in cook, cleaner, helper and nanny. These weren't just jobs you did for a few years. To be a ma jie was to dedicate decades of your life to another family, leaving your own children to be raised by someone else so you can send every cent you earned back home.

Every Sunday Mrs Lee would journey to Tai Po to visit her mother and attend Mass. Fate would have it that she went to the same church as me. And every week after Mass, this kind woman would greet my children with oranges and White Rabbit sweets as she insisted I called her Ah Wing but I never did. She will always be Mrs Lee to me.

Over the weeks and months, we became close friends, sitting beside each other in church as we mouthed along to words we couldn't read, praising Mr God with all our devotion. There was something comforting in that – our shared illiteracy, our shared shame.

After Mass, as my children devoured their citrus treats, the two of us would exchange small snippets of our lives: hers as a ma jie and mine as a naai gong worker. I never had the courage to tell Mrs Lee about Zeoi Mao and the beatings, afraid she would judge me for it, but I think she knew. We shared an understanding in the things we didn't need to say to each other, in the spaces of our silence.

***

'Can I hold her?' asked Mrs Lee.

'Yes, of course,' I said.

I handed over my baby girl, who had been napping in my arms. It was 1969, and I had given birth to my ninth child.

'Oh, isn't she precious. What a cutie, and look at those little cheeks!'

Mrs Lee's face radiated with joy and her eyes glimmered as she held my seventh daughter in her arms. It was a face only a mother could make, a face of love.

For the next six months, Mrs Lee would ask to hold my daughter every Sunday after Mass. I happily obliged, but when I saw my friend's eyes damp with tears, I wondered what kind of emptiness burrowed in her heart? At first, I didn't think much of it, but the more I watched Mrs Lee gently rock my daughter side to side, the more I saw a mother who was still lamenting the loss of her son. She craved children so badly it was as though her whole body ached for them. This is a mother without a child and a pain I can never understand.

'You must miss him a lot, your son, I mean,' I said, as Mrs Lee cradled my daughter.

My friend's eyes flicked up at me before turning away with a deep sigh.

'And what if I did? It wouldn't matter,' she said.

'Would you do it again? Have another child?'

'Well . . . I don't know. My husband passed away and I'm on my own. Besides, that's up to God. I can only pray.' Her smile was strained, as if it hurt her to admit she had little control over what happens.

Maybe I can help her.

I had no intention of selling my daughter. The memory of selling Saam Mui had left such a void that was too much to bear, but I couldn't stop thinking about Mrs Lee and the way she looked at my baby girl. I knew Mr God had put this childless mother in my life for a reason, and that was to help her and alleviate her suffering. I knew exactly what I needed to do.

'Why don't you raise her? You could raise my daughter as your own?' I said.

I stared straight at Mrs Lee as she cradled the baby, who was about eight months old at the time.

'Ha? What? No, you can't be serious?' She laughed, dismissing my suggestion. But her eyes lit up, betraying how she really felt.

'I'm serious. I have thought about it for a long time. You think I don't notice how much you long for a child? I see it in your eyes, in your face. I know what is in your heart.'

'But I can't . . . she is yours. How could I possibly keep her? Really, you shouldn't joke about these things.' She shook her head and handed the baby back to me.

'I'm not joking. I am being completely serious. Mr God has crossed our paths together for a reason. You are a mother without a child, and I have a child. Don't see how much we struggle? You can give her a better life, a normal life.'

'But . . . are you certain that this is what you want? Have you really thought this through?' whispered Mrs Lee.

I looked up at the sky and sighed.

Mr God, I hope I'm doing the right thing.

'It is what needs to be done,' I said.

I held her gaze for as long as I could before taking a last look at my daughter. With both hands, I offered her up to Mrs Lee.

Little one, you are truly a gift, one that will make this mother so happy. And really, you are so very lucky, you will always have two mothers.

This was how my ninth child was given away, not sold, on a mid-Sunday morning in a church courtyard. From that day, she became Mrs Lee's daughter.

***

1970. The Year of the Dog and the year I gave birth to my tenth and final child – a daughter. I was thirty-eight. The moment I caught sight of her face, I gasped at the resemblance.

Look at her! That big round face, those almond-shaped eyes. She is the spitting image of Saam Mui.

Zeoi Mao must have also noticed the uncanny similarities, and he spared Ah Yin from his violent outbursts. He never hit her. Ah Yin would become the most successful of all my children.

Do you believe in Mr God's mercy? I do. And you know why? Because the year after Ah Yin was born, my monthly bleed finally stopped, and I could no longer have any more children. Thanks to Mr God for giving me only twenty years of fertility.

I never wanted any children with Zeoi Mao but didn't have the means to prevent or stop it. Zeoi Mao didn't know anything either and even if he did, he wouldn't have cared. All he knew was how to take, how to violate, how to tear open. I may as well have been an animal. There is no such thing as rape in a marriage because how can you rape something that you already own? Property has no status, has no rights. When your body doesn't belong to you, how do you say no?

I was soaked in a culture that expected me to be a good daughter, an obedient daughter-in-law and a submissive wife – that was my role. I had to be a good cook, clean, take care of the house and children. Doing whatever my husband demanded and giving all of myself to my family are the expected minimum of every dutiful woman. And if your husband treats you badly, if he beats you, you are the one to blame.

You cannot cook or reproduce your way out of abuse . . . if only someone had told me that long ago.

He will win who knows when to fight and when not to fight.

—Sun Tzu

Video call 11 : 7 March 2021
Paupau's 89th birthday, 4:30pm Hong Kong time

'Paupau! Have you eaten yet?'

'Eh, Didi! You're a good girl for calling me. Yes, yes, I ate. Your cousin brought some spareribs, very yummy. What else did he buy? Some other stuff – dumplings and . . . I don't remember, but it was all very good.' She licks her thinning lips.

'How was your birthday? I saw from the pictures you had your usual mango pudding cake with lots of cream! It must have been delicious.'

'Ah yes! It was my birthday, wasn't it? Do you know how old I am now?'

'Of course, I do. You're now eight-nine! Born in 1932, which makes you a cheeky water monkey,' I wink.

'You remember? I am so pleased you still remember my birthday.'

'Who else's birthday am I supposed to remember? Ha? You raised me.'

'Eight-nine! I can't believe it! I am almost ninety – that's so old. Thank Mr God for giving me another year, but how did I get this old? It's like poof! And the decades have disappeared, just like that. Where did all the time go?' She scrunches her face as she scratches the back of her hand.

'I wish I knew. I'm nearing forty myself,' I add.

'What?' Paupau jumps back. 'Forty? Ha? Impossible! How are you forty?' she exclaims.

'Almost. I'm thirty-six, I'll be thirty-seven soon.'

'Ah-yah. I still remember when you were a little girl needing to take a shit at North Point MTR station before nursery!' She chuckles.

'Paupau, you're hilarious. You can't remember what you ate for lunch today, but you remember that?' I laugh.

'Who can forget? Every day, always at the same station, at the same time, you needed to shit.' She stomps her feet in a fit of giggles.

For some reason, my bowels were set on a timer and as soon as we got to North Point, I needed a shit. At four years old, I was a chonky and heavy kid but that didn't stop Paupau from piggybacking me and sprinting up two escalators to the McDonald's next door. She never complained, only ever teasing me for it even to this day.

'Thirty-six. Hmmm. Didi, do you ever think about having children?' she asks, her tone now serious.

Paupau has never asked me such a direct and personal question about my life before, and it takes me by surprise. Up until now, as long as I was happy and healthy, she never seemed too bothered about the other stuff. This is the first time she has ever asked me about kids.

I pick at the skin around my thumb. Do I tell her the truth and risk her scolding me for not doing what 'every woman is supposed to do'? Or do I spare her and blurt out a lie to keep her happy?

I take a deep breath.

'No, Paupau. No, I did not want to have children.' I prepare myself, waiting for her to admonish me with one eye squinting open.

But there was nothing, except a long silence. Did she hear me?

'Hmmm, I see. But who will look after you when you're old?'

'Good question. The home for the elderly. Having children doesn't guarantee they will take care of you when you're old. Besides, it's not so easy to raise a child.'

'That's true. Having children isn't simply giving birth. It doesn't stop there. You need to teach them and raise them correctly to be useful people. The raising is the hardest part, lots of ma fan.' Her voice is calm, almost forgiving.

I wonder if Paupau had ever wished for her life to have been different, if she had ever thought about what she could have done instead of having so many children.

'You had ten, right? Ten children?'

She nods. 'Yes, ten. But not my choice. It was never my choice. Zeoi Mao forced me, every time.' She looks down at the floor.

Paupau doesn't need to say anymore. She had never used the word 'rape' but it doesn't take much to piece it all together. It is in what she had never said, never spoken openly about, that I know the truth behind the number of children she was forced to have. Those are the dark corners of her life that she would never take out, always kept hidden, with glossed-over parts to protect me and to spare herself from having to relive her trauma.

'He didn't care. He only took. Take, take, take. Ah-yah. That pok gai Zeoi Mao. And I was too useless for being stuck with him for so long and not having the guts to fight back or leave. Don't be like me, Didi. You must promise me that! Never let a man hit you, not even once, because once is all it takes – he will hit you again and again!' She roars with such ferocity, such bottled-up rage.

'Don't worry, Paupau. I'll kick him right in the dick!'

'Ah-yah! So aggressive,' she scolds, but it is a pretend scolding, as I can see her lips curl as her shoulders relax. She is proud because she can see in me the ability to fight back.

Paupau had ten children in total. Out of those ten, seven remained. That's at least ten counts of sexual assault. Knowing this – the bitterness of this truth – it eats away at me every day.

It can get better

I had heard somewhere a saying that to repeat the same thing over and over and expecting something different is insanity.

Soon after Ah Yin was born, Zeoi Mao had once again attempted sobriety. Was I crazy or stupid for clinging tightly to the hope that his violent fits would one day be a thing of the past?

Why has he stopped drinking? Is he finally bored with poisoning himself every night?

It was strange and unsettling because I knew these periods never last, and yet I still wanted to believe another life was possible.

Zeoi Mao tried to play father to Ah Yin, often staying at home to take care of her. He even prepared the only meal he knew how to cook: steamed rice with luncheon meat drenched in soya sauce. It would become a meal that Ah Yin hated – a meal that tasted of her father, of poverty and of the salty, bitter memories of her childhood.

Those quiet periods when Zeoi Mao was sober was like living with a bomb at home, never knowing when he would blow up and kill us all. It was terrifying.

'Sei Mui, take care of your sister Ah Yin today,' Zeoi Mao instructed one morning.

Why is he awake? He never gets up this early.

'Where are you going? Sei Mui has to go to school. She can't stay at home,' I said.

'I'm going to find work. Is that okay with you? Ha? Do I need to report every part of my life to you simply because you can make a few dollars? Ha?' he grunted.

Sober or not, he is still a pok gai.

For the next ten minutes I watched Zeoi Mao fuss over his clothes, his hair, his slippers, trying to making himself look presentable.

You look ridiculous! Who on earth would hire you? A lazy, drunk forty-something nobody. No education. No skills. If someone hired you, you'd lose the job in less than a week.

Words I wish I had the guts to spray out at him, but never dared. Instead, I nodded, trying not to snigger.

When Zeoi Mao was done, he stormed out of the hut and slammed the door so hard I thought it was going to come off the hinges.

***

'Eh, stop. What are you doing? What are you looking for now?' I asked Zeoi Mao.

It was after dusk. I had just returned home from work to find Zeoi Mao rummaging through the hut in a frenzy. The same familiar routine, the same sight. Nothing ever changes.

'Where is it? Ha? Where's the money?' he asked. Frantic hands chucked our possessions on the floor, turning things upside down and inside out.

'I thought you went to go get a job today? Stop! There's no money here. You know there isn't. Stop it!'

Zeoi Mao ignored me as he continued his frenzied search for a coin, a note, anything.

I should have known this was going to happen. It was always going to happen.

'There's no money here. Stop, you're destroying everything!' I screamed, but as soon as those words slipped out of my mouth, I regretted it.

Zeoi Mao stopped and turned around with a feverish glare, waiting and ready to devour me.

'That bracelet. Give it to me!' His hand went to grab at my wrist.

He wanted my jade bracelet – the one my mother had given to me when I was twelve, right before being sent back to Tang House. It was the only thing I had left of her and it now fitted snuggly around my left wrist. Even if I wanted to give it to him, there was no way it would come off.

'What are you doing? Stop it! You're hurting my hand!' I jerked my arm back.

'Give me that bracelet, now!' he shouted as he got right up in my face. His breath reeked with the familiar stench of alcohol.

'No! I won't give it to you. You know it belonged to my mother. You can't have it.' I shuffled backwards, tiptoeing towards the door.

I have to get out of here.

'No? No? You don't get to say "no" to me. Give me that bracelet or I'll chop off your hand and take it myself!' He inched closer. His nostrils flared and eyes glazed over like a deranged monster. It was so easy, so quick for his period of sobriety to be over.

'Run! Get out of here! Now!' I bellowed at my children, who scrambled out of the hut, their footsteps vibrating through the air.

The instant as I was about to sprint out and follow them, I felt Zeoi Mao grab me by my hair and yank me back inside. With his other hand, he pulled at my wrist, trying to force the jade bracelet off me.

'Let go! Get off me! You're going to break my wrist!'

How easy it was for a man's ego to shatter and crumble. How easy it was for him to lose face, and yet women go through everything and still we stand. We are torn, broken and bruised but we keep living for our families. I had worked my entire life, my body repeatedly violated and still, it was not enough.

Suddenly, something in me snapped. In that moment, my rage exploded, ready to gauge Zeoi Mao's eyes out. My arms, made strong from years of naai gong, pushed Zeoi Mao with full force. As he fell onto the ground, I grabbed the tin tray we kept on the dining table and smacked him across the head with it. I did it over and over and over, as hard as I could.

'Eat shit, you pok gai ham ga chaan! Eat shit!' I roared. My body wanted to throw up everything Zeoi Mao had ever done to me as I hit him repeatedly with the tray.

Suddenly Zeoi Mao leapt up and grabbed me by my neck, hurling me across the hut. His hands pressed against the back of my head as he smashed my face against the wall, again and again. Hammers of fists thumped into my body. The more I tried to fight back, the harder he hit me, fuelled by his thirst to punish me. For a split second, I broke free and made a dash for the door.

What was that? I can taste blood.

My legs gave out and then I felt the familiar cold, hard surface of the floor as I fell. No matter how far I ran, I always ended up back here – a victim. Everything went blank.

***

I have been here before.

I don't know how I ended up in the hospital. The smell of bleach and sounds of tired nurses shuffling from patient to patient brought me back to consciousness. My head felt like the size of a watermelon, and I no longer knew which bruises were re-etchings on old ones and which were breaking new parts of my body. I took a deep breath to check if Zeoi Mao had broken any of my ribs. There were too many to count. The pain didn't get any easier.

'Dear Mr God, in my next life, I beg you, please do not bring me back as a woman. Anything but a woman,' I uttered through my cracked, swollen, bloodied lips.

Through my blurred vision I could make out the silhouette of Second Daughter, now a grown, married woman standing next to my bed.

'Ah Ma, you're awake! Thank God. Do you want to drink some water? Let me get you something to drink.' Her voice shook as she tried to hide her heartbreak.

'No, I'm fine,' I said, patting the bed for her to come sit next to me. 'What are you doing here?'

I didn't want her to see me like this. She had escaped this life by getting married and moving out with her husband and infant daughter. She had carved out a better life for herself. I couldn't bear to drag her back into mine and force her to confront monsters she had since fled.

'Sei Mui told me what happened. She was the one that called for an ambulance that brought you here. She said Zeoi Mao . . .' Second Daughter began to weep.

I hate seeing you cry. I hate being so useless. I hate having to accept that perhaps this is my life and that nothing will ever get better.

'Don't cry. What are you crying for, ha? Crying cannot solve anything. What did I teach you? Ha? Besides, it's not the first time he has done this to me.' I tried to comfort her.

'But Ma, how can I see you like this and do nothing? Why don't you leave? How many more times does he need to do this before he finally kills you?'

Her tears made a large wet patch on the bedsheet, tears stained by her black mascara.

'Maybe it's better he kills me, then at least I can have some peace. I am useless anyway.' I sighed.

I tried to roll onto my side to avoid her gaze, but the pain of my broken ribs wouldn't let me budge.

'And what about the others? Sei Mui, your son? Or Ah Yin? She is just a little girl. Who would look after all of them?'

There was a long pause. I knew she was right and that I couldn't leave the others behind. I had made a promise on Tai Po Bridge that Zeoi Mao can't win.

'You should come and live with me. Take Ah Yin and the others,' said Second Daughter.

'And then what?'

'I am serious, Ma. Take them with you and you all can come live with me. I'm making money now. You have been taking care of us all for so many years and suffered so much. It is now my turn to look after you,' she said, placing her hand gently on top of mine.

I turned my neck to meet my daughter's gaze, my eyes still pulsating and swollen, barely able to make out her face.

'We'll see.'

***

Three days in hospital. Two cracked ribs. A half-closed left eye. But I didn't have much time. I had one chance to pull this off. It was going to be now or never.

'Oh. You're back. Still alive, I see,' Zeoi Mao grunted the second I stepped into the hut.

Keep silent. Don't provoke him. It's not worth it.

I went straight into the kitchen area, pretending to rummage around.

'We don't have any luncheon meat left,' I said.

'So?'

'You know how much your son loves luncheon meat for dinner? Why don't you buy some for him whilst I cook rice?' I said as sweetly as I could.

It was Second Daughter's idea. We needed to get Zeoi Mao out of the house long enough, and the only way I knew was to involve his precious son. He would do anything for that boy.

'Fine. Give me money,' he grumbled.

I made sure he had enough, not just for luncheon meat, but for a detour to get some of his favourite cheap double-distilled rice wine. The instant I pulled out a banknote from my garment pocket, Zeoi Mao snatched it out of my hand and slammed the door.

The race was on between how fast I could gather my essential belongings and the children and how quickly Zeoi Mao would return.

'Children, pack your belongings. We are leaving. Hurry! We don't have much time before Zeoi Mao returns.'

I grabbed at my belongings, stuffing them into the large red, white and blue plastic bag Second Daughter gave me at the hospital.

'Come on, children! Hurry!'

'Ma, where are we going?' asked my son.

A HAKKA WOMAN

'No time for questions now. You need to get ready to go!'

With my bag filled and my children and I waiting anxiously by the door, my heart raced. Second Daughter said she would come with her husband – a stocky man over a head taller than Zeoi Mao – for protection.

Where is Second Daughter? Why aren't they here yet? What if Zeoi Mao comes back?

I was breathless. My head spun, and knots formed in my stomach, churning nausea with each passing second.

If he comes back, we are all dead.

'Oh, thank Mr God you are here!' I cried out.

Second Daughter and her husband had finally arrived.

'Here, take her,' I said and handed Ah Yin to Second Daughter to piggyback.

I scooped up my son and strapped him to my back. My son-in-law carried our only bag of possessions. Sei Mui clung onto her two younger sisters, one in each hand.

'We must leave now, Ma, before Zeoi Mao comes back!' shouted Second Daughter.

All of us fled. It was the sprint of our lives, running out of the hut, down the mud lane through the village until we got to the bottom where we crossed the bridge. We ran, and we ran, not once looking back.

We can't look back, we can never look back, ever.

We were fleeing for our lives, petrified if we stopped even to breathe, Zeoi Mao would suddenly catch up with us.

When we reached Tai Po bus station, the world was spinning around me as my chest constricted tighter and tighter. I was heaving.

Don't die now, you're almost there.

'Get on,' said my son-in-law.

We clambered onto a double-decker bus and spilled out onto the top deck. It was the first time any of us had been on a double-decker. The bus zigzagged through the streets like a rollercoaster towards our freedom and that freedom was in Sham Shui Po.

I had never been to Sham Shui Po until that day. It was a poor and less developed area of Kowloon, but compared to the quiet and rural Tai Po, it felt like a different world. The streets buzzed with commotion from the various shops, stalls, street hawkers and people. But at the time, I couldn't care less where I ended up. All I wanted was for me and my children to be safe and if it meant being on the other side of the planet, then so be it. I wanted to be where Zeoi Mao could never touch me or my girls again.

'This is it, go in.' Second Daughter led us to their 200-square-foot flat in one of those tong lau buildings. 'This is your new home now.'

'You'll be safe here,' said my son-in-law.

The flat was twice the size of the hut we had fled, but now there were nine of us.

I hope the son-in-law won't change his mind.

1974. This is the year I finally got my freedom. I was no longer a san pou chai, no longer Zeoi Mao's punching bag, and no longer a naai gong worker. With Second Daughter as the main breadwinner, I stayed at home to care for her daughter and my other children. This was how we lived for many years. If I had wanted to return to work, my body didn't let me – it was never quite the same because some parts could never heal.

I always had a fear that nibbled at my mind every day. What if Zeoi Mao found out where we lived? He could wait until everyone was at work or school, when I was all alone at home, just to chop me up into little pieces. He could wait outside my children's school, beat them, kidnap them. Maybe he'd set the whole flat on fire. Variations of the same theme where Zeoi Mao finds us, and wins. That fear never went away, it merely got lugged around like our luggage.

We had to move so many times over the next ten years, bringing true meaning to the word 'Hakka' – 'a guest family' unable to plant roots anywhere. I had become an expert in packing up and unpacking our lives, fitting an entire existence into a single red, white and blue plastic bag. Most of the flats we stayed in were illegal structures – rooftop slums built on top of social housing with no safety protocols. No one bothered with things like that back then. Some of the other places we lived in were crammed bedsits with landlords that would hike up the price at any time, forcing us to eviction.

We didn't move solely out of necessity. I didn't allow us to stay in one place for too long. I was always worried that somehow Zeoi Mao would find us. No matter how far we went, no matter how many times we moved, I could never rid myself of Zeoi Mao's shadow. Any time I saw someone that vaguely resembled him, my legs would turn to silken tofu and my mouth tasted of stomach acid. I would crumble.

Every night during the first year, Zeoi Mao haunted my dreams. Nightmares where he would find us. Yellow teeth, alcohol breath, the roar of his voice, and his hand holding a cleaver ready to chop us all up. Every morning I bounced up drenched in sweat, praising Mr God that they were just nightmares. My wounds may have healed, and the scars may have smoothed over, but what he did to me will never be forgotten.

My feet were never bound, but no one told me I could run. It took my daughter, a girl, to set me free.

Notice that the stiffest tree is most easily cracked, while the bamboo or willow survives by bending with the wind.

—*Bruce Lee*

Spit on His Face

I had imagined Zeoi Mao dying many times, each more elaborate than the last.

Choking on alcohol, getting hit by a bus, pok gai down the street and cracking his skull open, beaten to death by a group of thugs, suffering a mysterious illness that would one day kill him. Those are some of the scenarios I would imagine.

I cursed his existence every day for decades without remorse. I wanted Zeoi Mao to suffer and to die alone. Like his mother before him, someone somewhere heard me and in 2009, Zeoi Mao was diagnosed with kidney failure and liver cancer.

It was my son, the only one Zeoi Mao had loved, who broke the news to me over the phone.

'He's sick? Really? Well, he can't be that sick if he can pick up the phone and call you,' I snapped.

'No, Ma. He really is sick. I had to take him to the hospital for a check-up and that's when we found out. It was the doctor who told me that Ah Ba is dying. His kidneys aren't working, and he has cancer – liver cancer.'

I tried to imagine what Zeoi Mao dying would look like. I hadn't seen him in decades – the last time was at my son's wedding banquet and even then, I avoided him. Luckily for me, my children were as tight-lipped as I was and kept my home address and telephone number a secret.

So, you're finally dying. You can't even die like other people and have to drag it out.
My jaw tightened, thinking of him.

'Good. Better he dies faster, so he doesn't waste people's time.'

'Ma, don't say that. You can't mean it. He's all alone in that tiny hut. He doesn't have anyone.'

I have never seen Zeoi Mao's hut. I'm told it's a bedsit with four wooden walls, a bench for a kitchen, and no indoor plumbing somewhere on the outskirts of Tai Po. My son was the only one who visited Zeoi Mao regularly, while my daughters did so once a year out of a sense of duty. He is lucky to have such filial children – if it were up to me, no one would ever see him.

'And whose fault is that, ha? That piece of shit beat me all my life, ever since we were children. He never did a single nice thing for me! He only knew how to hit, how to violate. Better he dies so everyone can finally find peace!' I slammed the phone down before my son could respond. I was exhausted, so tired of having to recount to my children what Zeoi Mao did to me.

A few months later, my son called me again.

'Ma, Ah Ba is in hospital. I think you should go and see him. The doctors say he doesn't have long.'

'You mean that pok gai hasn't died yet? Better he dies soon. He's just wasting people's time and hospital resources. What a waste of oxygen!' I gripped the phone receiver so tightly my knuckles turned white.

'Ma, don't you think you should at least go and say goodbye to him? It's your last chance.'

'Last chance for what? Ha? Have I taught you nothing, son? That damn Zeoi Mao beat me all my life. I will put it behind me when he is finally dead!' I screamed.

'Okay, okay, Ma. Calm down. I won't ask again, but I want you to think about it so you don't regret it later.'

'I'd rather eat shit than see that son of a bitch!' I smashed the phone receiver down so hard, the plastic on the back snapped off.

I sunk onto the leather sofa and pictured Zeoi Mao lying in hospital, feeble and in unbearable pain as the cancer wreaked havoc through his body.

Are the Heavens finally trying to balance the cosmic score?

A part of me wanted to see him. I wanted to stare into his eyes so he could know that did I outlive him and he didn't win – as I had promised myself on that bridge in Tai Po.

I wanted him to know that whilst he spent his life in a bedsit in the poorest part of Tai Po to be forgotten, I was living comfortably in modern flats surrounded by people who loved me. Whilst he had to live off the meagre government social welfare, I could buy as much food as I wanted, and my rice bucket was always full.

As satisfying as it would have been to see how the monster of my past wither into a sickly nothing, I didn't go see him in the end. He had taken so much of me, so much of my life, my time. Time was all I had left, and I refused to waste it on him. Hadn't he taken enough? There was nothing he could do that would atone for all he did to me and my daughters, nor the marks he left on all of us. It would be pointless to see him.

My children, however, saw things differently. Out of some sense of moral obligation and filial duty, my daughters went to visit him, but it was my son who spent the most time with Zeoi Mao, sitting by his bedside for a few hours after work. It was to be expected, I guess. After all, he was Zeoi Mao's bo bui – the son who was never beaten. Some of my daughters urged me to go say goodbye to Zeoi Mao. Perhaps they thought if he saw me, he would have a chance to say sorry and I could put the past behind me. Ha! Zeoi Mao could say all the sorrys he wanted, it would change nothing. I didn't need his penance, nor did he deserve it.

In 2010, the cancer that had ravaged Zeoi Mao's liver had spread throughout his body. He was seventy-eight when he died. He was alone, without a single close relative next to him in Tai Po Hospital. For a short time after hearing about Zeoi Mao's death, I felt a sense of euphoria, a lightness of spirit I had never felt before. I could breathe, really breathe! But those feelings were overshadowed by another feeling that crept in. It wasn't grief, nor melancholy but rage.

Pure rage.

This was the man who was my childhood bully, who beat and raped me. This was the man who beat my children, stole from us and dehumanised me over and over. And now that he was dead, what did he have to show for it in the end? He had achieved and accomplished absolutely nothing. His life was as meaningless as the abuse he inflicted upon us. Utterly senseless suffering. Did he learn anything from it? No. Did he ever show remorse for what he did? Not until he was lying in his own piss and shit, waiting to die.

What about my daughters? Innocent lives and minds forever damaged because of how he treated them. Some ended up with deep, long-lasting mental health repercussions and who can I hold accountable for that? Not him! Zeoi Mao was already dead and got off lightly for everything he had done to all of us. Oh, how I would love to spit on his face.

And then, a small slit of a smile appeared as I realised that he really was gone. He couldn't hurt me or any of my daughters ever again. Knowing he was dead was as sweet as sucking on dried plums and I savoured it. There was no guilt, none.

Zeoi Mao's body was taken from Tai Po to Tung Ping Chau Island, where he was buried in the Tang family gravesite next to his parents and ancestors. My daughters and son went. I didn't attend the funeral.

There are so many terrifying and awful things that I wish I could forget, but despite my old age, I can't shed those memories. Too many have been etched, carved and burnt into my mind. Deep wounds, and even deeper scars that I carry with me every day. The sad thing is, my happy memories, those I wish to keep, they are slipping away so quickly. They become so muddied by the passage of time that I can't remember them anymore, like my mother's voice or the recipe for your favourite braised soya bean duck. Why does our mind seem to remember the things we want to let go of the most?

Video Call 12 : 5 April 2021
4:30pm Hong Kong time

'Paupau, have you eaten yet?' I ask.

Paupau is wearing dark colours today, which is unusual for her.

'Eh, Didi. It's you.' Her voice is quiet.

'You okay? You look rather pale, everything all right?'

'Yes, I'm fine. High blood pressure again today. I took my medication but it's still very high.' She rubs the back of her neck.

'What could have raised your blood pressure? Have you been eating too many salty foods again? Maybe you didn't get enough sleep – I bet you've been listening to the radio next to your bed at night again.' I smile, trying to lighten her mood.

I have never known Paupau to sleep in silence. She has always had a small radio next to her head on the bed, playing Cantonese opera through the night.

'No, it's not that. They all went to Tung Ping Chau for Ching Ming Festival yesterday. Why would anyone go all that way just to sweep Zeoi Mao and his family's graves?' She huffs and her nostrils flare.

'They? Who's they?'

'Your Auntie Yin and a few others. Why go all that way? Ha? What for? Sweep or not, they are all dead anyway,' she snaps as if arguing with someone – that someone being generations of Chinese tradition and customs. It is rare for Paupau to dismiss them completely, especially this one. But some rituals simply aren't worth it to her, some are utterly meaningless.

'Don't be upset, Paupau. It's not good for you.'

'Upset? Who's upset? Ha? That damn Zeoi Mao drank himself to death, so it served him right!'

I can hear her stomp her feet.

'No, I mean, being upset they went to Tung Ping Chau.'

'What can I do or say? Ha? Tell them not to go? They are all adults, they can do whatever they want. Besides, he was their father. But why ask me to go? What for? I'll never go back there, ever. I'd rather eat shit than go back to that island!' She clenches her fists.

'Do they go every year?'

'Don't know. And I don't care. That Zeoi Mao beat me all my life and still he is lucky enough for someone to go visit his grave. He took everything from me! Good that he's dead.' Paupau's eyes widen.

I remember the day when I was told Zeoi Mao had passed away. Yes he was my grandfather but he was a stranger whom I've only seen a handful of times. To me, he would always be the man who abused the one person I love most on earth. Some things I can't forgive. When I heard the news, I was almost glad because at least Paupau would finally get some kind of release, some closure.

'You know what, Didi?' Her tone changes as she stares straight at me. 'I'm afraid that when I die, I will see him again. I am afraid I will see all of them – Ga Pau, Gong Tau – and my afterlife will be them beating me over and over and I can't escape,' she mutters, biting the side of her cheek.

Even after all these years, Paupau is still haunted by Zeoi Mao, Ga Pau and Gong Tau. They are monsters in her personal Hell, which she carries with her every day.

'Don't say such things, Paupau. When you die, you'll go to Heaven for sure! You're Mr Jesus' number one fan. They have a place up there waiting for you when it's your time. And I am certain that pok gai Tang family are rotting and screaming in Hell for what they did to you.'

I don't tell her I don't believe in God, because it's enough I believe in her.

'Who knows? It's not guaranteed. Only Mr God knows what's going to happen to me.' She sighs.

I wonder if this is the reason she spends so much time praying – if it's because she is terrified of where she will end up.

'Well, I'm certain if anyone is going to Heaven, it is you. Besides, you have plenty of years left. You're not going anywhere yet, Paupau! We still have so much to do together when I'm next in Hong Kong.'

In that moment, I want to be selfish and put her on the next flight over to London and move her here so I can have her next to me and to know she won't be going anywhere. I can't tell her when I'll be back because I don't know. I don't know when I will be able to hug her and feel that jade bracelet pressed against my back as she asks me if I've eaten yet.

A book holds a house of gold.

—Chinese Proverb

LITERACY IS FREEDOM

As a little girl, I loved nothing more than listening to my father recite proverbs or poems. Then when my brothers started school, I would make them draw out characters they had learnt that day on the ground with a stick whilst I copied them. I would never forget the moment I learnt how to write 'mother' and 'father'. Learning the strokes was like having access to a magical script, and I wanted to learn everything. I had even fantasised about becoming a teacher like Second Brother. Silly, isn't it?

Being illiterate is like living inside a cage with an impermeable barrier between myself and the world. I can see the world outside, hear it, smell it, taste it, but I could never really touch it. The world was and has never been accessible to someone like me because the wall of illiteracy always lay between us. Today I can recognise only a few simple characters and write out my name but that's about it.

To possess the skill of reading and writing is to open that cage to the world and the incredible freedom, power and independence that comes with it. I have often imagined what that world would be like, one where I never needed to ask anyone to help me decipher a letter or a landlord's eviction notice. A world where I could read the order of service at Mass or the Bible. A world where I didn't need to be at a person's mercy and have to worry if they were going to take advantage of me. I would not have to be self-conscious whenever I met someone new, fearing they would look down on me for being illiterate because it's the same as being stupid. Or to live in a world where I could switch on the TV and DVD player and watch my favourite operas without having to wait for my grandson to come and do it for me.

Literacy is power, and it is freedom. Never forget that.

I never got that freedom. It was Fate that had me taken away from my family – starting with the Japanese and then being sold to the Tang family as a san pou chai. I wonder what would my life have been like if the Japanese never came? Would I have been a different person? If I had an education, would I have had the confidence to leave Zeoi Mao and the power to provide a better life for my children? I think so. Perhaps I could have lived a life for myself? For myself – that sounds so selfish, doesn't it? But I could have worked in a market stall or even a bakery or restaurant. My children would have been able to inherit my love for learning because there would be so many books at home instead of being forced to go to work at such a young age. No one has time for an education if they're starving. Perhaps more of them would have turned out like Auntie Yin with her PhD.

Education is a ladder to climb to a better future, and I barely got to make the first step on it.

As I think back to my past, I have grown to be afraid of my memory, not for what I remember, but for what I cannot. My memories are like ghosts that drift and wander without direction. The older I get, the louder they cry out, but when I try to listen to them, when I try to locate where they come from, I can't. This is what is so terrifying about growing old – my memories have become misplaced. My happy memories have started to fall out of my head as if there's a little hole that grows bigger with time. If everything kept falling out, there would be nothing left, and I would not be me. But if I knew how to write, I could have written everything down and read it back to myself instead of feeling my memories wander away into the darkness.

I want to only remember the things that matter, the things that brought me joy. Perhaps you can remember all of this for me, so there would be something left when I'm gone?

Paupau's stamp. As she doesn't know how to write, she was issued a stamp as her signature which she kept in her purse. The ink was always red.

A GRANDDAUGHTER'S REGRET

If nagging was an Olympic sport, Paupau would hold an unbeatable world record. In fact, she could probably resurrect the dead from sheer will. But her level of nagging wasn't random, it was on a gradient that depended on how much she cared about you. The more she cared, the more she nagged.

Here are some examples:

Ah-yah, too skinny, you need to eat more. You look like a dried cup noodle! Here, eat a bite. Just a little bite, it's nothing. Doesn't matter you had dinner already. See, I bought these oranges – very good price. Eat them or they will go to waste and wasting food is a sin. Cannot waste food!

Ah-yah! Forecast to rain tomorrow. Bring an umbrella just in case. If you get wet, you will get a cold and then get sick. Waste money on seeing a doctor for nothing. Doesn't matter your bag is full, put it on the side or hold it like this. Sunny later? Okay, take the umbrella anyway. Can't get too dark or you'll look like a roast pig. Where is your umbrella? Ha? Where?

Ah-yah, it's nine o'clock, very late! Time to shower and go to sleep. Go and shower now. Don't forget to wash your face and brush your teeth too. Here – use this towel, I bought it in the market only ten dollars for two. Look how pretty and pink it is – absorbs water very well, dries quickly too. You can use this after your shower. Come on, time to go to sleep. And don't forget to pray before going to sleep, ha! Mr God is watching. He sees everything.

Ah-yah, what do you mean you don't go to church? What? You live where? England with the Queen? Yes, I know what it is. I am not stupid. Don't they have churches there? Must find one, must go every Sunday. You've been baptised! You are one of Mr God's people. Must go otherwise you will let Mr God down.

The list is possibly infinite and the times when you could get out of being nagged to death were limited to:

- you are sleeping
- you are sick
- you are sick and sleeping
- you are studying
- you are working.

The first two didn't always work. If I had slept too long, Paupau would wake me up worried I was sick. If I was sick, she'd nag me until I got better, which oddly seemed to work as my colds and flus never lasted long as a child.

The only time Paupau was silent was when we were studying or reading. I had discovered this wizardry when I was little. Auntie Yin, who lived with us, would lock herself in her room for hours to study for her nursing degree. Paupau didn't bother her once, not even to knock on her door, and left Auntie Yin in complete peace, often turning down the TV in case we disturbed her.

Whenever my auntie crawled out of her room for dinner and her appetite was poor, all she had to say was she wasn't hungry.

'Are you sick? Maybe you are sick? Why aren't you eating?' Paupau asked as she piled chunks of food into Auntie Yin's bowl.

'Ma, I am not hungry. I have too much on my mind and if I eat too much, I can't study properly because it makes me sleepy.'

'Ah! Okay. Then eat as much as you can.'

That was it. No follow-up questions. No further nagging. Nothing. It was magic.

I learnt two very essential lessons back then. First was Paupau could actually control her nagging if she wanted to and second, my grandmother's will was (and is) as strong as I imagined God's to be.

'Look at your Auntie Yin. You must learn from her. She studied very hard to get to where she is now. So, so clever! Now, you must do the same. You must,' Paupau would say.

It was never a request, but a command. My grandmother rarely made any demands of me. As a child, I got away with pretty much anything with her, but not this. Paupau expected me to grow up, become an educated woman and be free from the same cage she had been trapped in as an illiterate woman. Being educated meant I wouldn't have to grow up with a life like hers.

Not all education comes from school or books. Some of the most valuable things I had learnt in my life were with Paupau or came from her. I remember watching her and how she cared for others, her ability to anticipate everyone's needs and put them before her own. It was in the little things she did, like buying my favourite mangosteens and putting them in the fridge so they'd be cold for desert – all just for me. I remember she never once counted how much money she had spent on her family because it didn't matter. So long as everyone was full and happy, Paupau would give everything she had. If she only had ten dollars in her purse, she would give it all to you without hesitation.

Through my fourteen years with her, spending every day consciously and unconsciously absorbing her, I learnt how to care for others and, most importantly, I learnt how to love. Despite all that she had to endure, none of it could take away her kindness and her ability to laugh.

I see it in old photographs of her that decorate my office and in my photo boxes, but there is one photo in particular that I always return to. Paupau is in her mid-sixties, wearing a royal blue silk blouse with her hair immaculately coiffed into a neat, permed bob. She is looking off to the side with a huge smile that radiates from her soul. Her entire body glows with love – innocence beautifully captured on film. This is what I love most about Paupau. She has every reason to be bitterly intoxicated with resentment and hatred, but instead she has found reasons to live, to love and to laugh. In recounting the story of her life, I have learnt the best form of revenge is to unlearn all the hatred your abusers inflicted upon you.

But in recent years, in the space where old age, politics and a pandemic intersect, that big banana smile I grew up with has started to fade like her memory.

'Ah-yah, your Paupau is getting so old. I can't remember anything. I don't know what is going on with me. I can't remember what I ate for breakfast this morning or what day of the week it is! What's going on with me?' Paupau's voice would break.

When that happens, I can barely hold back my sobs until our video call finishes and then they come all at once in loud cries and snot. I feel like I am losing her, that my Paupau is slipping away faster than I can hold on. Why hadn't I been writing down everything she's told me? Why hadn't I been recording her? And now it feels like I'm too late.

For someone who lives life with no regrets, this is my only one. I should have done this years ago.

Paupau holding Ah Lin (right). Big Sister with her first daughter (middle) and Jia Fu standing (left). Paupau was around 22 years old at the time. From what I gathered, Jia Fu wanted to take a professional family portrait. They travelled to Kowloon for this exceptional event. This is the only existing photograph of Paupau at that age.

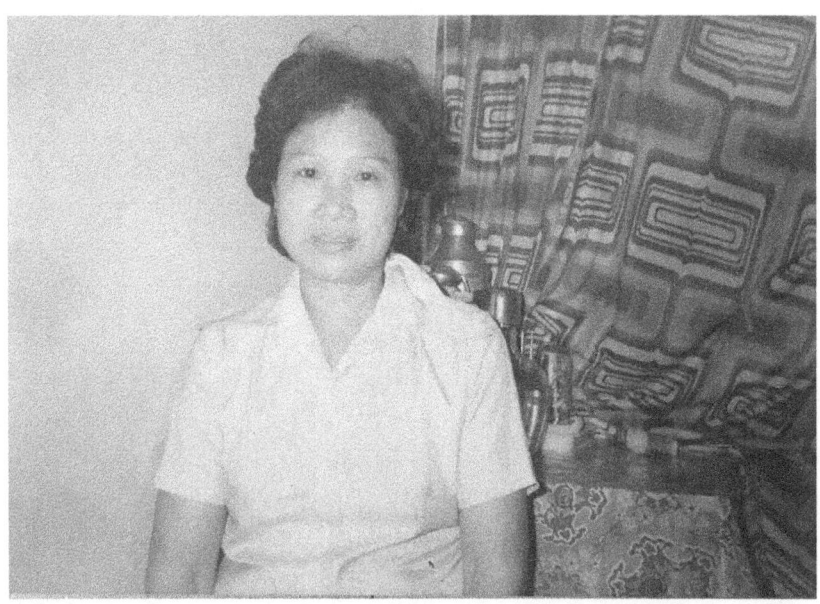

Mei Foo, Kowloon. Circa 1977.

A HAKKA WOMAN

Sham Shui Po, Kowloon. Circa 1982.

Paupau circa 1981–83.

Paupau circa 1982.

Paupau holding up her famous lo bak go that she used to make from scratch every year. Lunar New Year 2015.

A HAKKA WOMAN

Paupau on her 86th birthday enjoying her favourite type of cake – mango pudding sponge with a ridiculous amount of cream. Her memory at this time was still exceptional.

Paupau wrapping zhong (gluttonous rice dumplings) for Dragon Boat Festival, June 2021. This was the last time she made zhong.

Paupau and I in Hong Kong in August 2023. I had not seen her in four years.

POETRY

I didn't realise until I finished the manuscript, but this is a book I had been writing all my life. Paupau's story is so entwined with my childhood and who I am as a woman today. In many ways this felt like a journey of memory – the painful acceptance that my grandmother is losing hers whilst I got to recall so many exquisite moments from my childhood with her. Those moments are expressed in a small collection of poetry included in this book which I wanted to share with you.

FAITH

- *i thought you don't believe in God?*
- i don't
- *then why did you pray with me?*
- because i believe in you.

MANGOSTEEN

red plastic bag overstretched
sagging and heavy
too many mangosteens
picked out one by one with care
no, not that one, this one – check the bottom – give it a little squeeze – old ones aren't as juicy – old ones are dry – no one likes old ones like me
bundled into the fridge
squashed against other forgotten treasures
grown with extra layers of blue and green
here, eat.
her thumb and forefinger press
into the mangosteen
cracking its shell bursting
white flesh
exposed
tiny segments of juice too big
for small hands too weak
to break shells myself
ah yah, let me do it for you, you'll make a mess. code for let me feed you
gobble-gobble
slide them down one by one
kilos of fruit vanish leaving only sticky smiles.
she nods approvingly.

MTR RIDE

the slow steady sound of her heartbeat
dut dut
dut dut
dut dut
ear pressed against her back
floral silk blouse creased with sweat pressed up against my face
squashed up against her in the mtr
crowds of adult humans towering over me like skyscrapers
the smell of her
fish
tiger balm
imperial lather soap
so accustomed to hard labour
what are a few flights of stairs
carrying a chubby granddaughter
weighing less than two woven baskets
filled with cement and stone?
hurry! hurry!
jump out of the train
always rushing to get somewhere twenty minutes early
everywhere we went.

REUNITED

getting off the school bus my eyes
searched for hers
how they widened and lit up
hers mine
different eyes but the same.
the clank of her jade bracelet against my forearm
as she linked her arm in mine
hooking my school bag with the other
like it was nothing
not even half a bag of rice
so many questions
none about school
only food
all about food
because food is what nourishes
it is what heals
what connects
it is our language of love
a Hakka grandmother and her gwai mui granddaughter.

THERAPY

the sound of meat against wood
upside down cleaver
pounding against flesh battering it into soft paste
beating it into submission
almost a lifetime of being thumped
scrapped
scooped
chopped
hacked
the quiet power of a woman who never got to fight back
pounding meat cakes for her granddaughter
this is what we call *therapy*
meat cakes never tasted better.

BUBBLED CLOTH

the sound of her washing her face
violent thrashings of a ten-year-old cloth
splashing against the water
in loud slaps
rubbing away the day
of salt
and
oil
and
grief.

INHERITANCE

the roughness of her hands
skin like leather coarse and thickened by years of labour
rubbing tiger balm
in the small hours of the morning
onto smaller ankles
swollen and sore from childhood arthritis
inherited from her father long not seen
whispers that cut through the night
whispers of stories about monsters pretending to be people acting like monsters
whispers like the ointment rubbed into my skin
deeper and deeper
until all of it's absorbed
until it's in my blood
a part of me.

DRESS REHEARSAL

what terrifies me is knowing
that one day i will pick up
the phone to call you
and you won't be there to pick up
i won't hear your voice
asking me have i eaten yet
and what time is it in the UK
over and over
i know some time in the future that day will come
it is just as inevitable as breathing
but i don't want it to
i want to believe you can and will live forever
to always be there
that age and death could never touch you
i go through scenarios in my head of how it might happen
how i might get the news
what i would be doing at the time
what i would even say
i practise it in my head over and over
a dress rehearsal for what i know will be the worst day of my life
i don't know why i do it
they say practice makes things easier
so if i practised losing you
maybe it would be less soul-destroying
i tell myself this is life
it happens
people die
and still i hope it never comes
i don't think i'd know how to be me
knowing you aren't there anymore.

Epilogue

Family events are an odd phenomenon. They are the intricate and sticky webs of people's decisions that lead to unpredictable outcomes. Out of Paupau's seven remaining children, my mother ended up being financially responsible for my grandmother for a time. In exchange, Paupau gave us the one thing she had – herself.

For the first fourteen years of my life, my grandmother was my primary carer. She never took a day off, never called in sick and never once had a 'personal day'. Paupau took care of my mother, Auntie Yin, and me by washing all our clothes, cleaning our apartment, doing all the food shopping and cooking. She spoiled us every dinner time with a feast of steamed fish, a meat dish, two vegetable dishes, steamed rice and soup – and that was standard. During festivals like Lunar New Year, my grandmother indulged us with at least nine exquisite dishes, each one a testament to her culinary skills. My favourite was her braised soya bean duck. And it wasn't only Hakka or Cantonese food. I don't know how, but Paupau had perfected steak with garlic sauce and spaghetti Bolognese, which she cooked in a wok. To this day I still can't make spaghetti Bolognese as tasty as her version.

Every morning, Paupau made sure I started the day off right by cooking me a hearty breakfast. It was usually spicy braised pork rice noodles with bamboo shoots or udon with sliced spam and Maggi seasoning. She sent me to school with a lunch bag packed with delicious goodies for break time and lunch. I never went hungry. Monday to Friday, Paupau dropped me off and picked me up from the school bus stop before buying me whatever I wanted to eat. Ballet lessons. Piano lessons. Ice-skating sessions. Play dates. School. Church. It didn't matter what it was, Paupau got me there, punctual and immaculate.

A HAKKA WOMAN

When I got sick, it was Paupau who took me to the doctors and ensured I took my medication on time. She cooked special soup to make me feel better and tended to my every need. The most amazing thing was, she did all of this without ever needing to read.

At night, when my childhood arthritis would flare up and the pain was unbearable, Paupau would get out of bed and rub my ankles with ointment without complaint. In those small hours of the night, in the silence, Paupau would recount her stories as she soothed me to sleep.

Paupau never said *no*. She never said *I don't feel like it* or *I'm too busy*. It wasn't in her vocabulary.

My grandmother taught me so much more than I had the patience to learn, like how to choose the freshest fish in the market, or cursing in Hakka when we played Chinese blackjack. She never tired of imparting her experience, generously sharing anecdotes from her past imbued with her wisdom. It was through my grandmother that I learnt how to stand up for myself. Having spent most of her life as a victim and later survivor of abuse, Paupau often reminded me to never let any man hurt me, even if it was too late for her.

Paupau is by no means perfect with her incessant nagging and deeply internalised patriarchal views, but she gave me the best years of her life. She gave me her. This book is my tribute to my grandmother and all the lessons she had tried to pass on to an equally stubborn and impatient granddaughter.

Initially, I wasn't sure how to categorise this book because it isn't a word-for-word biography and it shouldn't be read as such. Rather, this book is a retelling of my grandmother's life through me. Her stories have been filtered through her memories and mine. The events mentioned in this book are true, but I took some artistic licence when describing certain events or places either to help fill in memory gaps or to better structure the overall narrative. I changed the names of all people mentioned in this book to protect their identities, except for Paupau, deceased family members and my name.

Writing this book is one of the hardest things I have had to do. How do I capture my grandmother's voice when I'm writing in a language she doesn't speak? Even in her native tongue, her vocabulary is rather limited and to make things more complicated, I can only speak Hong Kongese, I can't write it.

By retelling her story in English, I have had to translate not just words but her thoughts, her feelings – I have had to translate her. But so much of her life lies in what she leaves unsaid, in the nuances of what she implies. Certain subjects remain taboo in our culture. Things a grandmother would never openly discuss with her granddaughter.

Sometimes it felt I was losing something of her: the authenticity of Paupau's voice by adding my own. Where does her voice end and mine begin? These pages have intertwined our two voices, now speaking as one. We have a saying in Hong Kongese, *two hearts, one beat*, and when I wrote as Paupau, I felt her, and I lived her. I could scratch the inside of her skin.

I don't want to remember Paupau as an old woman still struggling with PTSD or as a grandmother who feels she is useless, losing her memory and capacity of self. No, I want to remember Paupau as the woman who, despite all her trauma, rose above it with her compassion, generosity and love.

I want to remember my grandmother as feeling safe and mostly loved. I want to know she can go to bed at night with a full belly and will wake up in the morning to a stuffed fridge and bags of rice in the kitchen. I want to remember my grandmother as the woman who taught me what it means to be a Hakka woman – a woman of a strength that is fluid and gentle, a strength like water. This is how I want to remember my grandmother, this version of her.

I had Paupau pretty much all to myself my entire childhood, and now I get to share her with the world through this book.

Glossary of terms

Ah Jia	Hakka, for older sister.
Ah Mui	Young girl, little girl. Can refer to own little sister.
Ah Pau	An elderly woman, respectfully.
Ah Sim	Hakka, a middle-aged woman, respectfully.
Ah Sum	A middle-aged woman, respectfully.
Bo bui / bo	Treasure, precious.
Cha gou	Tea dumpling, Hakka dumpling filled usually with pork and dried shrimp. Sweet versions usually filled with beans.
Chaa lau	Tea house, usually serves dim sum.
Cheung fun	Chinese steamed rice roll.
Dai fu	Traditional Chinese herbalist doctor.
Diu lei lo mo	Fuck your mother.
Fun gee khan	Hakka, for a small woven sieve used to catch small fish; also used as a curse to say someone is totally useless.
Fu yu	Chinese fermented bean curd.
Gong hei fat choi	Lunar New Year greeting for 'wishing you great happiness and prosperity'.
Guk gong	To bow formally, usually at official events like weddings.
Gwai lo	Literally 'ghost man' to describe Caucasian man or white man. Considered today a slur by some.
Gwai mui	Literally 'ghost girl' to describe Caucasian girl or white girl. Considered today a slur by some.
Hakka	Literally 'guest family'. Han Chinese subgroup originally from Northern China that emigrated across Southern China in 1270s.
Ham sup	Perverted, sordid.

Ham ga chaan	Strong profanity. Literally 'may your whole family be bulldozed'. Can be used as a noun like *pok gai* and a verb, depending on context.
Jia Fu	Hakka, for older brother-in-law.
Kung hee fat choi	Hakka, for *gong hei fat choi*, a greeting said during Lunar New Year to wish recipient fortune and prosperity.
Lai see	Red pocket or envelope with money given by married people to children or younger (usually unmarried) relatives, often during Lunar New Year but also during special occasions such as birthdays, weddings or graduations.
Lo bak go	Turnip cake made with Chinese lardons, dried shrimp and spring onion. Customarily made and served during Lunar New Year.
Ma jie	Female servant, maid.
Ma fan	Trouble, troublesome.
Man tou	Chinese steamed bun, typically white, soft and slightly sweet.
Maa Maa	Maternal grandmother.
Miu	Temple.
Mong chaa chaa	Slang to have blurred vision, unable to see.
Naai gong	Construction work, literally 'mud work'.
Ngi ho	Hakka, for 'hello'.
Ngai hen Ah Ping	Hakka, for 'my name is Ah Ping'.
Pau	Old woman.
Pok gai	Literally, to trip on the street. Used as an insult or curse. Can be used as a noun to call someone a prick or can be used to mean shit, damn or fuck depending on tone and context.
San pou chai	Child bride.
Sit faan mao	Hakka, for 'have you eaten (rice yet)?' Way of asking someone how they are.

Si kor mor	Hakka profanity. Literally 'dead mole' or 'fucking mole'.
Tit da jau	Chinese liniment made from various herbs used to heal external injuries.
Tai Yee Pau	Maternal Great Aunt.
Tong yuen	Glutinous rice balls served with sweet ginger soup, usually eaten on Winter Solstice Festival.
Tong hua	Term for Chinese language. Informal.
Tong lau	Literally 'Chinese building'. Utilitarian shophouses built in post-WW2 Hong Kong for local Hong Kong people. Usually around two to four storeys high.
Yum cha	Literally 'to drink tea'. Meal eaten in the morning or early afternoon usually consisting of dim sum dumplings and tea.
Zeoi Mao Gong	Literally 'drunken cat man', derogatory term used for alcoholics.
Zhong	Glutinous rice dumpling usually stuffed with belly pork, mung bean, yolk, dried shrimp and cooked in bamboo leaf. Made during Dragon Boat Festival.

Acknowledgements

This book was due to have been published in spring 2023 however my publisher, Onwe Press, told me in November 2022 that they were going into liquidation. I was heartbroken. Thus started the frantic search for a new publisher or even an agent. Between the no-responses to being told by publishers they loved my compelling writing style but felt the story itself wasn't 'marketable', I decided to do it myself.

But I didn't do this myself. The reason you are able to hold this book in your hand is because of the many amazing and generous donations from friends, family, acquaintances and even strangers who contributed to my crowdfunding efforts. Many fell in love with Paupau from my first book and memoir. Some understood the importance and need to pass on our grandmother's stories. Others were fellow ESEA creatives showing their most appreciated support. To all who donated: I owe this book to you. I could not have produced it without your help, and I am truly and utterly grateful to you.

To my cousin. Thank you for your countless hours of support, of research, filling in timeline blanks, your feedback and encouragement. I may have written the words, but this felt so much like a collaborative effort. Thank you for having looked after our Paupau and bringing her so much joy over the years.

To my Auntie who feels so much like my Big Sister and half-mother. Thank you for believing in me and supporting this project. I hope I have written Paupau, your mother, with the sensitivity, authenticity and love she deserves. Thank you for taking such good care of her.

To my partner, Klaudiusz, for understanding how much getting Paupau's story out there means to me.

To my grandmother, my Paupau. You are my heart.

Dear Reader,

Thank you so much for your time in reading *A Hakka Woman*. If you enjoyed reading this book, please review it on Goodreads or Amazon. Reviews greatly help indie authors get visibility so more people can get to know my grandmother's story.

Please feel free to connect with me on Instagram @di.lebowitz

Warmest wishes,

Di

If we don't look back, how would we ever know how far we have come?

www.ingramcontent.com/pod-product-compliance
Lightning Source LLC
Chambersburg PA
CBHW022058090426
42743CB00008B/645